Contemporary Punk Rock Communities

Contemporary Punk Rock Communities

Scenes of Inclusion and Dedication

Ellen M. Bernhard

ENJOY!

♡ Ellen

LEXINGTON BOOKS
Lanham • Boulder • New York • London

Published by Lexington Books
An imprint of The Rowman & Littlefield Publishing Group, Inc.
4501 Forbes Boulevard, Suite 200, Lanham, Maryland 20706
www.rowman.com

6 Tinworth Street, London SE11 5AL

British Library Cataloguing in Publication Information Available

Library of Congress Control Number:2019949533

ISBN: 978-1-4985-9967-2 (cloth : alk. paper)
ISBN: 978-1-4985-9968-9 (electronic)

♾️™ The paper used in this publication meets the minimum requirements of American National Standard for Information Sciences Permanence of Paper for Printed Library Materials, ANSI/NISO Z39.48-1992.

Contents

Acknowledgments

Firstly, I would like to thank my committee chairs Dr. Ernest Hakanen and Dr. Jordan McClain for their support throughout my PhD study and related research, and for their continued feedback and knowledge. I would also like to thank the rest of my dissertation committee: Dr. Barbara Hoekje, Dr. Ronald Bishop, and Dr. Lynne Edwards for their insightful comments and encouragement, and for the questions which inspired me to widen my research from various angles. For their insightful perspectives and truly meaningful conversations, I would like to thank those who participated in the research for this book. Without your contributions, this would not have been possible. I would also like to thank my parents, Carol and Ken, for supporting me throughout this (at times never-ending) writing process, answering every single phone call along the way, and accepting all of the peculiar idiosyncrasies that result when you raise a kid who showed a love of punk rock as a weird teenager and eventually grew up to study it. I'd also like to thank my sister, Julie, for never questioning my interest in the at-times terrible music emanating from my bedroom all those years ago. I am also grateful to my fiancé, Allon, for putting up with the truly impressive quantity of papers, books, and Post-it notes that accumulated in our apartment throughout this time, and for always being my punk rock partner in crime. Last but not least, I would like to thank the punk rock community for the music, memories, and miles traveled. It's been a fun ride.

Introduction

My long-term relationship with punk rock began as many introductions to music do, in middle school. A neighbor burned me a copy of Blink-182's 1999 album *Enema of the State* in seventh grade, and from there, I spent hours scrolling through poorly organized websites searching for any information I could find on the genre. For the next several years, a growing collection of CDs (compact discs) towered my desk in my bedroom, often accompanied by handwritten track listings of the albums for the mix CDs I made for myself and my friends. Bands like Bad Religion, Millencolin, Rancid, Pennywise, Less Than Jake, The Bouncing Souls, and Alkaline Trio were some of the first that caught my attention. For whatever reason, I was particularly drawn to Epitaph Records' catalog of 90s-era skate punk, and to this day, I still wonder as to what about Pennywise's *Land of the Free?* resonated with me at the age of thirteen. As an indifferent teenager from the suburbs of Billy Joel's Allentown, this was not the kind of music that many of my peers found inviting, which meant that I, with my studded leather belt and Dead Kennedys back patch, stood out among the kids who swore by country music and showtunes.

The first concert I ever attended was Blink-182 and New Found Glory at the Great Allentown Fair in 2001. Friends and I sported matching homemade t-shirts emblazoned with iron-on printouts of the band, with the phrase "Crappy Punk Rock" written around the edges. And the shirts had fringe. Yes, fringe. I am thankful that social media did not exist back then to record such a fashion faux pas, because that was the first and only time I ever wore fringe in public. While the concert itself took place in a large stadium and we sat in seats a good distance from the stage, I knew right away that there was something special about seeing a live performance. To witness your favorite artists performing their music, engaging with the crowd, and basking in the

1

energy of hundreds, or even thousands, of people who are there for the exact same reason is a feeling that is hard to replicate. Blink-182's show at the Allentown Fairgrounds was the first in a long procession of shows I attended, though (much to my disappointment) I have yet to return to the Great Allentown Fair.

My parents were enablers. In the spring of my eighth grade year, my mother lied to the school nurse about my having a doctor's appointment so I could skip a softball game to instead travel down the turnpike to Philly to see Face to Face, Midtown, The Movielife, and Thrice play at the Trocadero at 10th and Arch. My father, an avid fan of jazz and Bruce Springsteen, used to take me to Best Buy on the weekends, where I would flip through the endless rows of CDs and buy albums to fill my collection—long live the Best Buy CD selection of the early aughts. By this point I knew what I was looking for, and this process usually entailed searching for albums to fill in the missing gaps of albums from bands I already liked, or to find actual copies of beloved albums that I had acquired through burning copied CDs from friends. On some visits, Epitaph's *Punk-O-Rama* compilations were the album of choice. There was a lot of bang for your buck in those albums: 25ish fast and loud songs, clocking in at 4 to 6 dollars apiece, featuring bands familiar and unfamiliar in the Epitaph roster. Like *Punk-O-Rama*, the Warped Tour compilations also had a similar impact—they included many of the Epitaph and Fat Wreck Chords bands that became so integral to my understanding and appreciation of the music.

Through high school, I experimented with other nearby genres such as emo and pop punk, but regardless of subgenre, always felt a strong connection to the values and messages found in the music itself. Promotional posters and fliers for local shows adorned the walls in my bedroom and the collection of CDs kept growing. Our parents would drive us to shows at The Grange, a church basement far too small to fit the numbers of people that showed up to see local and touring bands perform on the weekends. Shows at The Grange were short-lived—too much violence and evidence of drinking on the property shut the space down. Your typical Lehigh Valley VFW hall, Friday night church youth group, or local firehall also pulled the weight to host some of these shows, which often attracted kids looking for something to do on the weekends whether they were into the music or not. Living on the East Coast, however, meant there was never a lack of shows. By the time I was in high school, friends and I would travel to Philadelphia and to New Jersey to see some of our favorite bands, and if we were lucky, those tours would come through Allentown to play at the now defunct Crocodile Rock Café, a smoke-filled dive of a music venue that somehow managed to score some really good shows over the years.

By the time I had a driver's license in 2004, skipping class in high school meant afternoon trips to the diner and the small record store on the other side of town. Double Decker Records took most of my money junior and senior year: While I wasn't buying records at the time, the store's used CD collection was a goldmine for low-stakes exploration into punk rock. Friends and I would peruse the collection and leave with two or three CDs at a time, often chosen at random, to listen to when we got home. Used copies of albums like Against Me!'s *Reinventing Axl Rose* and Against All Authority's *The Restoration of Chaos and Order* would blare through the crappy speakers in my green Mercury Sable station wagon while five or six of us would pile in and head off to the mall or the diner. While I haven't looked through my CD collection in years, this assemblage of relics has traveled with me from apartment to apartment. And while it now resides in cardboard liquor boxes in the back of a closet, it stands as a towering testament to a longtime love of a music genre that since informed my own philosophical outlook on life.

Moving closer to the Philadelphia area for college gave me even more access to shows, and I, often by myself, would trek into the city to see bands play smaller venues such as the North Star Bar, Starlight Ballroom, and the First Unitarian Church, and larger ones like the Trocadero and the Electric Factory. College was a weird juxtaposition to my punk rock persona—if I thought I was in the punk minority in high school, I was most definitely in that minority in college. I'd still attend shows in Philly whenever possible, but a scene of any kind barely existed on campus. Aside from some classmates who sporadically listened to Blink-182 and may or may not have heard of Less Than Jake, college was not exactly the epicenter of punk culture that I had hoped it would be. Thanks to social media, I was exposed to more of the smaller, local, punk scenes in the Philadelphia area and would frequent house shows whenever something good came through town. Thankfully, I was never too far from a punk scene, even though my college years often led me to believe that punk was dead after all.

I decided to attend graduate school in Philadelphia in 2011, not entirely sure for what purpose, but made my decision to study punk rock and punk culture after browsing a popular culture conference's website. Until then, it never occurred to me that studying punk rock—especially contemporary punk rock—in an academic fashion could be viable. My only experience with academic studies of punk rock largely emphasized the impact of bands like The Sex Pistols and The Clash, not what kids in New Jersey punk bands in 2017 were doing to keep their scenes afloat today. While there is no doubting the cultural impact of bands such as these, I felt that my own experience with punk rock had very little to do with bands like the Sex Pistols—it's very likely that my awareness of them did not occur until much later, many years after Sum 41 and Blink-182, with their catchy riffs and songs about unrequited love, caught my attention. Surely, I wasn't the only one who was exposed to punk rock through MTV and VH1, the pop culture arbiters of all things trendy and cool. And with that, I began my exploration into contemporary punk rock scenes in America today.

From there, I spent the next five years combining a love of punk rock with my own academic research and attended conferences each year to present on some punk-related issue or another, justifying my research to old-school naysayers along the way who would often ask—and at times tell—me whether or not my research was actually about punk. Semiotic analyses of music videos and band t-shirts. Fest, the annual Gainesville, Florida, punk-centric festival and the experience economies that surround it. Bad Religion's infamous crossbuster logo and do-it-yourself co-creation. The Menzingers and the existential grief of growing older as evidenced on their 2017 album *After the Party*. Yes, the topics I investigated often addressed what was going on in punk scenes today, but as far as I was concerned, it was still punk—it still embodied a particular ethos that resonated within the music and culture that I considered to be such an integral component of my life.

When I began teaching in the spring of 2012, it was often difficult to separate classroom conversations from my own experiences in punk. As it is a style of music that built its foundations on questioning the status quo, I often use various examples inspired by punk rock culture to help students see the value in critical thinking. Henry Rollins's spoken word often appears as a source of critique in public speaking classes, and rhetorical analysis is not complete without an examination of music videos from bands like Hot Water Music and Rise Against. Recently, students caught me off-guard during class and asked my thoughts about whether or not Green Day and Nickelback are punk (my answers: Green Day—yes, under certain conditions, Nickelback—a resounding no). And with each semester, I continue to explore ways to introduce my students to the ideological perspectives and emphasis on social issues that often exist in punk scenes today. I do this not because I want to introduce them to punk (that's my secondary goal), but rather, I believe it is important to show students the ways that grassroots efforts often result in big changes, or at the very least, that these efforts can bring about a conversation that puts the gears in motion to spark change. And while these practices are often influenced by outside forces that play a huge role in the functioning of our society today, there continues to exist an effort and a drive to ensure punk scenes throughout the country remain active and involved.

This book is an investigation into those scenes. To explore the goals and trends of those who participate in their communities and dedicate their time and money to keeping their punk scenes alive. While this is by no means an exhaustive search to uncover the true definition of "punk" or to understand every punk community in every city across the United States, my hope is to shed light on some of the resonant qualities of these scenes, and to share the stories of those who, like myself, recognized their love of punk rock to be more than just a nostalgic memory of time spent in high school attending shows in church basements.

THE CHARACTERISTICS OF CONTEMPORARY PUNK ROCK SCENES IN AMERICA TODAY

The purpose of this book is to investigate some of the outstanding qualities that comprise contemporary punk scenes in America today. While this is by no means a definitive exploration into the dynamic and ever-changing communities that exist within the spheres of punk rock and punk rock-adjacent genres, the stories I gathered provide some valuable insight into some of the prevailing characteristics of those who consider themselves active within the community today. Chapter 1 provides a historical background of the rise of contemporary punk rock, addressing the varied perspectives on youth cultures, which began with the Birmingham School and Center for Contemporary Cultural Studies and continues today through the more postmodern lens of postsubcultural theory. Chapter 2 provides an analysis of the outstanding characteristics of scenes today, which include the ways in which participants relate their experiences within their scenes to a larger understanding of an identity and sense of belonging. These understandings tie into the norms and values that many participants see as integral components to a sense of belonging within the scene today. This chapter considers the importance of social activism and representation within the scene, and alongside interview content, I have provided some useful examples of contemporary punk festivals that use their platforms to spread awareness on social issues that impact scenes and their communities at large. This chapter also considers the ways in which today's participants, both those in bands and those who consider themselves fans, actively work to encourage diversity and inclusion within their scenes.

Chapter 3 identifies some of the external influences that participants identified as a means of introduction to punk rock. A common theme throughout my conversations included the prevalence of influence from family and friends and more mainstream outlets, including MTV and the radio. An example of a peak music experience (Green 2016), participants provided very detailed information regarding their introductions to punk rock and identified specific bands and albums that were key in this introduction. Discussion of the appeal of punk included thoughts on the ways today's scenes provide an understanding of a community that shares similar values, and many participants expressed the ways that they dedicate time and effort to attending shows and connecting with others within their scene.

Chapter 4 seeks to address two of the overlapping forces that exist within punk scenes today—the grassroots efforts of DIY production and mainstream forces such as Hot Topic and major record labels that frequently co-opt various elements of punk culture, such as style and the music itself. While scenes today place significant value in the ability to remain largely autonomous, there is an understanding that outside forces will continue to exist despite these efforts. With this awareness, the reaction to such forces was generally met with indifference, though there was strong support for the bands and musicians who have used such means to make a living from their music. As an example of one of these mainstream forces, social media is often used by bands to share their music and raise awareness about new albums or upcoming shows. Today's punk scenes exist as proof that both of these spheres can exist within punk rock, and efforts by today's community to remain autonomous can still succeed despite cooptation or the omnipresence of social media and the culture industry.

Using interview data collected, chapter 5 looks at two distinct, but critical, practices within participatory culture—the practice of belonging in a band within today's scene and the practice of consumption. In chapter 5, participants shared their own experiences of playing in a band and considered the dynamics of these relationships as they relate to an understanding of identity and belonging. A large factor in any type of scene, levels and types of commitment varied among participants, and this was evident in the examples provided by those who play in bands today. This chapter also provides some insight into the commodified aspects of contemporary punk culture, and participants provided some insight into how their money is used to support scenes today. Band merchandise expands well beyond the minimum of t-shirts and albums, and this serves as evidence that today's scenes are highly commodified spaces where dedication to one's scene is demonstrated through the ownership and display of such goods.

Lastly, chapter 6 reflects on what participants hope to see in the future of their scenes. Tied to a current understanding of punk rock communities as sites where social issues can be addressed and improved upon, today's scenes wish to see more progress in this field and remain optimistic that further inclusion and diversity continue to be influential tenets in the future of punk to come.

Chapter One

A Brief History of Contemporary Punk Rock and an Overview of the Theoretical Considerations on Subcultures

This chapter will provide an overview of the history of contemporary punk rock in America while seeking to clarify some of the theoretical approaches and terminologies that surround the study of youth cultures. While punk rock's history goes back several decades, contemporary punk rock was largely influenced by the popularization of the genre during the mid-90s and early 2000s, following the decline of grunge. Facilitated by exposure from music videos, movies, and video games, access to contemporary punk rock was accomplished with relative ease. Furthermore, music festivals such as the Warped Tour popularized contemporary punk rock by bringing it to cities and small towns across the country for twenty-five years. While Warped Tour is ending its run in 2019, other festivals such as Fest and Pouzza Fest act as current examples of the prolonged interest in contemporary punk rock.

Following World War II, The Birmingham School and The Center for Contemporary Cultural Studies (CCCS) sought to understand youth cultures and the participation within through a critical lens that focused on the imbalance of hierarchical systems of power between youth and other forces within society. Participation within subcultures was observed to be a working-class phenomenon, where fashion choices, consumption habits, and all-or-nothing approaches to subcultural commitment were each considered as relevant components in the investigations of youth cultures. Moving forward, post-subcultural theory criticized the CCCS approach, arguing for more subjective, ethnographic investigations into the motivations behind participation in youth cultures, asserting that participation within such groupings exemplified more fluid levels of involvement, and a more ambivalent relationship toward social structures such as the media.

POP GOES PUNK: A BRIEF HISTORY
OF CONTEMPORARY PUNK ROCK

While many historical and sociological accounts of punk rock begin at the early onset of the genre's beginnings, this book will focus specifically on the more recent understanding of contemporary punk rock and its impact for those who were introduced to the genre in the 90s and early 2000s. Though it is important to acknowledge the role that bands such as The Sex Pistols, The Clash, and others played in introducing the world to punk rock, the contemporary and mainstream recognition of the genre was largely due to the rise of grunge in the 90s, and ultimately the "break" of pop punk into the mainstream in 1994. Furthermore, awareness of such punk bands after 1994 was facilitated by popular culture outlets, which included MTV, VH1, and the radio. By the turn of the millennium, digital filesharing sites such as Napster and Kazaa became common ways to download and sample new music. While illegal and with its own set of ethical concerns, filesharing offered users the opportunity to download endless numbers of songs and albums from other users for free.

Prior to Green Day and Napster, there was grunge. When discussing the rise of contemporary punk rock today, it is necessary to acknowledge grunge's role in the genre's success. On January 11, 1992, Nirvana's *Nevermind* surpassed Michael Jackson's *Dangerous* on the US Billboard charts. Riding the trend that followed, bands like Soundgarden, Pearl Jam, and Mudhoney were popularized by outlets such as MTV and college radio stations, and their songs saw frequent airplay across the country. With grunge's escalating popularity, it was clear that the public demand had shifted from the pop sounds of Michael Jackson and Madonna to the raw, organic qualities of grunge. Grunge appeared to be an ideal precursor to contemporary punk rock, as it provided audiences with a style of music very different from what dominated the radio airwaves at the time, introducing audiences to music that did not necessarily sound hyper-produced and perfected. With this success, Nirvana paved the way for the mainstream acceptance of punk rock, which until this time received almost little to no serious attention from MTV and the like. According to Tom DeLonge, former guitarist of Blink-182: "When Nirvana came on the map, they changed radio, got all the hair metal bands off the radio, and brought punk rock to the forefront [and] even though they weren't totally punk rock, they were a punk rock band, but just a different style of it. They brought back stripped down, raw, real music to the radio" (Al-Attas 2009).

Nirvana's success and countercultural appeal produced skyrocketing album sales, frequent radio play, several MTV Music Video Awards, and a Grammy Award in 1995 for their MTV *Unplugged* performance (Nirvana—Grammy n.d.). Nirvana's success continued but was short-lived: 1994 prevailed as a critical year for the alternative music scene as the world coped with Kurt Cobain's suicide in April. His death signaled the end of grunge in the eyes of many mainstream audiences. By this point, *Nevermind* had over two years in the spotlight, and as Green Day's *Dookie* came along, it was apparent that pop punk would become the next music style to capture mainstream attention. D'Angelo (2004) writes: "Until Green Day ushered in *Dookie* in early 1994, the mainstream rock marketplace had nothing in stock that could compare to the album's invigorating brew of disaffected young angst, teen rebellion and emotional confusion." With the success of *Dookie*, Green Day epitomized pop punk with their cartoonish looks and radio-friendly songs about boredom and girls; the band appealed greatly to younger audiences living in suburbia, who helped catapult the album to the number two position on the *Billboard* charts (Green Day n.d.).

As the new faces of a music style that had a large underground presence for nearly two decades, Green Day navigated this newfound fame while attempting to remain true to the DIY, antiestablishment ethos that punk rock has prided itself on since its beginnings. Their youthful, immature behavior channeled that of Sid Vicious and Johnny Rotten of the Sex Pistols, but Green Day's punk message was different; their music spoke to an entirely different generation living under vastly different circumstances: "soft-core potty humor became the social rebellion of punks tired of the boredom and apathy of the suburbs" (Chuang and Hart 2008). Punk no longer spoke solely to the working-class troubles of youth living through economic hardship and in many ways, made little effort to be political at all. *SPIN*'s portrayal of Billie Joe Armstrong spoke powerfully to the type of listeners the band attracted in the mid-90s—bored, juvenile teenagers persuaded by the omnipotence of MTV, many of whom sought to rebel against the status quo, no matter how insignificant and petty this rebellion seemed to be: "For a new generation of punks, the defining image of the music may no longer be Sid Vicious puking in a New York hotel room or even Fugazi's Ian MacKaye picking up litter in a theater lobby before his band goes onstage, but Green Day singer Billie Joe shredding his sofa with a bread knife because there's nothing good on TV" (*SPIN* 1994). Pop punk was more accessible to audiences than its punk rock and hardcore predecessors and this accessibility helped the genre maintain a lasting impact through the 90s and early 2000s. As the 90s progressed, other bands from the Southern California area saw success as well, including the Offspring, whose 1994 album, *Smash*, maintains the record for the best-selling album release by an independent label, selling over 10 million copies worldwide (Bienstock 2014).

By the end of the 90s, pop punk had solidified itself as a major genre, competing against other popular styles for audience attention. Blink-182, whose 1999 album, *Enema of the State*, produced three singles, all of which became mainstays on MTV and in the Top 40 charts, turned the three-piece from Southern California into the next Green Day (Anthony, Heller, and Ryan 2014). By the mid-2000s, pop punk became a permanent fixture on MTV, VH1, and on popular radio stations across the country. During this time, audiences couldn't escape the omnipresence of pop punk: it frequently made appearances in films and video games. Ska-punk band Goldfinger and Blink-182, whose members also had a cameo in the film, both had songs on the *American Pie* soundtrack, and The Mighty Mighty Bosstones performed their songs "Where'd You Go" and "Someday I Suppose" in the 1995 film *Clueless*. The soundtrack to Tony Hawk's *Pro Skater* video game series, which included songs from bands such as The Suicide Machines, Dead Kennedys, Avail, and Less Than Jake proved to be significantly effective in normalizing punk rock and bringing awareness of punk rock to the masses during this time as well (Mckenty 2019; Menapace 2018).

Movies and video games were not the only way punk was brought to the people. Referred to as a "roving punk-themed circus" by *The Guardian*, The Warped Tour, a cross-country skate and punk-centric music festival that began in 1995 and finished its enduring run in 2019, played a significant role in introducing suburban teenagers to punk rock and alternative culture for more than two decades (Pelly 2018). Each year, the festival hosted around seventy bands both large and small and made stops in cities across the country throughout the summer. The festival catered to fans of punk, ska, emo, and the smaller subgenres in between. Bands such as Anti-Flag, Less Than Jake, Fall Out Boy, and Motion City Soundtrack performed to excited and eager fans who would spend a day in the sun in parking lots, fairgrounds, and racetracks across the country. While the festival landscape has changed since Warped Tour's initial launch, and weekend-long, Instagram-worthy festivals such as Coachella are the new norm, Warped Tour stood by its original initiative: to bring punk rock and genres like it to the masses for a reasonable price. In recent years, Warped Tour garnered negative attention for its lack of diversity on the lineup and a failure to properly address incidents related to allegations of sexual harassment by performers on the tour (Brown 2018; Pelly 2018). The three final Warped Tour dates in 2019 signal the end of an era for a countercultural spectacle that, for over two decades, brought punk rock and similar-sounding genres into the parking lots of suburbia one sun-drenched July afternoon at a time.

Though it may be a long while before another pop punk band becomes influential enough to win a Grammy (Green Day—Grammy n.d.), contemporary punk communities continue to thrive in independent spaces around the world. Often inspired by the music they discovered through MTV and the internet during the late 90s and early 2000s, contemporary punk scenes have mingled their own musical interests with values that emphasize social awareness and independence, while acknowledging the impact this era of music had on the scene today.

PICKING UP WHERE WARPED TOUR LEFT OFF: FEST AND POUZZA FEST AS SITES OF CONTEMPORARY PUNK SCENES IN NORTH AMERICA

The first festival I ever attended was the 2004 Warped Tour at the Hershey-park Pavilion in Hershey, Pennsylvania. The sight was chaotic: kids from neighboring areas piled into cars and waited in line early to ensure first access into the festival grounds. Free CDs were handed out like business cards to those in line, with local bands hoping their latest album would be enough to get them on a stage next year. It was a scorching day in August, and once the gates were open, teenagers (and at times their parents) wandered through the pavilion while bands got ready to perform on nearly a dozen stages throughout the day. Sporting my "George W. Bush is Not My President" t-shirt and carrying an armload of posters, stickers, and free CDs, I have vivid recollections of waiting in line to meet Rise Against and the Bouncing Souls, and anxiously waiting among the crowd to see Bad Religion play songs from *The Empire Strikes First*, one of my personal favorite albums. MySpace reps were there handing out branded shoelaces, of all things. The carnivalesque atmosphere was palpable as you walked past merch tent after merch tent, and all of this spoke to the cultural stronghold Warped Tour had in alternative music during the early and mid-2000s.

While punk rock has waned in interest within popular culture since its heyday in the 90s and early 2000s and Warped Tour is soon to be a distant memory for many a punk, translocal scenes across the country persist as sites of continued production and consumption where punk is just as valued, if not more, than it was during the twenty-five years Warped Tour traversed the country. For example, punk-centric festivals in North America draw fans from around the globe and cater their lineups to both casual concertgoers and dedicated fanbases that return year after year. Festivals such as Fest (Gainesville, Florida) and Pouzza Fest (Montreal, Canada), as well as others, seek to attract graduate attendees of the Warped Tour, and while their efforts are accomplished on a much different scale, theses attempts have effectively turned contemporary punk rock into a profitable moneymaking venture. Fest and Pouzza Fest, which are consistently held in the same locations year after year, provide what is known as an experience economy, defined by Lorentzen (2009) as an "attractive atmosphere, which comes from place-bound activities, events and services, attractive places and diverse social spaces, which make visitors and residents feel inspired, involved and connected to the place" (840). While attendees visit Gainesville and Montreal for the festivals themselves, they often attend with a desire to explore the city-specific elements of each location and engage with local businesses such as restaurants, record stores, and bars. For these cities, these festivals act as important assets to their businesses—nearby restaurants may see an increase in sales as participants stop by as they travel from venue to venue on their way to see a show, for example. Festivals are an important asset to an experience economy, and a positive experience in this environment often determines whether or not attendees will return in the future (Cole and Illum 2006). If festivals cater to their attendees' needs by providing resources (such as nearby hotels, restaurant suggestions, and so on), there is a greater chance that repeat attendance will occur in the future.

In the case of these festival examples, which will be explored in more detail below, we see the ways that contemporary punk scenes often operate in spaces that are not scene-specific. In other words, while the main draw of the festival is to attend, it is naïve to suggest that participants do not visit these cities (as well as other punk-centric festivals in other cities) to solely attend the festival. In the case of Fest, for example, their website offers suggestions for "Local Eats" and information on nearby hotels that have partnered with the festival to offer discounted rates (Fest 18 n.d.). The venues themselves, while some may host punk shows throughout the year, do not operate as only catering to this particular style of music. Because of this, it is important to recognize the interplay between contemporary punk scenes and the spaces that operate around the scenes themselves. The examples provided here offer evidence of the "osmotic" relationship between scene-specific practices and the external environments in which they exist (Weinzierl and Muggleton 2003, 7), and further discussion of this relationship will be explored at length throughout the book.

Dubbed "the perfect music festival for people who hate music festivals" (Anthony 2014), Fest is an annual punk-centric music festival held in Gainesville, Florida, that proves to be a site where the punk scene continues to thrive. Sponsored by Pabst Blue Ribbon, Commonwealth Press, Orange Amplification, among others, Fest attracts fans from all over the world to spend three days checking out music from smaller, lesser-known bands, to the headliners, which included Against Me!, Jawbreaker, and Stiff Little Fingers in 2019. Held each year in October around Halloween since 2002, Fest invites over 400 punk and punk-adjacent bands, both well-known and up-and-coming, to perform in bars and music venues in downtown Gainesville. Of this style of festival organization, Anthony (2014) writes:

By adopting South By Southwest's model of taking over already-existing venues and allowing attendees to move among them, [Fest] allows fans a chance to see bands in intimate environments, while bands are able to play to packed rooms full of enthusiastic, passionate people. In other words, it's nothing like seeing a tightly scheduled lineup play in a field, amphitheater, or park.

In an obvious contrast to a festival such as Coachella, where the music can at times be secondary to the social media, brand influencer, and fashion aspects of attendance, Fest's focus is on the music, and this priority is reflected through the diverse and continually changing lineup that performs each year.

Along with the day-long festival model, Fest also hosts pool parties, wrestling, and stand-up comedy—it is also not uncommon to find yourself drinking PBR in a parking lot while consuming slices of Five Star Pizza on your way to the next show. There is also Yoga for Punks for those not too hungover for downward dog and warrior poses. In contrast to Yoga for Punks, The Great Canadian Beer Purge takes place on the final night of Fest, where festival goers do exactly that—offer sacrifices of leftover beer to others before traveling home the next day. While Fest may not have the same name recognition as a festival such as Warped Tour, it continues to be a site of active participation within the contemporary punk scene where the allure of attending the festival is not just to see one's favorite bands play—it's also to maintain and establish new relationships and connections with other who share similar tastes, all while chugging beers and reminiscing of Fests past while standing in line to buy a hot dog from the guy selling them from a cart outside the venue.

Similar to Fest, Montreal, Canada's Pouzza Fest attracts a similar clientele and a familiar lineup. Held each year in May, Pouzza Fest (a portmanteau for poutine pizza), operates in the same format—a several-day event where bands play short sets in venues and outdoor spaces, all walking distance from one another. Venues are located within the heart of Montreal, Canada, and like Fest, Pouzza Fest offers fans the opportunity to participate in the local economy through art exhibits, yoga, and barbecues. Pouzza Grand Slam is also a large event held during the festival—described as a baseball game with the goal of "help[ing] networking between professionals, businesses, partners and medias, while playing ball games in a friendly setting" (Pouzza Grand Slam n.d.). While Pouzza Fest operates in these non-scene-specific spaces, the DIY spirit can be found in the ways the festival is organized. With an aversion to large sponsors and emphasis on smaller partnerships with Canada-based organizations and products, Pouzza Fest strives to maintain an approach to organizing and sponsoring the festival that attempts to avoid a corporate atmosphere. Hugo Mudie, cofounder of Pouzza Fest explains this approach, stating, "We bring more of an indie feel to the way festivalgoers consume . . . we want to be more of a niche thing than a big rock festival" (Beedham 2016). With the pervasiveness of large-scale music festivals drawing huge numbers of fans across the country and the social media and branding hype that goes hand-in-hand with some of these events, Fest and Pouzza Fest provide fans the "anti-festival" experience, where the focus remains largely on the music and the communities that are built through the networks of fans that attend these festivals year after year. Festivals such as these act as current sites where contemporary punk scenes can be observed, and as it will be evidenced in the chapters that follow, participants were not only actively involved in the attendance at these festivals, they were also largely influenced by their exposure to and awareness of Warped Tour, long before their present day involvement at smaller festivals such as Fest and Pouzza Fest.

THEORETICAL CONSIDERATIONS: SUBCULTURAL THEORY AND POSTSUBCULTURAL THEORY

Cultural scholars have long explored the perpetually changing elements of youth cultures. Since its beginnings following the end of World War II, the Birmingham School and Center for Contemporary Cultural Studies (CCCS) sought to explore the motivations behind youth participation within such subcultures. While their investigations played a significant role in promoting the serious inquiry into subcultural participation, style, and motivations for involvement, the CCCS conclusions on the influence of class and their all-or-nothing perspectives on participation led postsubcultural theorists to take issue with this line of thinking, asserting an overemphasis on the effect these formations had on British youth (Bennett 1999). More contemporary investigations into youth cultures supported the claims that participation within youth cultures was more subjectively defined. Among these claims, postsubcultural theorists argued that participation within these spaces was flexible and not bound by age, gender, or class. Consumption habits were not viewed as semiotic resistances to the status quo but were embraced as a way for participants to display their identities, in-group status, and understanding of subcultural capital. As it will be explored within the contemporary punk communities investigated here, participants recognize the influences of outside forces such as the media and popular culture on the ways in which their scenes operate both with and against these forces.

Subcultural Theory: The Birmingham School and the Center for Contemporary Cultural Studies

While this theoretical perspective is not the one used to inform the conclusions made in this study, it is important to recognize the historical significance of subcultural theory on the timeline of studies in youth cultures. The Birmingham School and the Center for Contemporary Cultural Studies (CCCS) sought to understand youth cultures in the United Kingdom following the end of World War II. The CCCS saw society's problematic relationship with youth cultures and sought to address the ways that youth cultures resisted "parent" cultures and the status quo. Influenced by neo-Marxist thought, CCCS theorists asserted that subcultures arose from an unbalanced relationship within hierarchical systems of power (Debies-Carl 2013; Torkelson 2010). For many UK youth cultures such as the Mods, Teds, and Punks, consumption was purposeful and deliberate, and consumption habits and style (or lack thereof) became defining characteristics of subcultural values, prevailing as a way for youth to subvert the status quo and resist against hegemonic norms that existed within society. Because of this, the CCCS emphasized the importance of "appropriation and reinterpretation" (Debies-Carl 2013, 116) of everyday objects stylized in the name of fashion, the intention of which was to shock and offend (Hebdige 1988). Fashion remained an important indicator of subcultural participation for the CCCS; it was viewed as vital for the establishment of one's identity, but only if the commodities served a particular purpose and conveyed a distinct message. Furthermore, CCCS theorists saw these deliberate fashion choices to be an act of "resistance to capitalist incorporation" (Weinzierl and Muggleton 2003, 8). Postsubcultural theorists later criticized these conclusions, recognizing the ways in which subcultural groupings do, in fact, consider their deliberate fashion choices, purchasing habits, and an acknowledgment of the capitalist economies in which they participate to all be indicators of involvement within a scene.

To this day, consumption is important to contemporary punk scenes, and consumption habits act as a way for members to display insider knowledge and contribute to their scenes (Andes 1998; Force 2009; Fox 1987; Thornton 1995). It is the outward demonstration of appearance and ownership of goods that are still some of the most determining characteristics of identity for postmodern youth culture theorists today. This practice, and the significance for those who participate in scenes today, will be explored further in chapter 5.

While subcultural theory and the CCCS conclusions serve their purpose in the understanding of youth cultures, later theorists objected to the strict parameters set forth by this school of thought. According to Hodkinson (2002), subcultural theorists paint youth culture in broad strokes, and because of this, this school of thought identifies these subcultural groupings as monolithic and uniform: "there is a tendency to imply, without detail or evidence, that subcultures somehow originated through large numbers of disparate individuals all simultaneously and spontaneously reacting in the same way to ascribed social conditions" (11). As it will be evidenced by those who participate in contemporary punk scenes today, participation and involvement take on a variety of forms, and are often impacted by external forces outside of the scene itself. Postsubcultural theory, which will be addressed in the following section, seeks to dispel some of the totalizing assumptions set forth by the CCCS. Criticisms of the CCCS resonate strongly within the postsubcultural research published in recent decades, and there is support for the perspective that subcultures are not only inclusive, but participation remains fluid and generally free of strict categorizations based on demographics such as class, fashion choices, or gender.

Postsubcultural Theory: Beyond Birmingham

Postsubcultural studies, as a response to the CCCS and Birmingham School, provides a postmodern, and arguably the most subjective, approach to the analysis of youth cultures. Many of the theory's applications are understood through subcultures of music and music scenes, with a great deal of ethnographic research conducted on various music-related youth cultures of the past two decades (Shildrick and MacDonald 2006). Developed in the 1990s and 2000s as a critique of the CCCS paradigm, postsubcultural studies sought to understand the subcultures that did not meet the subcultural qualifiers established by the CCCS in the 1970s (Bennett 2011). For postsubcultural theorists, youth culture was reframed as a "dynamic and participatory process" whose characteristics expanded well beyond the underlying assumptions of CCCS scholarship (Bennett 2011, 28).

Postsubcultural theorists saw several flaws in the assumptions laid out by the CCCS, especially when looking at the manifestation of youth cultures through categorizations other than class and gender. Through this postmodern approach, the perspectives of the CCCS are viewed as "outdated and inapplicable to the current postmodern condition of social life" and therefore, a prime objective of postsubcultural studies is to reconsider these groupings and highlight the varied and unique ways in which membership is defined (Debies-Carl 2013, 117). Rather than maintaining an objective outsider's approach to youth culture, ethnographic and qualitative accounts of current scenes (Debies-Carl 2015; Force 2009; Griffin 2012) explore the phenomenon firsthand, providing dynamic accounts of the adapting and flexible qualities of these cultures today.

As argued by the CCCS theorists, subcultures and youth cultures of the post-war era were considered to be "necessarily urban, male-centric, and class-based entities that were only presumed to be non-contradictory, fully bounded, and authentic groupings which resisted hegemonic culture" (Torkelson 2010, 260). In other words, youth cultures were viewed as totalizing, all-or-nothing phenomena, largely driven by gender and class. Furthermore, these groups were defined by their resistance to the status quo, which included institutions such as fashion and the media. Contemporary examples of subculture, on the other hand, are viewed as inclusive taste cultures where participants demonstrate membership through a variety of methods, with many participants identifying with the subculture well beyond teenage years. While the CCCS scholarship provides us an understanding of the prevalence of youth culture within society, their conclusions become problematic when looking more closely at subcultural groupings that do not fit within the limits of their theoretical assumptions. Approaches to postsubcultural theory have considered the ways in which rave communities (Thornton 1995; Ueno 2003), heavy metal scenes (Brown 2003), and online fan communities (Bury 2003; Robards and Bennett 2011) among other scenes and cultural groupings embody the postmodern assumptions on participation, presentation, and representation. To add to this literature, contemporary punk scenes are an example of a cultural grouping that does not abide by the CCCS-defining traits of gender, class, consumption habits and so on. Rather, these scenes embody subjective properties that include varying levels and styles of participation, consumption habits, and dedication to the scene—all of which will be analyzed through the data collected for this book.

Within the last two decades, postmodern scholarship has frequently visited punk rock as a site for investigation. Studies have examined a variety of elements associated with punk culture, including ageing and subcultural participation (Andes 1998; Bennett 2006; Davis 2006), style and identity (Force 2009; Sklar 2013), punk aesthetics (Prinz 2014), issues of authenticity (Haenfler 2004; Moore 2002; Moore 2004; Williams 2006), and the cooptation of punk signifiers and the complicated relationship with mainstream culture (Clark, 2003; Hannerz 2013; Heath and Potter 2004). While this is by no means an exhaustive list of empirical research conducted on punk rock and its musically adjacent scenes, it is important to pay credit to the vast body of literature that exists to help us understand the always-changing norms and values that exist within translocal punk scenes today.

SUBCULTURE, NEO-TRIBE, OR SCENE?
NAVIGATING THE TERMINOLOGY

As evidenced by the myriad terms postsubcultural theorists have posited in effort to define subcultural groupings in the postmodern age, identifying one catch-all term to describe these various communities and their characteristics has proven to be challenging, and there is much debate among scholars regarding how we are to define the population studied in this book. While definitions have sought to characterize subcultures and youth cultures since the Birmingham School, characteristics such as participation, consumption habits, fashion, and insider knowledge suggest that these groupings are nuanced and somewhat difficult to define.

Because today's punk rock community does not embody the class-based and strictly youth-oriented features put forth by the CCCS, use of the term "subculture" to describe this population is problematic and ineffective. Bennett (1999) argues that the term "subculture" has become a "convenient 'catch-all' term" used by scholars to describe any element of youth-related or countercultural practice (599). Throughout postsubcultural scholarship, terms such as "neotribes" (Bennett 1999; Heath 2004; Maffesoli 1996; Vorobjobas-Pinta 2018) and "scene" (Driver and Bennett 2015; Cohen 1995) are also used in effort to provide a better understanding of these groupings, wherein the free-flowing properties of participation, fashion, and insider knowledge are considered as important elements to the understanding of these populations.

For this book, I will proceed to use the postsubcultural term "scene" to describe the population investigated in my research. By categorizing these populations as "scenes," it is possible to consider the multifaceted worlds that make up the groups of participants in the United States who consider themselves active members through a variety of practices. Furthermore, it is the term that surfaced most often within my interviews—it was the term participants used when describing their own communities. To add, Harris (2000) offers a succinct and descriptive definition of "scene," one that appropriately reflects the highly subjective and individualized role participants play within their communities:

> The implication is that scenes include everything, from tight-knit local musical communities to isolated musicians and occasional fans, since all contribute to and feed off a larger space(s) of musical practice. Even the simple action of buying a CD means to become 'involved' in a scene, in however slight a way, by virtue of causing some sort of effect within it. One cannot make a rigid distinction between "active" and "passive" membership. It also follows that everything within a scene, and indeed scenes themselves, may exist within a number of other scenes. (25)

What is important to note here is that Harris's definition emphasizes the varied levels of commitment and understandings of in-group affiliation. Here, there is overlap between scenes—members can envision themselves as members of more than one scene, and contributions both large and small are considered legitimate. Similarly, this explanation of the term highlights the free-flowing, subjective quality of scene membership and participation. To add, Bennett (2004) acknowledges the innumerable ways one might participate within a scene, as the term itself "offers the possibility of examining musical life in its myriad forms, both production- and consumption-orientated, and the various, often locally specific ways in which these cross-cut each other" (226). As evidenced in Bennett's definition, both production and consumption are vital elements of scene involvement, and these elements are evident for the participants interviewed for this book. As a practice, DIY offers scenes the opportunity to create goods—this also means there is an abundance of goods to consume, and the goods themselves are often valued and acknowledged as integral components to keeping a scene alive, while acting as a way for participants to preserve autonomy through the means of production. Furthermore, the term also conveys an understanding that participation within a scene is not age-limited and that once a certain age is reached, involvement is no longer allowed. Rather, participants identify with their particular scenes well into adulthood (Davis 2012). While levels of participation and commitment may vary due to the pressing obligations of adulthood, it is evident that participants consider their involvement and participation within these scenes as a large indicator of a particular identity.

Lastly, the use of "scene" recognizes the translocal elements that turn these groupings from place-specific, insular practices, to ones that reflect and are inspired by others in places across the country (Kruse 1993). Of course, the use of social media and the internet provide scenes the opportunity to share their cultural knowledge with others not physically existing within the real-world spaces, and this ability to distribute content helps to transform these scenes into sites motivated by well-connected networks of members who share like-minded goals. With this in mind, the communities investigated in this book will be recognized as scenes, due to the emphasis on the production and consumption that occur within (Williams 2006), the understanding that participation is subjective and participant-specific, and the significant value placed on the various levels of commitment that are defined by participants themselves.

Translocal Scenes

While scenes operate and exist in a variety of spaces, recognizing the fluid relationship participants have with their scenes will help to further clarify the population that contributed to this study. According to Peterson and Bennett (2004), a translocal scene is one that is "connected with groups of kindred spirits many miles away" (8–9). In other words, scenes are not always location-based, fixed entities that are available only to those who are in the right place at the right time. Rather, translocal scenes operate through networks of communication which create "communities that transcend the need for face-to-face interaction as a necessary requirement for scene membership" (9). As explored in the Riot Grrrl scene investigated by Schilt (2004), practices such as zine publication and distribution allow members of this community to establish networks with others around the country, many of whom view their contributions on a spectrum of participation. Describing these varied characteristics of participation as "flexible self-definition," Schilt (2004) argues that the subjective nature of these behaviors results in "no manifesto or set rules for participation," representing a strong departure from the CCCS conclusions about subcultural participation, which argued for an all-or-nothing approach from its participants (120). To add, Glass (2012) argues that translocal scenes "are heavily networked, interlinked, and evolving" (697). With the help of social media and other forms of interpersonal communication, participants maintain interaction with one another through these platforms. While the physical presence of one's scene involvement may not occur on a day-to-day basis, frequent digital presence within a scene is a reality for many who interact with others to share information on scene-specific events and news.

As it will be evidenced here, participants interviewed for this book hail from a variety of locations (largely the New Jersey-New York-Philadelphia region), however, this did not inhibit participants from sharing similar experiences and comparable details of insider knowledge about their understanding of the punk scene today. Moreover, the subjective qualities of participation among this population will reconfirm Harris's (2000) and Schilt's (2004) assertions that today's contemporary punk scene reflects postsubcultural claims which suggest involvement within a scene does not need to be fixed by location, and can be determined by a spectrum of practices and commitments that range from simply purchasing merchandise to organizing large-scale events such as shows and festivals.

Contemporary Punk Scenes and a Broader Understanding of Commitment Today

A great deal of recent research has explored some of the smaller, local iterations of punk and punk-adjacent communities around the world, including anarcho-punk (Drissel 2016; Dunn 2012a; Stewart 2017), Christian hardcore punk (McDowell 2017, 2018), emo (Allooh, Rummell, and Levant 2013; Sklar and Donahue 2018; Red 2014; Trnka et al. 2018) among many others. While these studies identify specific, smaller subsections within punk rock worthy of investigation, I have opted to address my studied population using broader terminology that understands an involvement as fluid and subjective. For this book, I use the terms "contemporary punk scenes" and "contemporary punk communities" to broadly describe groupings of participants who identify themselves as active within a punk community today. The use of such broad terminology allows for the acknowledgement that participants may consider themselves part of many different, more specific spheres within punk rock, and this terminology also supports my argument that today's scenes overlap with other spheres of commitment, which may include mainstream culture, obligations to lifestyle duties, and other hobbies that may exist outside of one's participation in a particular punk scene. Furthermore, its usage allows for an acknowledgment of the current general trends and popular practices that exist in scenes today. Because of this, I do not identify a more specific categorization of those who currently participate within the punk scene (such as anarcho-punk, pop punk, hardcore, straight edge, skate punk, and so on). While the terms "contemporary punk scenes" and "contemporary punk communities" may be representative of a range of practices and ideologies, some commonalities exist when considering what comprises a contemporary punk scene today. This position supports Bennett's (1999) argument that "coherent subcultures are better understood as a series of temporal gatherings characterized by fluid boundaries and floating memberships" (660). Rather than identifying the studied population through parameters set by specific definitions based on timeframe, location, and rigid requirements for participation, I will address some of the larger commonalties and trends that exist between members who participate in these scenes today. In doing so, I acknowledge that there are likely to be other nuanced and scene-specific traits that are prevalent within these groupings, but in this instance, I have identified some of the more general traits that are used to define one's involvement within contemporary punk scenes in America.

First, participants discuss their introduction to punk rock as largely influenced by an exposure to popular culture, the internet, and mass media. At the turn of the new millennium, punk rock and its subgenres were ubiquitous—the music itself was found in movies, video games, and at big box stores and the mall. Second, today's scenes place a strong emphasis on inclusivity and diversity. While this is not a phenomenon new to punk rock, the evidence here suggests that diversity continues to be an issue worthy of improvement, and those within the contemporary punk scene view it to be an important issue worth addressing today.

With these considerations, it is clear that today's punk scenes recognize their existence as one site influenced many spheres of external impact. While self-sustainment is valued in the practice of DIY, there exists an understanding among participants that external forces will continue to influence some of the aspects of the process itself. For example, social media is widely used within scenes today as a means to share information about shows, new music, and to discuss relevant social issues. Facebook, Instagram, and Twitter do not exactly represent a rejection of the forces that exist within mainstream society today. Likewise, participants applauded the bands who found success in making music. In what might seem contradictory, there was little derision directed toward bands who signed to major record labels or agreed to allow their music to be used in an advertisement. Discussion of such cooptation resulted in an ambivalent response—many participants credited their introduction to punk rock to retail stores such as Hot Topic, and there was a larger acceptance that Hot Topic's cooptation of various punk elements did not impact a personal understanding of what it means to be involved in a contemporary punk rock scene today.

By referring to the population studied for this book as a "contemporary punk scene" or a "contemporary punk community," I am also addressing the translocal nature of scenes today. Scenes are not location-specific and identified by physical locality, but instead exist in spaces where participants can interact with others, regardless of location. Those within these communities interact with one another in physical and digital spaces in real-time, and localities such as music festivals and Facebook groups provide interactions that help to generate a sense of belonging for members, despite the existence of large distances between those involved.

METHODOLOGY AND STUDY POPULATION

The study of contemporary punk scenes is important for a number of reasons. First, it is important to analyze contemporary punk scenes because this investigation shines light on how scenes operate today—interviews conducted with current members within these scenes provide firsthand accounts of the values, norms, and practices that resonate with those who are involved. While punk rock had its fair share of time basking in the pop culture spotlight around the turn of the century, it has largely faded from the consciousness of mainstream audiences. With hip hop and rap, pop, and rock rounding out America's top three most consumed genres of music (Share of Total Music Album Consumption 2018), punk rock exists in more obscure circles today, with smaller communities of dedicated fans working to preserve communities that remain largely autonomous, yet connected with one another through social media and other interpersonal networks of communication.

Second, the study of today's scenes will help us understand ways in which both the scenes themselves and the surrounding literature have evolved over time. As addressed earlier, postsubcultural theory sought to rectify some of the CCCS conclusions regarding youth cultures. This study further adds to the growing body of literature on contemporary scenes around the world today. As it will be explored, today's scenes embody many of the traits set forth by postsubcultural theorists, however, there exists is a larger emphasis on a scene's ability to use such spaces in constructive and purposeful ways—a phenomenon that has not be largely addressed by postsubcultural theory thus far. With this, it is useful to consider the ways in which the advocacy of those who identify as current members of contemporary punk scenes add an additional component to the existing literature on postsubcultural music scenes at large.

While a significant number of studies in the field of qualitative research (both academic and non-academic) have investigated the various aspects of punk rock's origins and history, a small, but growing, body of literature focuses on the significance of punk culture's more recent variations, specifically within the communities that exist in the United States today. In order to contribute to this body of literature, a discourse analysis inspired by Gee's (2011) seven meaning-building tasks and Hodkinson's (2002) "Four Indicators of (Sub)Cultural Substance" were used to examine fourteen semi-structured in-depth interviews conducted with participants who identify themselves as active within their particular scenes today. Gee's seven meaning-building tasks help the researcher address important reoccurring theme and help to "construct what are . . . the relevant parts of the context in which something was said or written" (102).

Most participants interviewed for this study participated in scenes that exist on the East Coast (specifically in the New Jersey, New York, and Philadelphia regions), though one participant identified his location in California, and another in Minneapolis, Minnesota. In-person, phone, and Skype interviews were conducted between May 2015 and October 2015. In-person interviews were conducted at a variety of sites which included coffee shops, classrooms, and in a tour van outside of the Asbury Lanes in Asbury Park, New Jersey. Hodkinson's (2002) "Four Indicators of (Sub)Cultural Substance," which were developed as an element of an ethnographic study conducted on UK Goth subcultures in the 90s, made a valid case for characteristics applicable to the contemporary punk scene investigated here, and were included as a coding scheme to assist in identifying reoccurring themes throughout the data collected in these interviews. Using Gee's meaning-building tasks as a primary coding category and Hodkinson's Indicators as a supplemental coding category, a discourse analysis was conducted on the interviews, and repeated themes within the interviews were coded as significant. By using discourse analysis, it was possible to recognize "patterns or regularities" in the discourse provided by the participants, and to understand "discourse as a socially and culturally organized way of speaking in which certain functions are enacted" (Baxter and Babbie 2003, 355). As a methodological approach, discourse analysis allows the researcher to analyze an interview and target specific instances of important or recurring themes across the discourse that will help to make some larger conclusions about the data collected. For the sake of anonymity, participants' names have been changed and any identifying information has been removed.

The population for this research consists of participants who consider themselves to be fans or active participants of today's contemporary punk scenes. Due to travel restraints, in-depth interviews were conducted with bands and fans that are active today and located close to Philadelphia and New Jersey. Ages of participants ranged from mid-20s to mid-30s specifically, because, as it will show in the data, participants shared similar experiences with regards to their involvement and exposure to contemporary punk scenes today. Likewise, participants considered themselves as active members at the time of the interview, and the data emphasized the ways in which concert attendance, playing in a band, purchasing merchandise, finding new music, as well as other activities, were behaviors in which participants continued to partake.

Conducting semi-structured in-depth interviews provides a thorough insight into the ways in which this population evaluates the scene in which they participate, and how this evaluation relates to identity and current values within the scene. With the data collected from the in-depth interviews, the research questions were best addressed by analyzing the recurring themes and common patterns within the interviews. Initial recruitment of participants was done via word-of-mouth communication through contact with members in the community in the Philadelphia, New York, and New Jersey areas. Recruitment was also accomplished through social media on local punk-centric Facebook pages. The process of gathering participants was not random; participants were chosen purposefully based on their contribution to their scenes. Due to the nature of a smaller research population, a predetermined method of participant selection was necessary in order to find participants with considerable knowledge of today's punk scene.

Again, the results of this study provide us with firsthand information about the lived experience and gave us a more well-rounded understanding of the phenomena. As a result, it's possible to understand further the attitudes and opinions of those who are involved with the scene. Likewise, because we are looking at a community, it is important to look at the culturally shared meaning that participants derived from associating with the scene, and how these meanings translate from scene to scene. In other words, it is important to ask, how do participants in their respective scenes establish meaning and how does that meaning present itself through the shared experiences described in these interviews?

CONCLUSION

Contemporary punk communities can be understood as sites where fluid participation and commitment are evident. Speaking to postsubcultural theory's emphasis of this trait, those who participate within these scenes understand their participation to be expressed through a variety of practices and belief systems. Today's scenes are not fixed by location, but instead operate through networks of well-connected individuals who use their involvement online and in scene-specific spaces to connect with others. As it will be explored in the upcoming chapters, this involvement and these connections facilitate a sense of belonging and an establishment of a community for those who remain committed to their scenes. With an acknowledgement that external popular culture and social forces impact and influence scenes within contemporary punk rock, participants remain aware that their own involvement with punk rock was likely influenced by such societal formations, and as a result, participants do not view these entities as largely detrimental to their own autonomous efforts.

Chapter Two

A Community of Punks

"Punk" is a broad term and it casts a wide net around a variety of timelines, ideologies, and practices. Since punk's inception, scholars and fans alike have debated the nuances of the term, citing specific bands, events, and moments in time that may or may not be qualified as "punk." Are the Sex Pistols' 1978 American tour, and their subsequent break-up, "punk"? Is Hot Topic, a countercultural retail store found in nearly every mall across the country "punk"? Is Green Day performing at the twenty-fifth anniversary of the original Woodstock "punk"? Fans who grew up listening to punk in Southern California in the 80s may have an entirely different definition of the term than someone who learned of punk in the mid-90s through a music video aired on MTV. Location is also significant—if you grew up in a working-class neighborhood in the United Kingdom during punk's early years, how does your definition of punk and experience within differ from someone who lived in a middle-class suburb outside of Philadelphia in the early 2000s? How do we go about operationalizing a word with so many subjective associations not only in music, but in fashion, popular culture, location, and so on?

Attempts at defining a particular subcultural grouping and its characteristics can be challenging at best and inaccurate at worst. An issue that arises when talking about the contemporary punk scenes investigated in this book occurs when we attempt to conflate today's punk community with previous iterations of punk and punk-adjacent scenes. As addressed in chapter 1, my use of the term "contemporary punk scenes" helps to mitigate some of the issues that arise when definitions fail to categorize the current state of punk rock today. A broad term such as this seeks to contend with the overarching themes that exist within scenes today, while recognizing that one's participation may include involvement in several, more genre-specific scenes, such as hardcore, straight edge, or pop punk. Today's punk communities have their own set of characteristics, so it is important to acknowledge that what is investigated here are the experiences of current members within scenes who participate in their communities today, and were largely introduced to punk rock through highly publicized outlets such as MTV, *Rolling Stone*, the radio, and the internet. Likewise, participants grew up at a time when genres such as pop punk and emo were well-received by popular culture, which meant that awareness and exposure to such styles of music required little more than turning on a television or playing a video game. In addition, at the onset of the new millennium, these styles of music were large sources of revenue for various culture industries, which, according to Heath and Potter (2004), ultimately results in the cooptation of the signifiers with the greatest ability to be marketed, thus causing the normalization of what was once perceived as a radical and misunderstood genre of music. Because of this, access to the music and its commodified elements was accomplished with relative ease. Thanks to the internet, music videos, and stores such as Hot Topic, knowledge of punk during the 90s and early 2000s was not delegated as an interest strictly for "insiders," nor was it considered to lifestyle bound by location. If you lived in the suburbs or other locations far away from the urban epicenters of early punk rock in America, you still had access to the music through other avenues, including big-box stores and MTV. You did not need to be driving distance from the Los Angeles area or New York City in order to know what was relevant in punk rock at the time. While such a mainstream introduction facilitated participants' exposure to the music, scenes today operate at the grassroots level in an attempt to maintain autonomous ownership of the goods they create. Using their resources to promote awareness of social issues, with a focus on inclusion within their scenes, today's contemporary punk scenes function as spaces where community values and minimal gatekeeping prevail.

CONTEMPORARY PUNK ROCK AND THE MAINSTREAM

While various moments in punk rock's early history often navigated a complicated relationship with popular culture, many of today's punk scenes acknowledge the complex and inevitable connections between their scenes and what cultural studies scholars call the "mainstream" (Baker, Bennett, and Taylor 2013). Like many other words associated with the issues addressed in this book, what constitutes "mainstream" is often a contentious and never-ending topic of debate (Taylor 2014). As a concept, the mainstream is perceived as the "undefined, multi-purpose centre to the periphery, the 'other' to subcultural, alternative, underground, outside, folk and art cultures" (Huber 2013, 4). In other words, the idea of the mainstream acts as the hegemonic opposition to countercultural practice and can be positioned as a foe to anything considered even remotely countercultural. While punk is often posited as the antithesis to the mainstream, both parties exist within overlapping spheres, and without the existence of the mainstream, punk would fail to exist: "As much as participants in local punk scenes attempt to separate themselves from mainstream culture, or even seek to destroy it, their conceptualization of their social world is dependent on its existence" (Green 2018, 82). Because of this, the mainstream is often posited as an "us-versus-them" relationship between the larger forces that exist with popular culture and the scenes that wish to resist attention from popular culture (Thornton 1995, 92). As it relates to punk rock, the mainstream exists as an oppositional force to the grassroots practices and critical perceptions of hegemony that exist as some of the foundations of the genre. The mainstream, in a never-ending quest to popularize the countercultural, works to coopt and normalize various aspects of punk culture, which include the normalization of punk fashion, the music, and the punk lifestyle.

While scholars may argue that "the mainstream" is detrimental to the preservation of authenticity within a scene as it hinders a scene's ability to exist free of external influences and cooptation, I believe that the mainstream is neither bad nor good when discussing contemporary punk scenes. As it will be evidenced in my interviews, participants responded to the larger forces outside their scenes in a variety of ways, but there was always an understanding that these forces existed, for better or worse. In most cases, participants acknowledged the role that mainstream media outlets played in introducing them to the music they continue to enjoy today and did not consider the objectives of their own scenes as efforts to attack or destabilize these major hegemonic forces. Rather, the objectives of their scenes involved addressing some of the issues that result from what takes place within mainstream popular culture, such as issues of representation, sexism, homophobia, and so on. This approach gives scenes the opportunity to locally address issues within their communities, with an understanding that by working at the microlevel, these issues may be more easily corrected and rectified within these spaces. While DIY is used as a means to preserve autonomy within these scenes, no scene is truly self-sustaining, and assistance from some of these external forces is necessary in order to raise awareness, produce merchandise, and make connections. In the use of social media, for example, scenes use some of these platforms, such as Facebook and Instagram, to promote and raise awareness of their own scene-specific activities such as shows, flea markets, and festivals.

COLLECTIVE IDENTITIES AND THE TRAITS OF
CONTEMPORARY PUNK SCENES IN AMERICA

Aside from the obvious associations through my years of research, my participation within the Philadelphia and surrounding punk scenes continues to
remain consistent. Though I've never really played an instrument, and stage
fright would get the better of me if I thought my voice were good enough to
sing in a band, I have always felt strongly about the importance of showing
up. To me, showing up does not mean arriving to the show three hours late
just to see the headlining band. Showing up does not mean buying tickets to a
sold out show and flipping them for a higher price. Showing up means
contributing to your community in positive and constructive ways. It means
thinking critically about the structures within society that keep certain groups
of people from achieving their goals and working to actively tear down these
barriers. It means applying your talents and resources to better your community in whatever ways you deem appropriate.

While I was never one for team sports (or any sport for that matter),
sororities, or youth groups, I generally found punk rock to be a welcoming
place that echoed my own personal and political beliefs, and spoke to the
indifferent teenager that was once sent home early from softball practice for
giving the coach "attitude." Today, I may still be indifferent about a lot of
things (see: team sports), but I continue to go to shows and follow the goings
on within the punk scene today. It may not seem like much, but for punk
communities around the world, these small and seemingly inconsequential
actions make an impact, and contribute to the larger efforts that help scenes
exist long-term.

The purpose of this chapter is to identify some of the significant characteristics and values of the contemporary punk rock scenes in America, as told
by those who participate within these scenes today. As it will be evidenced
here, participants interviewed had strong personal associations with their
scenes. Various scene-related activities such as attending shows, working to
promote progressive change regarding important social issues that affect the
community, and finding connections with others, were continual themes that
prevailed within these interviews. Participation was viewed as an active
means by which participants could work with others to improve these spaces
and address the issues that have faced these communities for decades. Today,
scenes actively work to oust some long-held stereotypes regarding representation within the community and wish to see their scenes as sites of acceptance, diversity, and connection. While this is the goal, there is an understanding that scenes have a lot of work to do in order to become the progressive and inclusive communities they wish them to be.

In general, participants' understanding of subcultural affiliation within a
community is profoundly tied to identity (see: Hodkinson 2002; Wheaton

2000; Williams 2006). Music, in a variety of ways, also plays a large role in one's understanding of an identity. According to Hancock and Lorr (2013), "More than just products for consumption, musical practices, whether intentionally or unintentionally, are part of the constitution of self, social interaction, social settings, and social worlds" (323). In other words, the act of involving oneself within a music-centric community will have lasting impacts on one's perceptions of self and this participation will proceed to influence the ways in which that person interacts with others in these spaces. In the case of contemporary punk communities investigated for this book, fans admitted to having strong affiliations to their scenes, and viewed their participation to be a positive use of their time and money. Sklar and DeLong (2012), in their study of the relationship between punk's sartorial expressions and workplace expectations, argue that "subculture is one portion of [a punk's] existence and acknowledge it in terms of the salience of that identity measured against the other life identities" (286). Once again, it is important to acknowledge there is often an overlap between one's identity within a scene and one's obligations in other aspects of life—participation within a scene is often influenced by outside forces, relationships, and obligations. Because of this, elements such as scene-centric values, fashion statements, and personal beliefs on social issues, become values that exist within non-scene spaces and as a result, we see an intersection between one's understanding of self within these scenes and outside of these spaces as well.

A sense of community and the resulting affiliation to these groupings manifested themselves differently for all of those I interviewed for this book. While some participants played in bands and actively contributed to the commodity side of scene development, others viewed their efforts in combating social issues as a means by which to display commitment and involvement. Through these actions, participants believed their efforts to be positive contributions to a larger community. Although commitment itself was varied among participants, dedication to one's scene was viewed as a strong component of identity, which meant that it was not short-lived. For these participants, their participation and association with their scenes was not fleeting, nor was it a practice that only took place from time to time. Rather, scene affiliation and a sense of self were viewed in tandem, and the visible display of commitment and continued involvement within these communities were viewed as ways to outwardly express a dedication to their scenes.

While commodities and the lived experience of participation were important factors for long-term identification within a scene, the adherence to scene norms and values was also important for participants, who acknowledged that inclusiveness and diversity prevailed over exclusionary practices. As observed in Haenfler's (2006) investigation of straight edge communities, contemporary punk communities also largely rely on "a set of fundamental principles" (63) that help to delineate the norms and values for the group.

Among them, norms and values within today's punk scenes include the scene's willingness to make shows and other scene-specific spaces welcoming and inclusive to people from all backgrounds, and to actively speak out against other social issues that face scenes today. With the efforts to combat punk rock's stereotype of largely operating as a white and male-dominated space, contemporary punk communities use music, social media, and the platforms within these spaces to denounce issues of racism, sexism, homophobia, and encourage others to actively support such positions on these issues.

BELONGING IN TODAY'S PUNK COMMUNITY

As a community that prides itself on the tightknit aspects of interactions within these spaces, a sense of belonging prevailed as an important theme with those interviewed. Studies show that not only is a sense of belonging a basic human need (Maslow 1962), it is also an important factor in the construction of relationships with others (Hagerty et al. 1996). A sense of belonging prevails when one feels a connection with others (Rosenberg and McCullough 1981). While this understanding can manifest itself differently for each individual, belonging within a group prevailed as an important element to the larger understanding of scenes in America today. As related to today's punk scenes, a sense of belonging and the connections one feels to one's community, however these concepts are defined by those who participate, play an important role in participants' positive affiliations with these groups. Furthermore, participants' sense of community acted as a determining factor in their likelihood to engage with their scene in the future.

For Justin, participation within today's punk scene offered him the opportunity to self-reflect on particular values and norms that he wishes to see thrive within his scene. For many, scenes were viewed as sites where moral behavior prevailed, and an emphasis is placed on "doing the right thing" to others within your scenes. While Justin's example of falling in the mosh pit acts as a literal example of the proactive ways in which scene members act toward helping one another within these communities, it also represents a metaphorical example of the philosophical stance that many abide by today. Contemporary punk scenes are not viewed as sites of hostility and aggression toward others (though a rowdy mosh pit may look like that to the untrained eye). Rather, they operate as spaces where, ideally, participants respect one another and look out for each other, as supporting one another is commonplace:

> Just in this community there's so much . . . no one really gives a shit about the menial things that are really getting in your way, and this gets celebrated more in general alternative culture I think . . . but I think if you're like, if you're involved in that kind of mentality, you can really focus on your core mentality

and who you are as a person, your character, your morals. You can spend more time emphasizing on that than the minutiae of life. And I think that's an opportunity you get with punk rock. Not that you can't have it elsewhere, but it's easier here because you can really think about your morals, and it's probably instilled in you pretty early on to be like. . . . I mean what's the first thing a lot of us learned at shows was like "this place is nuts, this is mayhem, there's people running around in a circle trying to kill each other." But as soon as someone falls over, stop doing it and pick them up and make sure they're okay. And I feel like that's been accelerated through the punk scene better than in other subcultures and in culture in general where you are looking out for the wellbeing of other people and celebrating diversity and celebrating independence and I think that punk rock is going to have to keep being a pioneer in that arena.

Here, we see an example of an unspoken rule that is followed within many scenes today. Those who participate within these communities understand that there are certain explicit and implicit rules that one must abide by in order to be perceived as an insider. In the instance here, the unspoken rule of picking someone up when they fall in a mosh pit at a show demonstrates an example of a universal ethical practice that can be viewed at punk shows throughout the scene today. Andrew echoed Justin's thoughts on the ways that contemporary punk scenes operated as sites where proactive outlooks on the world were encouraged and accepted, which prevailed as an important factor for his continued participation within his scene as well. While specific examples are not explicitly discussed here, there is an understanding that a specific set of values exists within scenes today, and any participation within these scenes assumes that your values reflect those of the community at large:

> To be honest most of the friends that I have are through punk. People that I met in high school, we were similar, we were friends but we weren't really that similar in a lot of ways, and I think when you listen to punk you already sort of have, a lot of times you have a certain set of ideals, and thoughts about how the world should be and how we should treat each other, so you already kind of have this base-level understanding with most other people who listen to punk.

These ways of knowing are understood throughout the contemporary punk community and are reinforced through the behaviors and belief systems that are shared among members. Because they are oftentimes reflected in the commodities and music that are produced, values of kindness and acceptance are important examples of the ways in which these scenes emphasize the significance of following these rules. With a small-town upbringing, Andrew addressed the ways in which involvement in a contemporary punk scene has afforded him the opportunity to meet a diverse group of people. Furthermore, Andrew acknowledged the importance in creating a space with values that reflect an openness and acceptance for anyone interested in participating within the scene:

> [Punk has] definitely opened me up to a lot more experiences that I would have never even considered and a lot of friendships that I would have never even considered when I was younger, and I think part of that too comes from that I grew up in a fairly homogenous, white area, and then when you get involved with punk, you meet people who aren't necessarily exactly the same as you, and that's a really good thing. And that's really my goal, is to take as many people in as . . . you know, punk is supposed to be the refuge of the outcasts, well I want that. I want them to come to my shows, I want them to come talk to me, and I want to be their friends because I'm an outcast too and I understand what it's like, and I want them to feel like they belong to something, and to feel the way that I feel about my punk community. So that's what I want. I want everybody to stand in a circle holding hands and be friends.

While the prospect of a community of hand-holding sounds a bit utopian and romanticized, the idea of inclusivity resonated strongly throughout my conversations, and presented itself as one of the most significant issues that faces the contemporary punk scene today. Members of various scenes across the country recognized the importance of providing all-inclusive spaces for those who wish to participate and hoped to see their scenes work toward making such spaces inclusive, rather than exclusive. While punk rock and its subgenres are often characterized by their propensity to attract disproportionate numbers of straight, white men, today's scenes are actively trying to dispel these stereotypes by providing space (either on stage or elsewhere) for those with different backgrounds and experiences. Further discussion of this activity will be discussed later in this chapter.

Like Andrew, Anthony expressed thoughts on the welcoming qualities of his scene, stating that his perception of his scene allowed anyone to join, regardless of certain financial or social limitations that may exclude one from joining a particular group. In this instance, punk was viewed as a sanctuary for outsiders who feel they are unable to fit in elsewhere. Furthermore, Anthony viewed his own involvement in a scene as a means to self-betterment and acceptance:

> Come with us if you don't belong. If you don't feel like you belong, we will accept you. If you don't feel like you can fit in. If you don't have enough money to fit in. I think money has a lot to do with it. I think that social status has a lot to do with it. I think that people who are well-off generally feel connected to other people and they have connections like families have connections. I think that it's basically saying, if you are broken, come with us. Come here because we will accept you. And that's where people who are broken can come to connect. To try to be better . . . which I feel inherently everyone wants to feel part of a community. That's how we evolved as human

beings. People don't take that kind of stuff into account. We've lived in communities for thousands of years, and now we live in a society that's very
broken up.

For Justin, Andrew, and Anthony, a resonating theme in their thoughts on
their communities included low barriers to entry. Scenes were not viewed as
places of exclusion or privilege, and those interested in participating did not
have to "prove" themselves in order to participate. Rather than operating
through such exclusionary tactics and practices, participants within contemporary punk scenes preferred these spaces to be open and accessible to those
with like-minded views on social issues and problems that face their scenes
at large. Furthermore, there was little, if any, discussion of authenticity—a
term that often surfaces when discussing punk rock and ways of knowing a
scene. While determining authenticity in punk can take on many forms, punk
scholars have debated the nuances of how membership in a scene can appear
authentic or inauthentic to those who participate. While factors of authenticity within punk rock may be determined by one's levels of dedication (Andes
1998), range of insider knowledge (Force 2009), comparisons to others
(Widdicombe and Wooffitt 1990), and through the cooptation of signifiers by
the mainstream (Clark 2003), those who I spoke to did not advocate for such
qualifiers when describing who can and cannot participate in their scenes.
What we see here is evidence of a preference to avoid exclusionary and
gatekeeping practices, and the belief that scenes should be open and inclusive
spaces that reflect the views and values of those within the scene itself.
Emily, whose experience served as an example of the ways contemporary
scenes operate as welcoming spaces, shared thoughts on her immediate attraction to the inclusive nature of the punk scene itself: "One of the first
things I picked up on is, even though at first I wasn't into all the music I was
hearing, but the camaraderie and the vibes that you get at these punk shows
are . . . it's hard to describe, but it's just like a big gathering of people and
everyone is mostly happy to be there, and it's hard to not like being there."

When asked why a sense of community within her punk scene is important, Emily provided further insight into her opinion on the subject, identifying the hard work that is involved in maintaining the particular scene in
which she participates. Here, she identified the ways in which an outsider
status became an insider status—the once-labeled outcasts now saw their
involvement within their scenes as a way to maintain an insider status and to
interact with others who possibly shared a similar experience growing up.
The early influence of punk rock was also identified as significant, as an
early introduction to a particular genre of music can have lasting impacts on
the listener's tastes and identity as that person grows up:

[Punk rock] is people who genuinely work really hard and are just average guys and gals and they work their asses and they work and they play and it's something that they're super passionate about and it's mostly just genuinely great people, and a lot of the same type of upbringings you've had. Everyone's came from different areas, but most people who are in the punk scene were the odd kids out growing up and all that stuff, and that's definitely brought the group together in general from that scene. . . . Instead of joining a sorority I would rather go to punk shows, I would rather be a part of a community that cares about each other, cares about the music, cares about other people, there's such a good . . . there's just really good people, I feel like I'm repeating myself, really great people and people really care about each other.

Additionally, the welcoming nature of the contemporary punk community was also identified as a positive feature of her scene, and Emily saw these characteristics to be admirable and preferable to those of other groups that involve similar levels of association, dedication, and commitment. In this description, Emily's scene is not portrayed as a site where participants are only participating for selfish or self-motivated reasons. Rather, any involvement within these scenes was viewed as a proactive effort by participants to improve their communities at large.

Elizabeth's introduction to her local punk scene was not a positive experience at the start. Prioritizing a sense of belonging over the music itself, Elizabeth described the ways that the connections made within these spaces were more important than the music that was performed. Eventually, this relationship developed into an interest in the music along with the community aspects, but what is evidenced here is the power of belongingness and feeling part of a community, even if the style of music is not preferred:

I had a very brief phase with local Christian hardcore, which I hated, but my friend's boyfriend was in a band and it was just a way to be in someone's scene. And it wasn't mine, but it was a step. And so I felt like I went from, kind of being like "I'm going to these shows and I'm not really enjoying them, but I like these people and I like what this is" to now being like "I'm going to see this band, I'm friends with everyone in the band," and stuff like that, and just knowing a lot more people, like I said how I used to go to shows alone, and now it's like you know half the people there, even if you don't know them, you've seen them before.

For Elizabeth, her involvement within her scene eventually evolved into one where important connections and relationships developed within these spaces, and her understanding of this affiliation became a long-term membership with a contemporary punk scene. What is significant here, however, is the understanding that a sense of belonging prevailed over the music itself. While Elizabeth expressed disinterest in Christian hardcore, the community-focused efforts of the scene were recognized and understood as significant.

Those within today's scenes view their involvement as a contributing element of an understanding of an identity. Belonging is crucial—for many, it is not enough to enjoy the music or attend a show every once in a while. Rather, participants expressed a valued investment in making connections with others in their scenes and prioritizing their involvement. While these factors remained important as they contribute to an understanding identity, making today's scenes accessible and inclusive can be viewed as a way today's members use their efforts to ensure that anyone, regardless of insider knowledge or connections to others, can participate if they choose to do so.

INCLUSION AND REPRESENTATION WITHIN TODAY'S PUNK SCENES

Thirty years ago, there was still some romance in the figure of the punk singer, glistening with sweat, seizing the microphone to scream truth to power. But now that figure seems like another iteration of a loathed archetype—the all-purpose angry white guy—and in his yelling there's less incitement than entitlement. (Piepenbring 2017)

In a 2018 study conducted by Pitchfork, 70 percent of all musicians performing at the twenty-three largest American music festivals were male (Mitchum and Garcia-Olano 2018). More specifically, Warped Tour, America's largest punk-centric music festival, included only six bands with women out of eighty-four bands and musicians featured in their lineup in 2018 (Knopper 2018). While the concept of inclusivity is not a trait unique to the contemporary punk scene, its importance was emphasized heavily in the interviews conducted. Furthermore, a strong emphasis was placed on keeping scenes open and available for those who wish to participate, regardless of gender, race, socioeconomic status, and so on. While no scene is perfect, these practices represent a strong departure from the claims that punk rock communities continue to be largely dominated by straight white men—today, participants actively attempt to dispel these notions through practices that include diversifying lineups at large festivals and local shows, and promoting voices and perspectives that do not always endorse the opinions of a straight white male majority.

As the discussion of inclusivity was a reoccurring theme evident across several interviews, Hodkinson's (2002) indicator of subcultural substance, consistent distinctiveness, is appropriate to reference here. Defined as "the existence of a set of shared tastes and values which is distinctive from those of other groups and reasonably consistent, from one participant to the next, one place to the next and one year to the next," consistent distinctiveness acknowledges the translocal properties of beliefs and values within today's punk community (30). As observed in participants' discussions of identity,

we saw a continued trend on an emphasis of community and the low barriers
to entry into these communities. Again, Haenfler's (2006) "fundamental set
of principles" (63) is apparent here—there is a consensus among those interviewed that scenes should operate as sites of inclusion, and when rules toward promoting inclusion are not followed, these infractions should be acknowledged and corrected by others within the scene. While scenes may
exist in locations across the country, values and norms often transcend these
distances, and issues of inclusion and representation have become important
issues for various punk scenes today. Today's scenes often embody a progressive, liberal stance on social issues, and use their music, social media,
and public platforms as avenues by which to express their thoughts on how
they hope to see their scenes improve.

An example of the values represented in today's scenes can be found in
my interview with Justin, who discussed the ways in which today's scenes
have made strides in terms of diversity and inclusion, however, there is still
more progress to be made. Here, he argued for a proactive approach to
stopping undesirable behavior at a show:

> If someone's being shitty, like if your friend is being shitty to a girl, if he's
> harassing a girl, that's not okay, call him out, tell him to stop doing that. At
> shows now if you see girls being harassed, they'll leave, and I've seen a lot of
> really upsetting posts online and tweets about minorities whether they be
> women, or gay, or not white, or whatever it comes down to, they still don't feel
> included, and that breaks my heart. . . . So the fact that I usually feel included
> in the punk scene, just like everyone else, that's all I really want at the end of
> the day. The fact that it still can't be provided for everyone upsets me, so I
> think that the future of punk has to be more inclusive actively.

Furthermore, Justin addressed the importance of sharing scene values and
practices with others when these rules are not followed. By continuing to
reinforce an inclusive atmosphere and acting upon behavior that isolates or
discourages others from participating, members within a scene can, at the
very least, attempt to eliminate actions of others that do not align with the
values of the scene.

Elizabeth expressed similar sentiments with regard to inclusion within the
scene. For Elizabeth, it was important for her scene to practice open-minded
behavior, and she encourages others to actively pursue music that does not fit
punk's traditionally male-dominated, heterosexual stereotype. She supports
the repeated assumption that punk continues to be very much a "white guy"
subculture:

> I just think it's really important to keep it this open space where people can
> come and feel welcome and feel as good as I do, and make sure that we are
> trying to be inclusive as a group. You know, I see a lot of discussions in punk

communities about "oh, punk has always been this way and we're trying to open it up more" and I feel like, one thing I try to do is definitely try to make it a more inclusive space. Like I try to see more bands that have more women in them, more LGBT bands when they're around and stuff like that because I think that it's really opening up, it's not just a bunch of white guys and I think it's really important to keep bringing everyone in and seeking out bands that maybe aren't in the spotlight but are out there.

The active pursuit of alternative perspectives demonstrates efforts on behalf of the community to dispel previous assumptions about what punk rock was, and its stereotypical portrayals throughout history. Later in the interview, the issue of punk's white male demographics arose, and Elizabeth appeared optimistic, recognizing the ways that the scene has certainly made progress in addressing these issues, though there is still more progress to make:

Right now, I've literally been at shows and someone's like "oh, there's the one black kid at the show," and I would like it to not be like that, I would like anyone of any race or any sexuality or whatever to be able to go to a venue and feel like they're accepted and safe. I think that there's definitely still a lot of "bro punks" that aren't super nice and I would like less of those people. But I feel like it'll get there, I feel like at its heart, punk is really just about supporting each other and fighting for what's right, so I think it will get there.

She continued this thought further in the interview by emphasizing the importance of actively pursuing alternative music, and using resources to search for bands with women or queer members, for instance: "So, I really think that part of it is the consumer-based, so the fans, you know—if you can't find any bands with women in them, or any bands with people of color in them, or any bands with LGBT people, find them. We have the internet, look for them. Usually they'll tell you 'queer punk band from Philly' or 'queer punk band from Brooklyn' because that's a thing."

In these examples, we can see the ways that scene members are actively trying to make their scenes more diverse and inclusive. By addressing rule-breaking behavior and using resources to explore new perspectives, today's contemporary punk scenes operate as sites where active involvement is used to transform the outdated assumptions regarding punk's narrow demographics. An acknowledgment of inappropriate behavior, for example, demonstrates evidence of a proactive approach to advancing these scenes, with the hope of progressing toward a reputation of inclusiveness and diversity.

Greg echoed a similar sentiment regarding the prevalence and importance of other voices within his scene. Acknowledging the shift in perspectives, Greg recognized the ways that the increase in diversity has helped to dilute the narrowed perspectives sometimes found within punk rock. Furthermore, the rise in interest in these voices demonstrates the ideological shifts that are occurring throughout contemporary punk scenes today:

> I was talking to a friend of mine, and I was like "what's big now? Indie rock was big for so long, what's the big thing in music now?" And he's like "not guys—[it's] women and queer people." And that's what's interesting now, so I think [the scene] is moving there, I don't think it'll ever totally move there, but I really like that people have more of a voice and there's less of the white male perspective. You get to hear other voices.

Both Elizabeth's and Greg's thoughts on inclusive practices and the prevalence of this issue throughout these interviews reinforce the translocal characteristics that are prevalent in today's punk communities. Through the use of streaming platforms and social media, fans can access music featuring a range of voices, perspectives, and ideologies from places near and far. With this immediate access, the punk message is not confined strictly to one location or another. Furthermore, these ideologies may be varied and based on individual experience and belief, but it is evident that the specific values of various scenes are similar to those in other scenes, and these perspectives are often evident in the music that is produced and distributed throughout these communities.

Along with the emphasis placed on inclusion and diversity, the larger topic of social awareness was a prevalent one within the community today, and issues range from the importance of diversity within the scene to gender equality among participants. In Joe's interview, he discussed how participation in his scene opened his eyes to issues that need advocacy. For Joe, the music and scene itself brought awareness to certain issues and motivated him to remain conscious of the various concerns facing the community today:

> A lot of people are very outspoken about feminism, and a lot of social issues in general. I find that great. I know there's people speaking out about assault at show, or in general in the scene, calling people out about it, and I don't think I would be quite as aware about any of these things if I had not found punk. I probably would have gone through my life like "this shit doesn't happen," when it really does and it's a scary thing.

When asked about the issues facing today's punk subculture, Joe provided insight into what the scene considers important today, noting the ways that the scene's major concerns have changed with time. Like others interviewed for this book, Joe acknowledged the positive aspects of progress within his scene, but was hesitant to say that all of these issues are on their way to being resolved:

> In general, feminism is probably the biggest . . . it's like the frontrunner right now for the scene. In the past I think it might have been more like anti-

government, or like anti-The Man. Now it's like "well, in order to really tackle that, we kind of have to get past a lot of other areas that we have against each other." There's a lot of hang-ups that we have that we may not even realized, that we've learned, and if we really want to like, tackle bigger problems, we have to not quarrel among ourselves. So, I feel like it's a good gateway to get involved in that.

To conclude this thought, Joe advocated for more action on behalf of the members in his community and described the concept of slacktivism an example of a well-intentioned, but essentially ineffective, effort to change larger social issues often stop after sharing information about said issue on social media. The term "slacktivism," is defined as the use of social media to bring about awareness to an issue while asking little physical action on behalf of the participant (Lane and Dal Cin 2018). While Joe expressed optimism in his scene's ability to raise awareness on certain issues, he admits the passive nature of social media allows for these issues to fail to be appropriately addressed:

> In some ways I do think it becomes easy for people to say they're a part of something and then not do anything. But I don't think that's quite as common. I think people like to become complacent, but I feel like a lot of people do care, I think people do want to make a change, but you know, it does require a little more than Facebook activism. And that's the thing, I see people really passionate about a lot of things, but I don't see people saying "hey, volunteer time at this organization" or maybe donate whatever you can to this. I would really like to see people do that. I'm guilty myself, I really should be more involved, but I see punk sort of as a catalyst for that. And if people can take what they've learned from that, and maybe think about how they spend their money, or think about how their actions affect other people, then I think it's done its job.

Alex also confirmed the ways that today's scenes continue to focus on social issues and inequality. Punk rock has always had a history of challenging the status quo, and evidence of this conviction can be viewed in contemporary examples of bands who use their platforms for speak out against social issues and inequalities. With the help of social media, scenes today can disseminate information and raise awareness in ways that were not possible decades ago. In this example, Alex references Rock Against Bush, a movement initiated by NOFX front man Fat Mike (aka Mike Burkett) in 2004, which aimed to use music and other efforts to speak out against the re-election of President George W. Bush. The Rock Against Bush campaign was comprised of a cross-country tour, two CD compilations featuring nearly sixty bands, and Punk Voter, a grassroots effort designed to register voters and raise awareness at festivals and concerts (Punk Voter n.d.). According to

Alex, these efforts, and those that preceded Rock Against Bush, were integral in furthering the politically minded message of punk rock:

> Punk rock started as a reaction to the homogenization of rock and roll music, and major labels, and all that stuff, and also a reaction to the political climate at that time, both in the UK and eventually in the US. The Dead Kennedys were writing songs about Ronald Reagan, and through the 90s where we had Rock Against Bush, and all this other stuff. It's still happening, and now there's even more because of the internet and social media. There's even more of this stuff being talked about that we know about than in previous generations, and that's what I love about it so much.

Here, we see evidence of a shift in objective: while the CCCS argued that subcultures used their countercultural position as an oppositional statement to the presence of the status quo, today's punk scenes seek to actively address concerns that may immediately affect their communities—in this case, issues of feminism. While punk rock has always included an element of civic action and resistance against various hegemonic forces, encouraging action on behalf of participants to change an issue that directly affects a scene demonstrates the need for this practice to continue. By tackling scene-related issues through music and discussion, rather than through hypothetical antiestablishment rhetoric, contemporary punk communities can advocate for change through specific courses of action.

As it is observed here, contemporary punk communities actively work to make their scenes more accessible and inclusive, and participants rely on the efforts of both casual and devoted fans, current musicians, and social media to raise awareness for the issues that directly face these scenes. In addition, it is important for participants to follow both the explicit and implicit rules within these scenes, and an understanding of these rules acts as a way for this insider knowledge to delineate between those who value the norms of the scene, versus those who do not. Participants stressed the importance of a low barrier to entry into their scenes for those who may be interested. Furthermore, scenes acted as sites of change—an emphasis is placed on actively, not passively, advocating for these changes to take place, as it is commonplace for these issues to be addressed head-on as they are witnessed in real time. While social media is viewed as a positive method by which to advocate for these changes, there is hope that slacktivism will transform into actively working to address some of the issues that face scenes today.

PUNK FESTIVALS AND THEIR
EFFORTS TO MAKE AN IMPACT

While it is possible to observe the ways in which contemporary punk bands and musicians use their platforms to speak out about issues facing their scenes and the world at large, punk-centric music festivals have prevailed as a viable opportunity where these messages can be amplified to larger audiences. Both Fest and Pouzza Fest serve as contemporary examples of punk-centric music festivals that are representative of the norms and values prevalent in punk scenes today.

In an effort to give back to the Gainesville, Florida, community at large, Fest 18 has partnered with several nonprofit organizations that exemplify the community-driven ethos of the festival at large. With these organizations' focus to address social change, environmental issues, and homelessness, it is evident that contemporary punk communities actively consider their impact on the populations that exist nearby. While Fest provides links on their website for participants to learn more, the festival also takes on initiatives to allow festival attendees to give back to those in need. For example, $1 from every Fest ticket goes to some of these organizations, and attendees are encouraged to donate hygiene items and learn more about how they can reduce their carbon footprint as they travel to the festival by plane or by car (Social Impact n.d.). By providing these resources to fans on their website, Fest actively uses their platform as a means to raise awareness of the issues that impact the communities that exist around Gainesville. Feed the Scene also has a large presence at Fest. A volunteer-run organization based out of Baltimore, Feed the Scene is described as a "Band and Breakfast" that offers traveling bands and musicians a meal and a free place to stay while on tour (About Feed the Scene n.d.). In the past, Feed the Scene has provided festival attendees with Fest safety kits—small bags that contain some of the necessary items to survive a three-day festival, including ear plugs, condoms, and reusable water bottles.

In a similar fashion to Fest, Pouzza Fest offers fans another site by which community building and progressive stances are welcomed and expected. In addition to their emphasis on collaborating with smaller, Canada-based sponsors, Pouzza Fest explicitly outlines the expectations making the festival an "all-inclusive space." By their definition, Pouzza Fest operates as a "safe space" with a commitment "to providing a welcoming and safe environment for everyone, regardless of gender, sexual orientation, disability, gender identity, age, race, or religion" (Safe Space n.d.). Similarly, Pouzza Fest underscores the importance of a welcoming atmosphere where those in attendance should be expected to behave in a manner that reflects the inclusive nature of the festival. Failure to abide by these policies could result in consequences, which include warnings or expulsion from the festival. Through this example, we can see one of the ways in which rule-following prevails as significant within scenes today—if a rule is broken by a festival attendee, there are repercussions. This practice speaks to the active ways in which scenes today address the problems that threaten a scene's ability to function as a place for everyone.

With these examples, it is evident that contemporary punk scenes are taking a proactive stance toward ameliorating the issues that face their communities today. These practices speak to the heart of DIY (do-it-yourself) practice that will be explored in more detail in chapter 4, as they are enterprises that are taken on by those within the community and by those who have an active hand in organizing these festivals. Fans are encouraged to participate in these endeavors as well. In promoting the egalitarian practice of DIY through these altruistic endeavors, Fest and Pouzza Fest emphasize the effect and impact of grassroots organization—even a $1 donation to an organization can make a lasting impact for those who need it. By partnering with organizations that reflect the values of their festivals, Fest and Pouzza Fest can use their platforms to raise further awareness of issues that directly face contemporary punk communities today and the world at large. Similarly, by asking participants to actively participate by donating products or acknowledging the festival's definition of a safe space, festivals such as these can reify the norms and values that participants feel strongly about within their scenes. What is observed here is not a scene that wishes their communities to be exclusionary, stagnant, or static—rather those within these communities see their positions within these spaces as a means by which change and progress can take place.

ADVOCATING FOR REPRESENTATION IN SCENES TODAY

Addressing the issue of representation in punk provided insightful reflection on what steps the community is actively taking to tackle these issues. For many punk scenes, association with diverse bands and musicians allows for greater acceptance and awareness of perspectives throughout these scenes. One way for this goal to be achieved is by recognizing the viewpoints and behaviors that do not align with the ethos that is evident in today's scenes. For Jamie, members of today's scenes need to be open-minded and supportive of a variety of progressive perspectives, and to abandon the outdated, racist ideologies and aggressive behaviors that have plagued punk rock in the past. Here, they reference the controversial behaviors of Joe Queer and Ben Weasel, which will be explained further following the quotation:

> I do hope that progress does come to the forefront. You realize, if you're going to claim to be a progressive music movement that includes everyone, then you need to really actually make good on that. You want to make this inclusive to

women; you have to listen to women about what they need to feel included. You need to listen to people of color . . . so I hope that keeps happening, I hope that it becomes where it's not even a question of this is punk—not that asshole up on stage making jokes about kids being shot by cops. Not that guy. That's not who we're about, that's not what we're about. And that's the thing . . . you'll see these dudes on stage making racist jokes or whatever. And you have Joe Queer saying "yeah, Darren Wilson's a great guy, he should shoot more black kids." And crap like that. And people—and I even liked The Queers. You have the Screeching Weasel controversy, and stuff like that. And people still try to defend them and you can't. . . . Sometimes you can separate those things, and sometimes you can't. . . . Joe Queer, Ben Weasel, they're still around, there are kids that still look up to those guys and that's what scares me. That's where I get concerned about it. . . . Punk is a lot safer and more inclusive than it used to be, but there's still such a long way to go.

In 2011, Screeching Weasel front man Ben Weasel (aka Ben Foster) was accused of punching two women who came up on stage during the band's performance at South by Southwest (SXSW), a festival held annually in Austin, Texas (Aswad 2011). Following the incident and the resulting public backlash, four of the five members of the band quit, and in a personal statement published by PunkNews.org, the members stated "the un-calculated act put forth by Ben Foster leading up to and including the violence that erupted on stage is seen by the band as shameful and embarrassing" (Aubin 2011). Following the event, Joe Queer (aka Joe King) of The Queers publicly supported Ben Weasel's actions in a detailed Facebook post, stating "The whole Weasel thing is way out of hand," suggesting people support Weasel despite the reaction and public outcry (King 2018). In 2014, Joe Queer made another controversial statement by thanking Darren Wilson, the police officer acquitted of shooting Michael Brown in Ferguson, Missouri, in 2014, calling Wilson "a man of peace in a world of mayhem" (King 2014).

By actively denouncing these controversial actions and statements, contemporary punk scenes work to condemn these types of behaviors and belief systems. While incidents like these stand out as reminders of the work that needs to continue to be done in order to move toward a more accepting space, examples of progressive ideologies can be found in the music of a multitude of artists that operate today. When asked about the bands that take an active role in advocating for progress, several participants cited a range of bands whose messages offer perspectives of open-mindedness and dissent toward perspectives reflected in the actions and statements of musicians such as Ben Weasel and Joe Queer. Again, we see evidence of progress with regards to diversity and representation, but Elizabeth provided some thoughts on the progress that needs to be made:

I would say that I feel that Plow [United] does a good job, I feel like they have a lot of friends, and especially because they're friends with Mikey Erg, who's in like every band, and knows everybody, so anywhere Mikey Erg is, you're automatically tied to a million other bands. And definitely Chumped and Cayetana. Gaslight [Anthem] does a really bad job with it. The only female they've been associated with in years is Laura Jane Grace from Against Me!, which is great, but also it's like, she's not your token female.

Jamie also discussed the importance of highlighting bands with different perspectives, and cited similar bands as Elizabeth as having relevant, contemporary messages within their music: "Even now I'm even more into like prioritizing listening to bands with female members, people of color, and queer folks because those are perspectives that are my perspectives and I relate to that a lot more. Recently I've really been into Worriers and RVIVR has been one of my favorite bands for a long time." They continued to discuss the importance of accepting and supporting bands that do not fit the stereotypical persona of a punk band, referring to punk's image as "white dude bro central":

> That's the thing—I can see a lot of, there's been a big surge in female-fronted bands or bands with women in them, people of color . . . there's been a bigger surge than there has been in the past, and that's amazing and it's because I've been focusing more of my time and energy on that, I see a lot of that and that's a great feeling, but then I go to a show where it's going to be white dude bro central, and I'm like "oh wait, yeah . . . the rest of us."

While Jamie acknowledged punk's progress within recent years, the notion that there was progress to be made was also addressed. They continued their discussion of whiteness and the importance of inclusion by acknowledging the fact that the importance of inclusion sometimes goes unnoticed by certain populations within the scene:

> When it rocks your world that the system has always been great for you, and wonderful for you, and people want to change it and you don't want it to change because it's great for you. That's the thing, even . . . there are some bands with people of color, but I wish that was . . . most of my friends that are people of color, they're not involved in punk and they're like "you're weird" . . . it's sometimes you feel weird being in a room full of people, of aggressive white people, when you're a person of color.

Though it is a commonly agreed upon statement that punk rock is now a scene working toward acceptance and diversity, it is up to those within these scenes to actively make such hypotheticals become a reality. While many bands have spoken out against issues of racism or sexism over the years, and there have always existed examples of progressive and inclusive spaces within punk throughout the decades, those without such a platform can also participate by supporting these viewpoints through attending shows or buying merchandise from artists who echo such ideologies. Elizabeth discussed this in her interview and encouraged others to seek out these perspectives:

> I just think it's really important to keep it this open space where people can come and feel welcome and feel as good as I do, and make sure that we are trying to be inclusive as a group. You know, I see a lot of discussions in punk communities about "oh, punk has always been this way and we're trying to open it up more" and I feel like, one thing I try to do is definitely try to make it a more inclusive space. Like I try to see more bands that have more women in them, more LGBT bands when they're around and stuff like that because I think that it's really opening up, it's not just a bunch of white guys and I think it's really important to keep bringing everyone in and seeking out bands that maybe aren't in the spotlight but are out there.

In addition, Elizabeth considered her own definition of punk today. While this definition does include some of the traditional characteristics of punk rock, such as a valued sense of independence and autonomy, there is also the sense that today's scenes work in unison to ensure that their own efforts are for the greater good, not just for the few at the top:

> I think in general, [punk is] about standing up for yourself and going after what you want, while at the same time not pushing other people down. I feel the older stereotypes are like "well, punk is violent" and whatever, but I really think now there's just a lot of support within the community and I think that a lot of people consider punk [as] using what you have to fight for what you believe in and bring other people up with you.

As evidenced here, participants within these scenes understand the importance of making their scenes inclusive for all groups of people. There is an understanding, however, that this change will not happen organically—those within these communities have to actively take part in addressing these issues, while also seeking out viewpoints from underrepresented or marginalized voices within the scene. By actively seeking out these viewpoints and supporting such bands through the purchase of merchandise and attendance at shows, scene members view their contributions a way to diversify the demographics of the scenes themselves. While these practices are common, and there continues to be enthusiasm for actively supporting bands and musicians that promote social awareness and equality in their message, there exists an understanding that more work needs to be done to ensure that these spaces continue to operate in ways that continue to uphold these progressive norms.

What to Do about "White Dude Punk"

In an article written in *The Guardian*, Kai (2014) writes: "If there is one ethos of punk, and especially DIY (Do It Yourself) punk, it is that the punk world is for everybody: anyone can sing, anyone can play, anyone can listen, anyone can participate. But in reality, men run the scene, men are the scene, and men always have been and probably always will be at the center of the scene." The matters of race and gender are contentious topics that have existed at the forefront of punk since its heyday, and scenes today have worked tirelessly to confront these problems and address them in constructive ways with the hopes of turning their scenes into sites where diversity becomes the norm.

In a subculture that is stereotypically assumed to be represented by a white, male majority, emphasis was placed on actively working to make punk scenes representative of people from all backgrounds. Further emphasis was placed on making punk scenes accessible to voices that represent perspectives that are not those of straight, white men. For many, contemporary punk scenes were viewed as spaces where these voices could be encouraged and promoted. While there was an understanding that there will always be an element of a white male demographic within contemporary punk rock and in punk rock's future as well, participants were enthusiastic to explore ways for other experiences to be shared, both on the stage and elsewhere. In their own efforts, participants expressed the ways that they actively seek out alternative voices, by attending shows or listening to music where diversity exists. The issue of the white, male majority within the contemporary punk scene was a topic mentioned frequently throughout the interviews, and participants recognize the traditional demographic as one that occupies a large space within the scene. Many acknowledged this positionality but have also pointed out that definite changes have been made within their scenes to encourage participants from all backgrounds to feel a part of these scenes. In his own experiences with his scene, Justin observed the ways that it has become more diverse, which can be viewed as a reflection of the ways in which society has progressed in general: "There's going to be the white dude punk over here and that's still going to exist always, but I feel like as society is progressing, punk is progressing in an even more outward way than it would have been even five years ago, which is awesome. It's really exciting." Justin's thoughts on inclusion suggested that the community needs to do more than just talk about this problem, but instead act upon the issues of representation within the scene. Furthermore, there is a growing movement toward advocacy for alternative viewpoints and experiences within these scenes:

> I think that there have been steps in this community, that have been moving a lot faster—than society as a whole, America as a whole—toward tolerance and acceptance of gay people and trans, and queer, and equal rights for women.

And I think that it still has to do a lot better, it's still a white male boy's club in many ways and I do think that the highest percentage ever is recognizing that, and that's awesome, but it's one thing to post that on your Tumblr and another thing to actually make that practice real.

Once again, we see the ways that participants acknowledge an issue exists within their scenes, and while steps are taken to combat these issues, there is an understanding that more needs to be done to tackle them. Again, this example demonstrates the existence of slacktivism within scenes today, and the acknowledgment of such reaffirms the need for participants to do more than use social media to advocate for change. While social media can be a valuable platform through which to raise awareness and start conversations about the issues that face those within these communities, active steps within scene-specific spaces need to be encouraged if change is to occur.

Like Justin, Andrew also observed the ways that contemporary punk communities have made progress with regards to representation and inclusion, but women and people of color are still underrepresented within the community, and for those who do not see themselves in the bands they listen to, it can be difficult to find the messages within punk rock to be relatable or welcoming:

> I see more women and I see more people of color at shows and that makes me really happy, but I also am of the viewpoint that you know every single show that I play there's not, if I don't see at least a couple of those people on stage, then I'm not going to be happy, but the other thing about it too is the more non-white men you get onto a stage, more people will see that. . . . It's really hard to say I'm gonna be the woman singer in this hardcore band if you've never seen a hardcore band with a woman singer in it.

In his interview, Andrew mentioned the significance of the progress made within these scenes, but also spoke of the response that this inclusion has encouraged, specifically citing what is referred to as the "PC Police," with PC being short for political correctness. Those who may not agree with the influx of diversity and other voices within the scene may sometimes refer to those who welcome it as the "PC Police." This response is often cited by opposers as a push back to the idea that punk should have a more constructive purpose than to shock and offend. The term itself is often used by those who see these diverse voices as a threat to the dominant position held by one particular group for an extended time. Andrew mentioned this growing issue in his conversation with me, and recognized the growing dichotomy that exists between generations of punks who see their involvement within these scenes, and the message of punk itself, very differently:

There's certainly a backlash against that going on right now. There's a lot of "oh you know PC Police are telling me what I have to do," but there's also a lot of us who are like "no, we want these people to be a part of our community, and we're just asking that you be nice." I definitely think there's tons of room for improvement, there's always gonna be room for improvement, no matter what. I definitely think we're getting a lot better.

Andrew continued to address the issue of punk's persisting stereotype as an offensive and crass style of music and expressed hope that with enough pushback from participants who wish to see their scenes as progressive and welcoming, that the future of punk rock will be less focused on shock and offense, and more focused on inclusion and representation:

I know a lot of people are getting down right now, are annoyed, or pissed off right now because of PC punks and feminists and stuff like that, and the only thing I would want to say is to kind of step back and think about the community as a whole. When you say certain words, they may not bother you, they may not upset you. When you make certain jokes, they may not bother you or make you feel bad or whatever, but like I said, punk is supposed to be this scene where we accept everybody, we accept all the outcasts and we bring them in with us. And a lot of times those outcasts have had those words and those jokes used against them to make them feel bad. So, all we're saying when we say, "don't use racial slurs or certain words for gay people or whatever," all we're saying is we want other people to feel accepted in our scene too.

Andrew's thoughts represent an interesting point of ideological departure within today's punk scenes. Recently, punk scenes around the world have found themselves at the crossroads between two outspoken groups with different perspectives on what punk's message should be. On one hand, punk's modus operandi, for as long as it has existed, was to shock and offend with its wild antics, crass lyrics, and juvenile behavior. Evidence exists in all aspects of punk culture—in the fashion, lyrics, stage antics, and elsewhere. Lecaro (2017) writes:

On one side, you have the old-school punk crowd: men (and some women) who argue that the purpose of punk rock is to upset the status quo, to cross the line, to fuck shit up and take no prisoners doing so. They say punk is about anything but being safe, and to police it so it's digestible to all is to strip it of its very essence. One should go to a punk rock show prepared for anything, even—and maybe especially—to hear offensive content. On the other side, you have feminists and younger music fans who feel that punk music and shows have long been breeding grounds for misogyny and hate against people of color, the LGBTQ community and other marginalized groups.

In my observations, younger generations of punks view their scenes as communities for everyone, and those within these scenes actively take steps to dispel the outdated and exclusionary ideologies that wildly contradict the beliefs of those who feel punk rock should be offensive and crass. Rather than using their platforms to insult, offend, or offer unconstructive commentary on the social issues that face the scene and the world at large, contemporary punk scenes want to see their platforms be used in a productive and progressive manner. An incident at the 2017 Warped Tour highlighted the disparity in these dichotomous ideologies during the Dickies' set at their Denver, Colorado, stop. Known for their raunchy and offensive stage banter, Dickies' front man Leonard Grave Phillips reacted with "a string of misogynistic obscenities" to a sign held by an attendee in the crowd, which read "Teen girls deserve respect, not gross jokes from disgusting old men! Punk shouldn't be predatory!" (Rife 2017). The incident brought to light two varying perspectives of what is considered punk today. Is it the continued argument that punk should shock and offend, and if it does, then it has successfully delivered its message? Or has punk progressed from this stance to represent a wholly different message, one that encourages scenes to be safe and free of unconstructive humor that at its core, is meant to exclude and alienate? Shawna Potter, organizer of Safer Spaces, an advocacy group that addresses the issues of harassment and discrimination in public places, saw the Dickies incident at the Warped Tour as an evident example of the paradigm shift that is taking place in punk rock today. In an article written for *Vice*, Potter viewed Phillips's tirade as emblematic of some of the larger issues facing America in light of the Trump era:

> Maybe "fucking shit up" at all costs was exciting and revolutionary in the conservative Reagan era. But now we have Trump, and while the white dudes in power are still conservative, they also look just like the Dickies or Phillips. Bands like this often look and sound exactly like the people they're rallying against—those who hate women and queers and people of color and refugees and people with physical and mental challenges, and they sound just like them to us. (2017)

The dichotomy between these camps represents a continuing struggle between two vastly different ideologies on punk's message. While some communities continue to support the belief that punk exists strictly to shock and offend, the evidence provided here demonstrates that we are seeing significant effort in many scenes toward transitioning these spaces from sites where offense and hostility are the norm, to spaces where minorities and underrepresented populations have equal representation. In the interviews conducted for this study, all participants took the position that punk rock scenes should be open and accessible and the idea that punk needs to be a site for shock and offense appeared as outdated and inaccurate. Another example of this can be found in speaking with Adam, who recognized the ways the

scene has become more accessible for minorities and women. He also encouraged others to actively partake in making scenes inclusive:

> I would hope [the punk scene] to be even more diverse than it is now. Being
> Hispanic in the punk community, even though no one really recognizes that, is
> sometimes hard, because the fact that nobody recognizes it is like "oh you're
> that white punk kid." No, not really. And not that I can see the problems
> inherent firsthand because I do kind of have that privilege of people thinking
> I'm a white dude, but I think there's a lot of energy to put toward making it fair
> and accessible and fun for everyone, where right now, it's not. But it's getting
> there and I'm hoping that's where it goes. I think the most important thing to
> do . . . I guess just encourage people to get into it, rather than keeping people
> out of it. if a bunch of girls come to your show, don't make them feel unwel-
> comed. If a bunch of people of color come to your show, talk to them. Don't
> let these weird groups start forming where it looks like a high school dance.
> You're all friends, you're all there for the same thing.

Elizabeth also expressed the importance of inclusionary practice and observed the ways in which her scene actively works to make the space available for everyone. We see evidence of the ways that punk rock has continued
to exist as rowdy and aggressive, but there is also evidence that practices are
transforming in ways that encourage constructive use of these platforms to
address the issues that face the scene today:

> Now it's still the shows I really love, like a small show that's really rowdy.
> Just the physical aspect of it and just the community too. I don't think that
> punk music, like I know that there's definitely things that are more common in
> punk, like the angst and the political stuff like that, but that's also in a lot of
> other types of music, but I think that the communities found at shows is really
> what I love, like I love that if you fall down in the pit, a bunch of dudes pick
> you up and stuff like that and I think that it was really dominated by a lot of
> men for a long time and now there's a lot more girls in the scene, a lot more
> diversity. A lot of places still aren't super diverse, but I think it's definitely
> getting there. And there are a lot of people really using their voices to bring a
> lot important stuff to the forefront, which I guess is always been the case. I just
> think that now there's a lot of room to focus on stuff for everybody.

While shows and music are two prominent locations where these issues
are addressed, it is important to recognize the ways scene-related media can
also provide a platform to not only confront the issues that face the scene, but
to also be an avenue by which these issues can reach intended audiences. In
discussion of his blog, Alex, the editor of a website that addresses various
issues within contemporary punk rock, stressed the importance of having
diverse writers to provide a range of perspectives on issues related to the
community: "I want more women to write for the site and people of color to
write for the site, trans people, queer people, anybody. Those people don't

write about stuff on the Internet, they have other stuff to worry about. Meanwhile, every white guy with a beard wants to write about this band they like, which is also great, but everybody else is doing that, and I want to do other stuff."

Alex emphasized the need to employ not only diverse writers, but also a range of topics on the website that address some of the pressing issues, such as racism or sexism, that confront scenes today. In this example, we see the ways that DIY efforts can work to bring these issues to the forefront. If those who have such platforms are willing to share these spaces with a variety of viewpoints, then it is possible to continue the conversation surrounding the topics that these communities wish to address.

While contemporary punk rock continues to be a site of diverging opinions and conflicting thoughts on its core message, it is evident that those within these scenes are actively working to transform their scenes into inclusive and diverse spaces where acceptance is paramount. Though it is understood that there is still much work to be done regarding these issues, participants view their scenes optimistically—while incidents such as Leonard Graves Phillips's response at the Warped Tour continue to be the exception rather than the norm, it yet again prevails as a contemporary example of the diverging opinions on the current status of punk. Participants are largely enthusiastic and willing to open their scenes to people from all walks of life, and actively seek out the opportunities to explore content related to experiences within the punk scene that do not reflect the "white dude punk" that has existed within punk for decades.

MAKING CONNECTIONS WITHIN THE PUNK SCENE

As with any community, making connections and finding similarities among participants is celebrated and these connections operate as an important element that helps a community survive. The shared experience of attending similar shows, listening to similar bands, and interacting with one another through various social networks provide participants with similar experiences that resonate positively, and prove to be a prevailing reason for why participants continue to partake within their scenes today. For Emily, her involvement within her punk scene served to be more than just an involvement with the music itself—the connections made served as a means of relating to others and sharing experiences related to mental health:

It's a support system that you have as far as if you just need a safe place to go, or someone to talk to, or understand that there are other people struggling with the same things or feelings. A lot of punk music comes from experiencing similar situations or having those different sorts of feelings and it's important to acknowledge that and understand that almost everyone experiences stuff like heartbreak and getting really frustrated and driving around at 3 am. It's a normal thing and it's just stuff people go through that the music talks about.

Like Emily, Joe placed great value in the friendships made within his scenes and described the way these friendships are representative of the larger community itself. Having used Facebook groups and social media to meet many of the people with whom he attended shows, Joe viewed his involvement as way to meet similarly minded people who share in the same values:

> It was always really hard for me to meet friends, so once I saw an opportunity, I was like, alright I'm going with it, so I went on Facebook, I met people outside of shows, or at shows, at bars, and it's just like, it's a really welcoming community. I feel incredibly comfortable around these people. In fact, more so than people I've known since elementary school. It's sort of weird to say because you wouldn't expect that, or maybe you would because that's . . . I'm into the same kind of music, the same kind of values, I guess it would make sense that I would feel comfortable around these kinds of people. It's really comforting being around people that are not only welcoming and friendly, but also care about the same sort of social values that I have.

Furthermore, Joe emphasized his own thoughts on how those within today's punk scenes work to use this space productively and constructively to improve the scene itself and communities that exist around these locations:

> That people want to better the scene, that people are aware, that people want to be progressive. And I can't speak for other scenes, but I don't know if that's even on the table. I don't know if that's a thing. I feel like punk has always been about, since the beginning, not that I was there, but historically that's what it's been about, and I feel proud to be a part of that. . . . That's always why I liked punk. . . . I felt like being involved in it, I felt like I was involved in something a little bit bigger than myself.

The notion that punk scenes were an accessible place where friendships could be made remained prevalent throughout my interviews, and participants stressed the ways their involvement within their scenes helped to assist in making these connections. Greg shared his own experiences with these connections, and thought that the underground or grassroots traits of contemporary punk rock helped with this process:

> I posted the other day it's really cool that your friends can make records that you can listen to. My friends do that and they're good and I like them and it's really good that you have that alternative to, I dunno, Mumford and Sons or Kings of Leon or just mainstream bands. It's cool that you have an alternative and it's cool that you can look locally and just really see what your peers and what your friends are doing, like that's so special to me.

The act of experiencing the music created by one's friends is a valued trait within scenes today. More value is placed in the music that is created in the bands that exist within scenes today than the music that is created and manufactured by well-known bands on major record labels. Likewise, musicians within today's scenes are also viewed as fans of the music, rather than as musicians who perform for the purpose of entertaining and making a profit (Haenfler, 2006). Participants see the music as a means to connect with others and expressed an interest in sharing music with those who are most likely to understand the level of commitment and dedication that is involved in creating music through DIY practice.

The desire to bond with others prevailed as a common theme throughout my interviews. Participation within the scene was not viewed as a solitary act—interactions with others and remaining up-to-date on the goings on within the scene were significant elements of an understanding of one's involvement. For Adam, attending music festivals such as Fest served as a way to make such connections, or to reestablish connections with scene members who live elsewhere:

> If I go [to Fest] this year it will be my fourth. I guess in a way it's a good vacation. And it's a vacation spending time doing what I'd rather be doing instead of being on a beach. I like being around people. Initially it was a real bonding experience for some new friends that I had who had just kind of asked me to go. I went and it was awesome I really made some solid friendships. Every time I go, I tend to meet new people, either if they're from New Jersey and I probably should've known them already. I do meet new people and a lot of times I go because I feel like I'm missing out if I don't.

Attending Fest satisfied a social need to interact with others, but going to Fest also reinforced Adam's understanding of his involvement within the scene—as a relatively popular punk-centric music festival, attendance (and repeat attendance) at Fest becomes a way for members within these translocal scenes to maintain their relationships and connections in a local setting. While participants may not live near one another, a lot of scene maintenance relies on interactions via virtual spaces such as Facebook, Fest operates as a physical location where these social media connections can exist in real time.

The physical space of a show acts as a location for participants to connect with others based on similar music tastes and an understanding of perceived likeminded values. Aaron and Jimmy both expressed similar sentiments regarding attending shows and making friends. The camaraderie that exists within these spaces prevailed as an integral component of furthering these connections and establishing a greater presence for the scene. For Aaron, attending shows became a valuable way to meet others and learn about new music: "I mean, you're screaming along to it but you go to a show, you can get into it, there are just people that are into it and it feel like you're actually part of this group with the songs. That's a lot of fun, you wind up finding a lot of good friends and actually end up turning you onto new music. Yeah, you see a lot more bands, you make a lot of good friends and hear good music at the same time." In a similar fashion, Jimmy shared a comparable anecdote, commenting on the fact that most friendships were the result of attending shows in Southern California: "Most of the shows that I go to are all, I mean, I'm pretty much half way between San Diego and LA, so the scene is really cool. . . . I've made a lot of friends just going to shows. . . . I don't know that's just how I've made a bunch of my friends now."

Emily's experiences within the punk scene reflected similar qualities with the experiences shared by both Aaron and Jimmy, but for Emily, the community aspect was prioritized over the music. Here, she explains how the sense of camaraderie was an attractive characteristic of the scene itself:

> I started going to local punk shows on Long Island. I became friends with a few people who are in different bands on Long Island, and really into the punk scene, and I became, I don't know, I really enjoyed going and one of the first things I picked up on is even though at first I wasn't super into all the music I was hearing, but the camaraderie and the vibes that you get at these punk shows are . . . it's hard to describe, but it's just like a big gathering of people and everyone is mostly happy to be there, and they just I don't know, it's just really hard to get, it's hard to not like being there.

For those who are active within the scene today, current and frequent participation within the scene was an effective way to interact with others and make connections. Though the music itself is an important aspect of any punk scene, there exists a strong emphasis on the value of the relationships that evolve from interacting with others who also display shared similar tastes in music. While scene maintenance often relies on the translocal connections that are facilitated by social media, physical spaces such as shows and festivals operate as locations where these connections can be reinforced, reignited, or established. Because of this, we can understand the ways that scenes today rely on both virtual and physical spaces to ensure that these connections continue to be made.

CONCLUSION

In referring to what she calls a "contradictory emphasis on inclusivity," McCormack's (2017) study of mountain biking communities addresses the fundamental issue that arises when a particular subculture demonstrates a desire for inclusivity rather than exclusivity (345). While it may seem obvious that a scene might revert to exclusionary tactics in order to maintain an inclusive reputation, this is not the case. Like the mountain biking communities, introducing new members to the norms and values within the punk scene prevailed over gatekeeping practices meant to narrow down only the most committed. Instead of making access to a scene difficult, time-consuming, or labor intensive, we see examples of the ways that scene members in today's punk community choose to portray their scenes as open, easily accessible, and welcoming to everyone. Unlike Emily's example of joining a sorority, which includes a time-consuming process where members are expected to demonstrate their commitment in ways deemed acceptable by sorority insiders, today's scenes see their spaces as sites where commitment can be self-determined and free of similar types of gatekeeping. Instead, older members use their insider status as a way to introduce newer members to the norms and values of the scene—by explaining these practices, older participants reiterate the expected behaviors within these spaces, and work to distance their scenes from the exclusionary practices that perpetuate assumptions that today's scenes are insular and unreceptive to outsiders.

The values and norms of today's scene resonated strongly throughout these interviews. Inclusiveness and diversity were priorities for today's scenes, and participants shared their own experiences in exploring new music and voices that represent the true demographics of the scene today. There continues to exist a contingent of participants who wish to see punk rock as a site where shock and offense continue to be the norm. This has created a discrepancy within the scenes themselves, and in some cases, this divergence in perspective appears to be generational, with younger generations of participants hoping to see their scenes become more inclusive, rather than exclusive.

Furthermore, participants describe their communities in ways that emphasized the people within. Insider status was not framed as a commodity-driven element, and participants did not express their thoughts on identity as they related to the commodities that are produced within the scene. While commodity consumption and production are important elements of scene maintenance, participants did not underscore the ownership of goods as a priority in their conceptualizations of identity. Rather, the interactions with others within the scene and one's understanding of dedication to the scene prevailed as reoccurring themes throughout these interviews. Included in this discussion is the understanding of punk fashion—while closely associated to specific sartorial elements, clothing and fashion statements were not topics that arose during my interviews. Participants did not express the importance of an insider's "uniform," nor did they mention brands or companies that were considered appropriate within today's scenes (Force 2009, 299). More exploratory research on the connections between fashion and today's scenes would provide further insight into the prevalence and importance (or lack thereof) of style and fashion choices within these communities today.

In an exploration of the windsurfing subculture Wheaton (2000) observed a similar trend with regards to low barriers to entry within a subculture—while commodity ownership was an important factor in involvement within windsurfing communities, dedication and commitment predominated as the more valued elements, and a continued involvement and allegiance within the windsurfing community was viewed as a more significant means by which identity is constructed. As evidenced here, commitment was valued by the individual, but also by the group—attending shows, staying connected with others, and remaining up to date with current events all worked to reinforce one's status as an insider within the scene. While these connections were highly valued, the involvement of newcomers was also important, and evidence here suggests that one's insider status should be used as a means to introduce new participants to the norms and values of the scene. Today's scenes place a great deal of value on the connections made with others within the scene—scenes continually work to encourage new members to take part, and value is placed on the relationships that are formed as a result of the networks that exist with these spaces.

Chapter Three

The Contemporary Punk Rock Identity

*Early Introductions, Values, and
a Dedication to the Scene*

Though I no longer sport my fringe-adorned homemade t-shirts to shows and I've put aside the studded Dead Kennedys denim jacket, punk rock continues to be an enormous part of my identity. While my continued research on contemporary punk scenes remains a large element of my life, an active involvement and participation within the scene continue to occupy a great deal of my time and money. The days of making mix CDs are over, but I always have time to listen to a new album or playlist featuring music from the punk bands that continue to play today. Though not uncommon, I believe it is important to stay up to date with the with bands I listen to, and to make sure that I catch their set if they come through town—I would not be who I am if I were not traveling down to Gainesville each year for Fest or waiting up until midnight to hear Bad Religion's latest album on Spotify. While my fashion sense these days looks less like your stereotypical punk and more like an aging fan of grunge who only owns gray t-shirts and flannel, my beliefs on social issues, inclusion, and questioning the status quo remain as dogged as ever. I do not doubt that my own early introduction to punk rock, and an immediate attraction to the socially conscious messages from bands such as Anti-Flag and Rise Against during the George W. Bush era, have impacted my continued interest in politics and social issues. As it will be explored, many participants shared similar stories to mine, and their stories underscored the importance of the ways in which an appreciation for punk rock assisted in instilling a sense of awareness and compassion for others within their scenes and beyond.

For many participants, practices such as these were viewed as defining elements of a greater sense of self—punk rock is not a hobby relegated to a weekend here or there when nothing else is going on. Instead, punk rock in all its forms existed in every facet of their lives—it was listened to at work, discussed in text messages and on social media, emblazoned on a denim jacket or backpack. Social issues such as racism and sexism were important issues to address, both inside and outside of the punk scene. Shows were attended frequently, and buying merchandise and albums continue to be methods by which participants demonstrate their awareness of subcultural capital. These signifiers and the displaying of them served as ways to make connections with others—seeing someone at a bar wearing a t-shirt of a band you recognize, for example, might compel you to approach that person to discuss their latest album.

For those involved in a scene, participation and involvement directly influence perceptions of identity (Glass 2012; Traber 2012). As explored by postsubcultural theorists, identity and its relation to scene involvement is multifaceted, abstract, and varies based on a range of factors. According to Hodkinson (2002), identity, as it relates to one's involvement with a subculture, refers to "the extent to which participants hold a perception that they are involved in a distinct cultural grouping and share feelings of identity with one another" (30–31). In other words, subcultures allow participants to see themselves as part of a community, and this community establishes itself based on the norms and values that are represented by members in the group. For postsubcultural theorists, the notion of age-based involvement in a scene is challenged. Rather than "aging out" of a particular scene, participants often remain committed to their involvement, though, the practices may differ as adult responsibilities become a priority (Bennett 2006; Hodkinson 2013).

Notions of belonging are crucial to the construction of identity, as Hodkinson emphasizes the importance of a "sense of affiliation with perceived insiders" and "feelings of distinction from those regarded as outsiders" (31). In-group association can present itself in a variety of ways and can include actively participating in a scene's social media presence, attending shows, or interacting with others within the scene. When these practices become commonplace and routine, they often become one way in which a participant acknowledges the influence of these activities on an understanding of one's identity. Largely subjective and abstract, these practices, as well as others, can be considered elements of in-group association by those who partake in these behaviors. As it was a prominent topic discussed in my interviews, the various manifestations of participants' understandings of in-group affiliation will be explored in the interview content provided in this chapter.

Postsubcultural theory suggests that a member's participation within a scene is not static but is instead just one component of the larger understanding of self. Therefore, levels of participation vary from fan to fan and involvement can manifest itself in a variety of ways. For instance, certain obligations such as homeownership or children might hinder a fan from attending weeknight shows, but that individual will find other ways to contribute, which might include buying merchandise or remaining active on a local punk scene's Facebook page. Either way, these forms of participation are viewed as legitimate indicators of participation within the community. Fashion, often cited as an important element of a punk identity and frequently the most obvious indicator of one's affiliation with a particular scene, can sometimes fall victim to the pressing obligations one encounters as an adult (Hodkinson 2011; Sklar and DeLong 2012). While the denim jackets and Doc Martens may be put away in lieu of collared shirts and ties, postsubcultural thought asserts that a punk identity can still exist despite a diminishment of external sartorial indicators. As a result, it is important to recognize the subjective and varied ways that a participant may envision himself or herself within their scene.

Subcultural capital refers to Thornton's (1995) subcultural perspective of Bourdieu's (1984) cultural capital. Subcultural capital represents the commodities and taken-for-granted ways of knowing that are inherent within a subculture, and an understanding of the ways these indicators operate within these spaces helps to confer one's insider status within a particular subculture or scene. According to Moore (2010), subcultural capital "is a scarce commodity that can only belong to a minority" (138). Once these experiences and goods become coopted by popular culture, however, they cease to exist as part of the countercultural experience (Heath and Potter 2004). The highly popular Ramones Presidential seal t-shirt is an example of how a subcultural-specific item, once coopted by fashion retailers such as Forever 21, JCPenney, and Nordstrom—who sells their distressed version of the shirt for a cool $200—becomes a good that does little to help the wearer demonstrate particular ways of subcultural knowing (R13 Ramones Print Tee, n.d.). Once the shirt is worn by Paris Hilton, Lindsay Lohan, and Demi Lovato, what insider status can the shirt truly possess?

While many elements of punk culture have made the transition to popular culture and can be observed on fashion runways and in shopping malls across the country, there will always be examples of products and ways of knowing that continue to persist as credible within these scenes. In the case of contemporary punk, examples of subcultural capital include tangible objects such as the ownership of rare albums or lived experiences such as attending a small basement show of a band that now performs in larger venues. Merchandise including t-shirts, hoodies, beer cozies, and show posters prevail as contemporary examples of commodities that are popular within scenes today. While the subject of band merchandise and the ownership of goods will be explored in chapter 5, it is relevant to note here that participants saw the ownership of these items as part of a larger understanding of their own identities and helped to assist in a participants' understanding of considering themselves insiders within their respective scenes.

Taking an early interest in a subculture is not an uncommon phenomenon for teenagers. In their studies of youth cultures, one of the strongest conclusions made by the CCCS asserted that participation in a subculture was a trait of youth, wherein younger members of a society explored ways to rebel against an older, hegemonic "parent culture" through practices such as fashion choices and consumption habits (Hall and Jefferson 2006). More contemporary evidence, however, suggests that participation in a subculture does not necessarily end when one gets older. Rather, participants continue to remain active within their communities, and envision their participation to be long-term and a large part of a constructed identity. As examined in Hodkinson's (2011) exploration of aging Goth communities, it is not uncommon for participation to continue, though this participation may be adapted to fit a lifestyle that must accommodate other responsibilities.

As it is witnessed in contemporary ethnographic studies of subcultures which include punk (Bennett 2006), straight-edge (Haenfler 2012), and Goth (Hodkinson 2011), to grow up does not necessarily equate to growing out of a scene. Participation is not strictly a trait of youth, and while many participants found themselves adopting subcultural practices in their teenage years, these practices often extended well into adulthood. While commitment styles and levels of dedication may change due to the demands of adulthood, participants in contemporary punk scenes viewed their participation to be an important component of their identity today.

In addition, the translocal qualities of today's scenes allow members to interact with other punk scenes across the country, and around the world. Through social media, these interactions provide connected networks of like-minded participants who share similar experiences regarding their own ways of understanding an affiliation within the scene. While scene members may exist in cities far from one another, there is an understanding that these similarities and shared interests are more effective in establishing a sense of connectiveness within these groups than with those who may live nearby, but do not perceive themselves as insiders within this scene (Hodkinson 2004). As a result, one's interest in a scene can be viewed as a cross-generational, translocal interest, and "can therefore be characterized as a cultural practice that seems to dissolve the borders between youth and youthfulness" (Klein 2003, 41). The postsubcultural approach, in other words, views participation as a practice that, for many, continues well into adulthood.

THE PUBLIC MEETS PUNK: GRUNGE, POP PUNK, AND THE MAINSTREAM'S ACCEPTANCE OF PUNK ROCK

One of the most important indicators of scene affiliation was an early intro-duction to punk rock. Participants shared their introductions to punk rock—many of which learned of the genre through mass media outlets such as MTV, VH1, or the radio, and this introduction largely occurred during teen-age years, which, for many, took place during the early 2000s. As explained in the introduction to this book, my initiation into punk rock took place during those awkward middle school years—I'd listen to AFI's *Sing the Sorrow* on a Discman as I rode the bus to middle school and would proudly draw the Pennywise and Dead Kennedys logos onto my math binder. *Sing the Sorrow* still maintains its presence in my music collection, and more often than not, I continue to curate playlists filled with songs that bring me back to those awkward years. Though the rise in filesharing allowed for near-immediate access to this genre for free during the early 2000s, it is important to acknowledge that age is also an important indicator of how significant this introduction proved to be at that particular time in my life. Research suggests that teenage years are a formative time period where music tastes are devel-oped (North, Hargreaves, and O'Neill 2000) and adolescence is a critical time period for the development of one's identity (Arnett 2007). As it will be evidenced here, the taste decisions made during the adolescent years often transform into strong markers of identity as participants grow older.

Many participants interviewed for this book were introduced to punk rock through relational means such as friends and siblings, or through exposure to television and radio, and it is evident that this introduction played an integral role in the identity-building process as participants aged. Interestingly, par-ticipants were able to provide very vivid and specific details of these intro-ductions and recalled the instances where friends and family members played a role in this introduction. Green (2016) refers to the meaning-making tied to these moments as "peak music experiences," wherein listeners associate strong emotional attachments to certain music-related moments in their lives. Attending a first concert or buying a favorite album from a record store are examples of these peak music experiences. These recollections reconfirm the assumption that music and one's involvement in music-related activities have a profound impact on one's identity, even as participants in a scene become older.

With most participants identifying as being in their mid-20s to mid-30s at the time of their interviews, participants shared similar experiences that largely referenced comparable timeframes of introduction to punk rock: the late 90s and early 2000s. I do not believe this to be coincidental, as this timeframe saw an enormous rise in interest in punk rock throughout popular culture. Punk rock was no longer only delegated to gritty basement shows and underground methods of commodity distribution, nor was it viewed as subculture that incited "moral panic" from the media (Clark 2003; Cohen 2002; Hebdige 1988). Rather, this style punk rock, which emerged into popular culture in 1994, was headlined by artists and cultural moments that reached an entirely new generation of bored suburban pre-teens and teenagers, and the music itself was met with enthusiasm and curiosity from popular culture.

Before any of this happened, however, punk was, as they say, dead—or at the very least, close to it. Though it caught the attention of popular culture throughout its heyday in the late 70s and early 80s, there was relative stagnation in punk scenes across America by the late 80s. By the mid-80s, the punk communities across the country began to dwindle, the result of both diverging beliefs about punk's ideologies and a waning interest in the genre (Al-Attas 2009; Sheppard 2012). The music itself saw a shift in style as well, as bands began to experiment with their musical styles. Bad Religion, known today as one of the most important and long-lasting contributors to American punk rock found themselves experimenting with their sound, releasing *Into the Unknown* in 1983. With its heavily synthesized tracks and slower tempos, the album was seen as a strong departure from the band's traditional punk sound and was considered a commercial failure by the band and its record label, Epitaph Records (Roche 2013). By this time, new wave, a style of music characterized by "a direct, danceable energy that had largely been abandoned" by rock music at the time, dominated the radio waves in the 80s (Cateforis 2011, 2). According to Cateforis (2011), new wave was "portrayed as a mollified, less dangerous version of punk's politicized confrontational rage," and bands such as Devo, a-Ha, and the B-52s caught the attention of the public with their synthesized, catchy beats (9). As new wave faded from public consciousness by the 90s, alternative music and grunge were next to have their moment in popular culture. In search of the next big thing, it was at this time that smaller, local alternative music scenes were sought after by the music industry (Moore 2010).

With its origins in Seattle, Washington, grunge found its footing on college radio stations and in indie scenes, and with that, the Pacific Northwest city eventually became what Azerrad (1992) refers to as "a rock mecca" for those who shared in the spirit of the music. Like punk, grunge operated as a DIY music scene—music was performed and distributed by those who knew it best, and functioned independently of the mainstream until Nirvana's *Nevermind* caught the attention of popular culture (Azerrad 2001). Nirvana's "Smells Like Teen Spirit" premiered on MTV in September 1991, and by the beginning of 1992, the song had made its way to the top of *Billboard*'s pop charts (Marin 1992).

By the mid-90s, and following the death of Nirvana's Kurt Cobain, punk rock would find itself back in the mainstream conversation. Described by

Spin Magazine as "The Year Punk Broke," 1994 introduced the world to Green Day's *Dookie* and The Offspring's *Smash*. Just a few months after the release of Green Day's *Dookie*, Orange County punk band The Offspring followed Green Day's success with their album *Smash*. The album set, and still holds, the record for the most units sold (16 million copies worldwide) by an independent record label (Epitaph Records n.d.). In an interview in *One Nine Nine Four*, a documentary chronicling the rise of pop punk in America, Epitaph Records owner Brett Gurewitz describes just how lucrative he believed The Offspring were going to be:

> I had a feeling about it. . . . I remember when I first got the finished mix and I was driving home from work and was listening to them in my car, which at the time was a, you know, a 1978 beige Volvo station wagon, and I'm driving home and I'm cranking this cassette tape and I was already into my home neighborhood and I just started circling the house. I didn't want to go in because I was listening to "Self Esteem" over and over. I listened to it like 11 times and I just kept circling the block because I didn't want to stop listening to it and I didn't want to look like a weirdo sitting in my car. And then I went in and I said to my wife, and this might sound really vulgar, but I said "Honey, I think we're gonna be rich." (Al-Attas 2009)

With the release of these albums, fans were reintroduced to a revived genre of music that largely faded from view in the 80s and early 90s. For many, punk was no longer about the Sex Pistols and the Clash, and while this new generation of punk rock may not have included as many leather jackets, safety pins, or proclamations of "God Save the Queen!," the music that emerged following Green Day and The Offspring proved to be defining elements in the identity formation for participants interviewed in this book. Punk was no longer against the status quo; it *was* the status quo. And though punk rock was arguably as popular as other genres of music, this was not always applauded by those who believed "authentic" punk rock could survive without the help of popular culture:

> The success that came from pop-punk was bittersweet. Sweet, because some bands made a ton of money; bitter, because a lot of pop-punk fans were looked down upon for liking the sub-genre. For the first time, punk was on radio airwaves, nominated for Grammys, and was promoted with events such as the Vans Warped Tour music festival. Success became associated with pop-punk bands, and yet, for some reason, it was too much for the original punk culture they had grown from. (Schmidt 2017)

While we have seen numerous examples of the ways punk rock entered mainstream consciousness, the consumerist cooptation of punk rock during the 90s significantly impacted the public's perception of those who participated in the subculture. With the continual airing of music videos from bands

like Green Day, The Offspring, Rancid, and Less than Jake, punk rock became just another music genre made familiar by popular culture. Clark
(2003) writes: "Not only are deviant styles normalized, but subcultural presence is now taken for granted: the fact of subcultures is accepted and antici-
pated" (231). What was once a style of music that intended to shock and
confuse grew to be one that occupied enough space in the public consciousness for *Rolling Stone* to award Green Day's *Dookie* the number one position
on their "1994: The Best Records from Mainstream Alternative's Greatest
Year" list, stating "If Pearl Jam were too epic for you, Nirvana to oblique, if
your suburban teen inertia sprang from tedium not trauma—well, these nag-
ging brats were here to spill hair dye on your living room carpet" (Harris
2014). In these depictions of punk rock during the 90s, we see the shift in
public perception—no longer is punk rock meant to be a working-class middle finger to hegemonic structures and capitalist ideologies, but instead, an
answer to the postmodern existential crisis of teenagers growing up under
vastly different circumstances.

PEAK MUSIC EXPERIENCES AT THE PEAK OF PUNK
ROCK: INTRODUCTIONS THROUGH THE MAINSTREAM

By the late 90s and early 2000s, contemporary punk was safely within the
public consciousness. It was accessible in ways that it was not a decade
prior—MTV routinely aired music videos from bands such as Green Day,
The Offspring, and Blink-182, and CD compilation albums such as Epitaph's
Punk-O-Rama saw immense sales in big box stores like Best Buy, selling
over two million copies by the end of their decade-long run in 2005 (Ozzi
and Bayer 2017). The Warped Tour, a roving festival of music and skateboarding culture, brought punk rock to the suburbs across America in the
summers between 1995 and 2019, and Tony Hawk's *Pro Skater* video games
combined the task of landing skateboarding tricks with tracks from bands
like AFI, Less Than Jake, and The Ramones. The accessibility of the internet
and digital filesharing also played a valuable role in bringing punk rock to
the masses. Before the time of YouTube and Spotify, illegal streaming sites
such as Napster afforded many an easily accessible and controversially free
way to find new music. As evidenced in a study of a Brazilian straight edge
subculture, Reia (2014) asserts that the accessibility of Napster helped to
assist in the establishment DIY communities during the early 2000s by providing users with a way to subvert the traditional mainstream methods of
music production, allowing for musicians to prioritize a DIY ethos that afforded users the autonomy to share and distribute their own music. Alex,
who learned of bands such as Green Day and the Offspring through the radio,
cited this source as one of his initial introductions to punk rock:

I was listening to the radio a lot as a kid and listening to quote-unquote modern rock radio, you know, I was probably . . . what year was this, I was probably 12, 13. I heard The Offspring, Green Day on the radio, and I was like "wow, I like this part of the music a lot more than all the other stuff they're playing." It's more aggressive. It speaks more to my sensibilities as a teenager in a lot of ways. So, I just kind of gravitated toward that, just kind of discovered it on my own through that.

As one of punk rock's most well-known bands, The Offspring was cited on several occasions as an important "gateway" band for many. Eric, a guitarist and vocalist for a current Midwest punk band, also reflected on this introduction, citing the Offspring's record *Smash* as one of the first albums that introduced him to punk rock:

Epitaph put out that Offspring record [*Smash*] and through that, I loved it. It just didn't sound like that stuff but still had its own thing. That was a cool time for music, I think, and I was like what is this, and then kind of did a little research and like bought the record, looked at the liner notes and then just checked everything out, got comp CDs, vinyl, and realizing there is a whole local scene, that's like, wait a minute, this is a way bigger than just some song on the radio.

Searching the liner notes is a popular practice that involves reading the "Thank You" section of any album's lyric insert. Usually, bands will include other bands in this section, giving them credit for assistance with various elements of the construction of the album. For many, the logic goes as follows: if my favorite band is friends with a band referenced in the liner notes, then I will probably like that band as well. A practice largely adopted before the age of streaming, social media, and digital playlists, reading the liner notes provided fans with insider knowledge of other bands that likely sound similar.

Because access to punk rock during the late 90s and early 2000s involved little more than turning on the TV or finding some songs online, many of the more popular bands such as The Offspring, NOFX, and Blink-182 proved to be "gateway" bands into the scene for many, including Greg. With the prevalence of Napster and free online music downloading services during this time, acquiring large quantities of music for no cost was simple, effective, and a questionable method to explore new music:

I think it was like 2001 or 2002 and Napster was a thing, and I had a bunch of cool camp friends and they were like "you should listen to Brand New" and for whatever reason it was the first album, *Your Favorite Weapon*, which was the first album I ever loved, and I was like this is great! So that got me listening to more pop punky stuff, which was very popular at the time. But then I went to my first show when I was 16 and it was—there was like 10 bands—it was so

stupid, but I loved it at the time. All these ska bands and, I'm still friends with
a lot of people who played that show.

With these examples, participants discuss their early introductions to
punk rock through avenues such as MTV or the radio, but it is important to
note that this introduction was often an impetus to finding smaller, lesser-
known bands—while the more mainstream examples of punk rock were
frequently the gateway to the genre, the lasting dedication and interest in the
music was frequently due to the research and investigation that resulted from
these early introductions. The early days of Napster facilitated this exploration for many as well. By 1999, music piracy was ubiquitous, and advances
in technology meant that more songs could be downloaded at faster speeds
(Witt 2015). It is not hard to make the connection between the greater access
to all conceivable genres of music and a desire to use this platform to inexpensively acquire songs from similar-sounding bands that may not have received the attention from other sources.

Jamie's experience involved an introduction through their parents. In the
quote below, they describe how their parents influenced their music tastes at
such a young age, and how that influence expanded into their current music
preferences. Jamie referenced *Headbanger's Ball*, which was at one time
"MTV's once flagship heavy metal show" (Martins 2012):

> I've been listening to music since I was really little. My parents were very
> young, so I grew up watching MTV and stuff with them. I'd watch *Headbang-
> er's Ball* with my dad and stuff like that. He was really into metal, but they had
> a few punk records at the time, they had *Dookie* by Green Day and they had an
> Offspring record and I really loved it when I was a kid, and I always liked that
> kind of stuff. But I didn't think it was punk, it was just music that I liked. And
> usually when you hit your pre-teens and start asking your parents for, at that
> time it was CDs, and stuff like that, I started getting into Blink-182, and all
> those gateway bands. I used to listen to Green Day, so it was, like most people
> you start out with like the gateway bands and then you get into it from that and
> that was even before the internet happened so, it wasn't as accessible as it is
> back then. I would read magazines with a crappy band that was on the cover
> and find all the really cool bands that the journalists were talking about inside.
> That's sort of how it evolved.

In their recollections, Jamie identified several punk bands in their introduction that made it to mainstream popularity during the 90s and early 2000s.
Bands such as Green Day and Blink-182 were identified as "gateway" bands,
and exposure to their music often led to exploration into the lesser-known
bands of the genre. Because access to these popular bands was facilitated by
mainstream exposure and the continual repetition on MTV and the radio,
they served as easily accessible methods by which many participants famil-
iarized themselves with the music. For Aaron, these bands also became a

gateway for an introduction punk rock. He explains his introduction in the 90s, and stating specifically how The Offspring and Green Day's *Dookie* played a meaningful role in heightening his awareness of punk rock:

> I guess if you consider them a punk band, I guess my first album is The Offspring when I was in 4th grade and I guess, they'd hit the radio pretty well back then. That was my first CD and my third CD was also, I guess, from the punk stream as well, is Green Day's *Dookie*. For a while, that had pretty much been, like most of the punk stuff that I listened to and then I stayed pretty much general rock and lot of my friends were really into hip hop and rap, and so, I kind of followed the crew there, it's what they were listening to until, I guess, my junior year of high school, sophomore or freshman probably. People started giving me albums like Alkaline Trio and Goldfinger and some pop punk bands, and [I] started going to shows, getting more back in the punk scene.

For Aaron, popular culture played a role in his introduction, but this introduction was also facilitated by friends who suggested other albums worthy of a listen. Friends play a valuable role in the introductions to music, and in a similar experience to Aaron, Emily described her introduction to alternative music as one having involved more mainstream bands and punk-influenced pop artists such as Avril Lavigne, but her introduction to punk rock was through a mix of friends and Tumblr, a popular blogging and social network site:

> Well I guess I started listening to it when, I guess the beginnings of being steered toward punk rock would be when I was in like middle school and high school, and I was listening to Avril Lavigne, and I was one of the few people that I knew who really liked her and I don't know, she just really piqued my interest as a musician and as an artist in general, like a song writer, and her style really got me into it a little more, and once I went away to school, I listened to a lot of her stuff and then I had a little phase of listening to Glassjaw and Slipknot and then I was like "eh, I don't really like that anymore," and for a while I was listening to Top 40s and stuff like that, but I was like "this is dumb, I don't like it," so I couldn't really discover a lot of new music at the time, I don't know why I just wasn't looking for it, so for a while I had a lull, and then when I went away to college, one of my friends who I met there, he— between him and Tumblr were the two things that got me into punk, especially Brand New was probably the first big band that I got into.

Like Emily, whose introduction involved friends and social media platforms as a means of learning about punk rock, Justin attributed his introduction to the influence of a schoolmate and Interpunk.com, a website that carries an extensive selection of punk-related merchandise, including records, t-shirts, stickers, and accessories. Self-described as "The Ultimate

Punk Music Store," Interpunk.com provides customers with an enormous selection of punk-centric paraphernalia and music (Interpunk.com n.d.):

> The other girl in my history class freshman year who would also always be asleep all class like I would be, she wore a Distillers shirt one day or something, and I was like "oh I know who that band is," and she was like "you're wearing a Common Rider shirt," and I was like "yeah, I found them on Interpunk, they're so cool." And we became friends, and we started finding shows. And we started going to the Trocadero in Philly. My parents would always be willing to drive us, and I think it's because they wanted me to go do something with my life. Like social-esque. So, I'd get whatever friends I could, and we'd go to the Trocadero. We saw . . . the first show I ever saw was Against Me! opening for Anti-Flag and Rise Against.

In this example, Justin identified an example of subcultural capital, which include subculture-specific commodities that confer an insider status within a particular community (Thornton 1995). Through the shared knowledge of these bands and Interpunk, Justin and his friend used this information to establish a relationship based on an awareness of these commodities. Through these ways of knowing, connections are established between those who consume these goods.

It is evident from the responses in my interviews that mainstream media outlets had a powerful impact on introducing this generation to punk rock. With bands like Blink-182, the Offspring, and Green Day topping *Billboard* charts, headlining festivals, and disrupting the pop-centric music world, it is obvious to see how this pervasiveness could influence listeners long-term. With the internet prevailing as a valuable resource in the exploration of new music, the timing was perfect.

ADOLESCENT INFLUENCE: THE IMPACT OF FRIENDS AND FAMILY

In many experiences shared by participants, the influence of friends and family played an integral role in their introductions to punk rock. During adolescence, there exists a correlation between the influence of peers and a need for approval from those peers (Burnett et al. 2011). Furthermore, evidence suggests that these adolescent connections are built upon an understanding of shared tastes and norms, with an emphasis on shared attitudes— as these relationships develop, adolescents use these shared peer groups as a locus for self-reflexivity (O'Brien and Bierman 1988). Because peer groups and the influence of such during adolescence are such powerful motivators for taste and decision making, it makes sense that many of my participants shared experiences of an introduction that took place during teenage years. For Andrew, his introduction to punk rock was facilitated by an older sister and further influenced by a participation in the high school band. The connection between the Mighty Mighty Bosstones, a ska band from Boston, Massachusetts, and the music performed with the high school band proved to be an appealing similarity: "My older sister had a Mighty Mighty Bosstones tape that she had made for me that was a mix of a whole bunch of different things that they had recorded off of different albums and . . . they had horns and stuff, and I was a trumpet player in school, and I got so excited because I didn't know you could be cool if you were a horn player so I was like wow they're in a band that's really cool."

Here, we see the ways that Andrew recognized an overlap between an extracurricular hobby and an interest in ska—this introduction to ska (and subsequently punk rock) was the result of both an introduction by an older sister, but also due to an involvement in hobby not directly related to participation within the punk scene. In a similar fashion, Anthony also shared information about an introduction to punk rock that was enabled by popular culture, but also participation in school band:

> I remember maybe 6th, 7th, and 8th grade, you know, middle school time I was into a lot of stuff like Weezer a little bit, again, influenced by friendships, people which, it was funny because I feel like a lot of getting into the music, again, came from friendships that I was making and the people, we were all kind of like, we shared that. And I think that we always talked about being in a band together and making a band together, and this is like 6th grade, 7th grade, you know, young.

For Anthony, participation in the school band was important because it instilled in him a sense of community, one that preceded his understanding of community within the punk scene:

> I played trombone in the school band. . . . I wasn't necessarily good in academics, and they actually wouldn't let you [play] unless you were getting certain grades, but middle school band was definitely something that influenced me to be a part of a band in general because I realized that it was a really good sense of—it was a challenge, and it made you feel like you were a part of something, which I think that a lot of people in our scene and in the community in general . . . everybody wants to be part of a community. I think that back then I was subconsciously wanting to be a part of a community and I saw what it felt like to be a part of a band through middle school. It's the collaboration of all these people who are basically inputting their energy into these instruments and making it together. And I think that music affects people on such a deep level.

Lastly, Joe shared his experiences of growing up listening to punk. Like many others, Joe's introduction to punk rock started with an introduction to music his parents listened to:

It was middle school for me, at some point. I don't know what was the first thing but I was listening to the Beatles and Jimi Hendrix CDs my dad had, and I kind of just stumbled upon it, and I don't know what it was but I just started listening to it a lot. I think the first couple CDs I bought were Bad Religion's *Stranger Than Fiction*, and Alkaline Trio's *Good Mourning*. So, from there I just sort of . . . it became my thing, I haven't really ventured that far from there, it's been punk, pop punk, hardcore, and I've been hooked.

While it is important to recognize the value of the ways that mainstream and popular culture venues introduce fans to punk rock, acknowledging the role of older siblings, family members, and friends demonstrates that these close relationships proved to have a long-lasting impact on many fans of punk rock. Green's (2016) discussion of peak music experiences is very prevalent here—not only were these introductory moments recalled in great detail, they prevailed as significant because participants identified long-term affiliation with their scenes, and a expressed a continued interest in dedicated time and effort into keeping their scenes alive.

LIVING IN PRE-PLAYLIST TIMES: THE INFLUENCE OF CD COMPILATIONS AND WARPED TOUR

My own interest in punk rock would not be what it is today were it not for the early influence of *Punk-O-Rama*. As a thirteen-year-old with no source of income, the price to track ratio on these compilations was perfect. For me, these albums acted as a catalyst to my introduction to punk rock—I'd pick up a *Punk-O-Rama* album at Best Buy, and through Napster and the like, would download hundreds of songs, compiling mix CD after mix CD of punk bands both new and old. While it may be a forgotten practice in today's streaming and digital worlds, punk CD compilations were a popular and readily available way for many fans to find current music that did not receive the recognition from more mainstream sources such as MTV or local radio stations during the late 90s and early 2000s. *Punk-O-Rama*, a series of compilations released by Epitaph Records between 1994 and 2005 featured a variety of punk bands and were often sold inexpensively (between $4 and $6) at big box stores like Best Buy. Because of their low-cost nature, they were frequently cited as an accessible introduction for those new to the subculture to become exposed to a large variety of bands for a low price.

Hoping to attract fans with the high quantity-low cost method used by Epitaph, other punk record labels, including Hellcat Records and Fat Wreck Chords, released similar compilation albums around the same time. While many of the albums included songs from bands that cease to exist today, they also included songs by some of punk's longest-running mainstays, including Bad Religion, Millencolin, and Dropkick Murphys. The selling point of these albums came from the instant recognition of these larger-name bands, with the hope that the inclusion of these names would be enough to introduce fans to some of the smaller names on the track listings. A precursor to streaming services such as Spotify, iTunes, and Bandcamp, punk CD compilations provided a wide range of music without the pressure of commitment and provided fans with a similar experience to the playlist curation features that exist on streaming service platforms today. Ozzi and Bayer (2017) write, "Cheap comp CDs soon became young punks' de facto tool for pre-internet discovery of new artists, offering suburban teens a gateway to the acts on the forefront of a revived genre." What is important to note here is that compilations such as *Punk-O-Rama* were not introducing fans to decades-old punk bands such as The Clash, Sex Pistols, or even influential 80s hardcore bands such as Black Flag or Minor Threat. These CD compilations introduced new fans to what was currently popular in the scenes around them. While these compilations provided contemporary artists for fans to explore, they often acted as a motivator to deeper exploration of punk rock. Andrew recalled the impact of *Punk-O-Rama*, and explained how these albums acted as a starting point for investigation into other albums and bands: "I bought a *Punk-O-Rama* sampler and kind of went from there, kind of picked the bands that I liked off of there and bought their CDs and took recommendations and stuff like that."

Here, it is possible to see the ways that *Punk-O-Rama* compilations provided a way for participants to explore the current bands in punk rock, while also using these CDs as a means by which to explore similarly sounding music. Though these compilations were released before the rise in streaming sites such as Spotify and iTunes, they offered a similar experience in the sense that they provided a "playlist" of sorts for fans to explore a wide variety of bands through a low-stakes method. Talking with Alex, he described how compilations like *Punk-O-Rama* offered an accessible introduction into punk rock:

> Once I figured out that I could discover those bands, I kind of moved onto all the cheap punk compilations that Epitaph, and Fat [Wreck Chords], and Hopeless were putting out. Every Friday I would get my allowance from my parents, and it was usually $10, so I would go to Best Buy, I would ride my BMX bike to Best Buy and find a compilation for $3 or $4 that I hadn't heard, pick it up and I discovered most of my first favorite bands that way.

It is also important to note the widespread availability of these compilation albums, which may have led to the success of the business model as a whole. Gaining access to *Punk-O-Rama* compilations did not require a great deal of work—albums were sold at big box stores such as Best Buy and F.Y.E. and acquiring these albums did not require traveling far and wide, or even resorting to making purchases online or through mail-order catalogs. At a time when CD prices were in the $15 to $20 range, cheap CD compilations were an ideal way for young people with little to no financial independence to gain exposure to punk rock.

Much like the allure of the *Punk-O-Rama* albums, Warped Tour introduced an entire generation of teenagers to punk rock, skateboarding, and counterculture. Under the similar philosophy of the low-cost, high-quantity philosophy embodied by *Punk-O-Rama* and Epitaph Records, the cross-country punk-centric summer music festival hosted dozens of bands at each stop and was an avenue by which many people were able to gain access to punk rock during the mid-90s and throughout the 2000s. Sponsored by the skateboard shoe company Vans, Warped Tour traversed the United States for twenty-four years before founder Kevin Lyman ended the cross-country operation in 2018. In 2019, the Warped Tour returned for one final celebration in honor of its twenty-fifth anniversary with three weekend-long shows in three cities in the United States. In its early days, Warped Tour hosted many popular punk bands such as Bad Religion, The Bouncing Souls, Less Than Jake, and Rancid, with more well-recognized acts filling the lineup in more recent years. While bands such as these performed during peak hours on the largest stages, lesser-known bands would perform on smaller stages scattered around the festival grounds throughout the day. Like *Punk-O-Rama*, the allure of attending Warped Tour included seeing your favorite big-name bands, but the hope was that you would leave the festival having learned of some smaller bands that may not have the instant name recognition. Like Epitaph, the Warped Tour also capitalized on the low-cost CD compilation as a means of introducing new fans to the genre, and released several albums featuring Warped Tour performers during their tenure. Jamie credited the Warped Tour compilation CDs with introducing them to new music:

> I was very much of the time of the early aughts, the child that liked Good Charlotte and Simple Plan and all those embarrassing bands, I don't really care. I'll admit it. . . . But at the same time I was getting into a lot of other bands, like I would get the Warped Tour compilations every year, and there would be Bad Religion on there, and I was really into Fall Out Boy and they covered a Jawbreaker song and I was like "oh, let me check out the original" and that's how I heard of Jawbreaker, they're like my favorite band to this day. It was kind of like a domino effect . . . it evolved.

Similar to the ways many people hear of new movies or music via word-of-mouth, Jamie drew like comparisons to this process in explaining their awareness of the Warped Tour compilations. Liking one song by a band on a compilation album will often lead listeners to actively seek the band's other albums, and through this process, are then introduced to current bands within the genre and older bands that are not currently performing or producing music.

While unlikely to be a prime method though which fans learn about new music today, the Warped Tour and the various record label compilations that emerged at this time were integral in raising awareness of punk rock to younger generations. With their low cost to access and high quantity of music provided, these methods offered participants a low-stakes opportunity to explore the current trends in punk rock, while providing an accessible gateway into other elements of the genre itself.

IDENTITY FORMATION AND THE POSITIVE ASPECTS OF BELONGING TO A PUNK COMMUNITY

As explored, many participants attributed their introductions to punk rock through means such as popular culture and close relationships with friends and family. While these introductions remained critical "peak music experiences," many participants also stressed the importance of community, and how a sense of belonging played a valuable role in an understanding of identity, both in and out of the scene. The sense of belonging that resulted from participation in a scene was often cited as an important factor in long-term affiliation with the punk community. Many participants, like Andrew, were drawn to the punk community at an early age and found it an accepting and open place for anyone who had an interest in the music. Andrew stressed the importance of community and the effect it had on him during middle school, as he found his scene to be an unbiased, welcoming sanctuary for outsiders at the time:

> The concept that punk is supposed to accept everybody—I was a big nerd in school, like I said I played trumpet, I was in marching band, and when I joined my first punk band, it was very obvious that it didn't matter. That they were all kind of nerds too and we were all kids that didn't necessarily fit in with mainstream culture, or we weren't interested in mainstream culture or mainstream music didn't do it for us.

Citing the "insider" status identified by Hodkinson (2002), which emphasizes one's understanding of an identity as it relates to a perception of shared tastes with others in the scene, Andrew understood his participation as a way to interact with like-minded individuals who shared a common interest in the music. Furthermore, participation in a band helped to contribute to a sense of belonging, which was not necessarily found in other traditional places such as a job or after-school activity:

> I think it's still important too because it gave me a place to belong when I was younger when I kind of felt like I didn't have a place and so at least for me being in a punk band, part of doing that is to provide a place for other kids who feel like they don't fit in, or they feel like high school's going to last forever,

and they're never going to make any friends. To have a place where they can go and they can feel accepted and they feel like they're a part of something is really, really huge. I think a lot of people search that out in other places of their life, whether it's through their jobs, or through their religion, or through different groups or community service, we're all kind of looking for where we belong, and punk gave us, at least when I was younger, it gave me a place where yeah, I was a weirdo, and I was a nerd, but it didn't matter because I liked the music and I was there for that.

Within the discussion of their roles in their scenes, participants often reflected on why they had joined in the first place, and how this involvement played a role in their identity formation moving forward. Many participants spent a great deal of time within their respective scenes, and this involvement played a significant role in their considerations of how this participation impacted their understandings of identity. As argued by postsubcultural scholarship, the punk rock identity manifests itself differently for participants, but many acknowledge their longtime participation within the scene, and how this participation has affected their personal values and ideals growing up. Here, Anthony credited the punk scene with affording him certain privileges, such as the opportunity to live on a farm and to meet friends with likeminded values:

And I for one am grateful, because I know that if it wasn't for the punk rock community, I wouldn't be half the person I am today, I wouldn't have any or most of the friends—I wouldn't be here on this farm right now, I wouldn't be a part of this. I met the people I live on this farm with in an underground punk rock community. Nothing here on this farm has anything to do with punk rock music, but it brought me here and so, if it wasn't for the punk rock community and it wasn't for punk rock music in general, then I might not be here. And I can tell you right now I'm a happy person and I'm grateful for it and I really hope that in the future that everybody gets to experience something along the lines of punk rock communities, you know, whether it's punk rock or electro-dance, or that bee-bop, or you know, any of that alternative music, that really just opens your mind and makes you think of things differently and makes you feel that other people out there feel the same way.

While he acknowledges the disparities between life on a farm and the signifiers of a traditional punk rock practice, the prevalence of community involvement resonated strongly for Anthony. As postsubcultural theory suggests, participation in a scene varies from person to person—and while one participant's understanding of involvement in a punk community may include more common practices such as DIY or particular fashion statements, we see the community-oriented values translating into other practices outside of one's direct involvement in a punk scene.

As with any scene that revolves around the production and performance of music, live performances and the roles participants play within this practice provide valuable insight into the values of a particular scene. Live performances are an integral element in a larger understanding of how music fans both define a scene and define themselves within this scene (Shank 1994). As an example of this, Cormany (2015) cites Coachella as a translocal music scene that prevails as a community through the shared process of attending a live music experience. According to Thompson (2004), the performance of live music serves to exist as a space for a community to exist and, the experience of a live show must be done in person due to the fleeting nature of a live performance: "[the show] it combines music and community and is an experiential and embodied phenomenon that can never be replicated or fully captured in live recordings, photos, videos, zine accounts, and/or personal narratives. It must be experienced directly, and unlike other commodities cannot be hoarded or accumulated" (123). Several participants interviewed for this book cited some level of involvement in at least one band, and for many, this participation was viewed as an important component of an identity that manifested itself in a variety of ways. For Greg, playing in a band was viewed as an important component of his identity, but his involvement in a band was also understood as a means to meet others and travel:

> For me, [being in a band] is an identity. Music's also a great pretense to do other things. Like I don't like to go on vacation. I don't want to go on a cruise, travelling to Europe is cool if you have the money for it or whatever, but I travel for music and I get to meet all these people, and I have friends around the country now that I get to see a couple times a year and it's really exciting and it's really cool. It's a great pretense to hang out with your friends and be social and travel.

As participants are forced to navigate the relationship between their scene-related hobbies and other adult obligations, there existed an understanding that finding a balance between both of these worlds is important. This sentiment was not unique, as Justin also grappled with his own positionality between performing music and having a job:

> I feel like being in a mildly successful band for a while, I have this kind of choice about do I . . . it feels you fall into mainstream society or you keep doing this weird thing for a while, and I didn't know how to deal with that, and I was privileged enough to go to college, and have a generally privileged experience there. I had a good education, I got a job, and there's this kind of middle ground in between where you just don't know which way you're supposed to go and I tried both ways legitimately. I guess I don't really know what it means that I did that, but I just remember thinking I have a job, just go to work every day, and I can go home, and I can go buy groceries, or I can buy

a pizza and do whatever I want and that's cool and then there's other times
where I'm like I'm going to go on tour for a month and see what that's like,
which is working for me, and what's kind of funny is neither really did.

As other participants have shared, belonging in a punk scene was an integral
component of an understanding of identity. While the reasons for participating within these scenes varied from person to person, many felt their involvement within their scene satisfied the need for belonging and an understanding
of what a community should look like. Below, Jamie echoed this sentiment,
expressing that an association with punk rock was large part of an identity—
involvement was more than just attending a show or two a month, or buying
a new album every once in a while. Rather, this involvement satisfied several
needs in one's life, including friendship, community, and an understanding
of perceived shared values: "[punk rock] is something that's been part of my
life for so long and it feels like a part of you. It's hard to even separate myself
from it because that's where 90 percent of my friends are, based in some kind
of punk community. There's very few people that I know outside of that. It's
enabled me, it's encouraged me to be the person that's always inquisitive,
always questioning things, I'm never complacent, not afraid to say what
needs to be said."

In each of these examples, participants expressed not only a strong connection to their scenes, but a strong connection between these scenes and
their own identities. For many, the punk ethos was represented in other
aspects of life and was not an ethos reserved for the time spent participating
within the punk scene. Participants acknowledged their existence within the
spheres of scene-related identity and adult life, and while certain obligations
may prevent them from fully focusing on a career in punk rock, many saw
their involvement within their scenes as a convenient distraction from the
responsibilities of adulthood.

CONTEMPORARY PUNK VALUES

Research shows that there is indeed a correlation between perceived shared
values and members' affiliation within a community (Breidahl, Holtug, and
Kongshøj 2018; Pirkey 2015). For many participants, subcultural scenes act
as sites where connections are made based on commonalities related to
shared tastes and beliefs. For instance, Haenfler's (2006) investigation of
straight edge hardcore scenes and Portwood-Stacer's (2012) exploration of
activists and anti-consumerist practices confirm that the overarching values
that resonate across a particular community will attract those who share
similar ideologies. A major tenet that has endured throughout the history of
punk rock is an emphasis on critical thinking and an encouragement to avoid
complacency with the status quo. Encouraged to question the hegemonic

practices that exist within society today, participants within contemporary punk scenes view these sites as places where constructive discussions can take place for the betterment of the scene and society at large. Jamie, who was intrigued by these ideologies and the messages within the music itself, viewed their scene as a place where they could find likeminded people dealing with similar issues related to anxiety and mental health:

> [Punk is] aesthetically pleasing, the music itself is aesthetically pleasing. Certain types of punk that's incredibly melodic and really harmonic, that appeals to me a lot. Just like from a musical standpoint. But also a lot of my favorite bands and most bands I like are incredibly political . . . it's sort of stuff I relate to because it's the type of people who write this music . . . they're people like me who are constantly questioning things, are never complacent, there's always like this . . . things should be better, they could be better. The other side of the coin I also like bands that are about having miniature existential crises and writing songs about anxiety and I feel like in a lot of ways, I guess punk music specifically is very bluntly honest about it . . . they don't have to worry about appealing to the radio, they don't have to edit themselves quite as harshly and that's even a weird thing when you see bands bump up to major labels and major labels try to fight them with their content . . . there is I think a big, honest element to that that I like.

In their discussion of an affinity to punk rock, Jamie emphasized the messages that exist within the music today and appreciated the straightforward approach to addressing some of the more pressing issues that face society at large. While many genres of music often highlight the division between musicians and fans, today's contemporary punk rock communities generally continue to be sites of equality between these two groups.

While becoming a more common practice in recent years, some contemporary punk bands have flirted with the hyper-commodification of their music, offering fans a VIP experience through the sale of tickets with exclusive privileges. Producing limited edition merchandise, exclusive access to the band's sound check, and selling meet-and-greets at each tour date are other examples of this practice. Following the release of their 2017 album, *After the Party*, The Menzingers offered their fans the "Before The Party" Upgrade, which featured early access to the venue, admittance to a six song acoustic set, a photo opportunity with the band, and an autographed version of their most recent seven-inch record (Before the Party n.d.). In celebration of their thirty years together as a band, The Bouncing Souls introduced their Hopeless Romantics Club in 2019, which gave fans access to a short acoustic set, digital downloads, and band merchandise, among other perks before each show on their Thirtieth Anniversary tour (Hopeless Romantics Club n.d.). Though growing in popularity, the majority of today's punk bands shun these ventures in favor of a more or less egalitarian relationship with their fans. For

Alex, one of the more important ideologies prevalent within today's punk scene emphasized the democratic relationship between artist and fans:

> The thing I like about it the most is that, as opposed to other subgenres of music, I feel like everybody's kind of on the same level in punk. There are no rock stars, there are no celebrities for the most part. Everybody's just kind of on the same level and you can get to know your favorite bands on a personal level. You can go and approach them and talk to them at shows and it's not weird usually. It's just nice. I can't think of another kind of music where it's like that. Everybody's just on the same level.

A current example of this philosophy can be found at Fest. Since its start in 2002, Fest continues to be a significant event, where up to three hundred bands perform at small bars and venues throughout the college town during a weekend in October. While the festival draws smaller bands on independent record labels or no label at all, more recognizable bands have headlined the festival in previous years. Joe discussed the important community-centric aspects of Fest that were appealing to him, explaining that by attending the festival, he was able to find a place with like-minded people who had similar opinions and shared similar values:

> Punk means a lot to me. It was always really hard for me to meet friends, so once I saw an opportunity [to go to Fest], I was like, "alright I'm going with it," so I went on Facebook, I met people outside of shows, or at shows, at bars, and it's just like, it's a really welcoming community. I feel incredibly comfortable around these people. In fact, more so than people I've known since elementary school. It's sort of weird to say because you wouldn't expect that, or maybe you would because that's . . . I'm into the same kind of music, the same kind of values, I guess it would make sense that I would feel comfortable around these kinds of people. It's really comforting being around people that are not only welcoming and friendly, but also care about the same sort of social values that I have.

The emphasis of community and the shared perspectives on values and ideologies is a theme that was evident for other participants including Eric. Eric, who plays guitar in a band, provided his example of a "peak music experience," which highlights the democratic nature of punk practice. Here, he describes his own introduction to live music and reflects on how this introduction fostered a lifelong interest in the punk rock. Again, in this example, we see how accessibility and egalitarian ideologies of punk prevail as significant:

> I think that the first memorable like actual show, like that, that I went to was kind of more of a hardcore mix of things, like Snapcase and Avail, and Kid Dynamite. . . . All on the same bill at this college day, and you had to be 18 to get in but I was only 16 and I just went to see and they're just like. . . . And that

was another thing that I thought was cool. The college girl running it was just like, I get it. I get it. Go in. Don't fuck up. And like that was cool to me. Again, mixed bill, bands hanging out, and it just seemed so cool that everything was so accessible, when you're a kid like that, these shows become addictive and you can't miss them like they're so important and that's all I did. I just went to shows nonstop.

When ideologies such as these present themselves within a punk community, it is not hard to see these values resonate for members in places other than the scenes themselves. For instance, while fans may feel strongly about issues such as social justice or inclusiveness within a scene, these beliefs tend to translate to other areas in their lives, including academia. Referring to the phenomenon as a "punk pedagogy," Torrez (2012) writes, "While punk philosophy frames how we interact with outside society, it likewise shapes our position as educators and the manner by which we construct the classroom (and other sites of knowledge sharing) as a learning environment" (135). This pedagogical approach is evident in Allie's identity as a teacher. While it may seem that punk rock and academia are "queer bedfellows" (Miner and Torrez 2012), there are often ideological similarities between these two camps—namely, the quest for knowledge and a resistance toward complacent thought. Here, Allie explained how a punk pedagogical approach impacted her own teaching philosophy, and credits an interest in punk to the role it plays in her job as an educator:

I'm a teacher, so [punk rock] has definitely guided how I teach. I definitely do not believe in just following authority because it tells you to do something. I feel like it has taught me to actually look deeper and question everything. I don't just take anything at face value. . . . I have never pulled the "because I said so" bit. I do not yell at my students the way a lot of teachers will yell. I prefer to teach my students as if they are young adults with opinions and feelings that deserve to be expressed and listened to. I am also very open. My room is always open for anyone I know or don't know. Even my kids have said that I teach differently. I don't judge anyone, any of my students. I can have a kid come into my room with the worst reputation, but I don't judge the kid by how they look, or what I've heard. I treat them based on my experience with them.

The concept of "doing the right thing" and treating others fairly resonated for other participants as well. While Andrew's experience with this philosophy did not involve students and teaching in a classroom, he explained his own thoughts on pay-to-play. While it can take on a variety of forms, in this instance, pay-to-play is an arrangement where a band is required to sell a certain amount of tickets in order to play a venue, and if the minimum limit is not met, the band has to pay the remainder out of pocket. Below, Andrew explains this process, citing the ways that pay-to-play is both unethical and fundamentally antithetical to a DIY ethos:

[Pay-to-play] is the exact opposite of DIY and I think that might be kind of why I have such a strong pull toward that stuff because I've done pay-to-play before. I've had to sell X amount of tickets and I sell a $15 ticket to my friend, and my band gets a dollar in return, whereas the venue is getting $14, I'm sure some of that goes to the touring band, but what's my motivation to keep doing that and to keep hustling when I'm not seeing any return on it? I might as well play in a basement where I'm not getting any return anyway, and then I don't have to bother my friends and try to sell tickets to them or drive around trying to sell tickets to fans. . . . I don't want to have anything to do with that. There's no guarantee that we're even going to play. And sometimes the monetary reward can be pretty good if you sell a certain number of tickets, but at the same time, you're the promoter, you promote the show, you sell the tickets. My job is to play the music. I'll post about it, I'll go flyer for it, but I'm not selling the tickets for you anymore, that's not my job. It puts way too much pressure on a bunch of kids when there's a fully grown adult whose job is to promote the show and get heads through the door. If you don't think these kids are going to draw to these shows, then don't book them. But don't force them to sell tickets. It's degrading when you're trying to sell tickets, you just feel kind of like garbage. This is what I have to do to get people to pay attention to my band? That I have to hang out in a mall to try to sell tickets until a rent-a-cop tells me to leave? That's not what I signed up for.

For Andrew, pay-to-play was viewed as an unethical exploitation of musicians, as it places responsibility on the bands themselves to invest their own money in the show, with no guarantee that a profit will be made. Furthermore, it blurs the boundaries between the responsibilities of the venue and the bands. In this case, it is the venue's responsibility to sell the tickets, not the bands themselves.

Interestingly, many of my interviewees did not address the contested relationship punk rock has with politics. While punk rock has always enjoyed voicing criticisms of politics, hegemony, and authority in general, participants rarely brought up their own political thoughts as they relate to punk rock. While larger social issues such as sexism, feminism, and racism made an obvious appearance, and these issues are of course inextricably tied to politics at large, there was little discussion of the current political climate in these conversations. While this was largely the case, Alex addressed some of his own thoughts on how ageing has impacted his desire to remain active within the punk community, stating that punk ideologies continue to align with his personal outlook on political and social issues:

I also feel like as I get older . . . it's funny because I have a lot of friends who are my age who are like 30, 31, as they've gotten older, they've gotten more conservative in every aspect of their life, not just politically, what they do, who they talk to, who they hang out with, whereas I feel I'm getting way more idealistic as I get older, so punk rock is the most idealistic form of expression in my opinion. That's another big reason I still identify with it and gravitate toward it.

Participation within the contemporary punk scene manifests itself in a variety of ways. For some, belonging within a community prevailed over the music itself, and this participation developed into a strong understanding of belongingness with others who share an interest in the music, as well as similar values. As explored here, there is at times an overlap between one's understanding of an involvement within a scene and one's responsibilities outside of the scene. Values transgressed these spheres of involvement, and the values that participants upheld in their experiences within punk often transcended into other realms of life. In general, these values underscored the importance of treating others fairly and with respect, and to help others when necessary.

FAN COMMITMENT AND THE FACTORS THAT CHANGE DEDICATION

As a teenager, I thought my involvement in the punk scene would never change—I believed that in my adult years, I would continue to travel far and wide (on weeknights, no less) to see my favorite bands play in big cities and middle-of-nowhere towns hours away from home. If the Bouncing Souls were playing in Reading, Pennsylvania, on a Tuesday night, so be it—I would be there. And like my views on attending shows, I foolishly thought that my spending habits would remain the same; that I would feverishly spend my hard-earned money on every album and every t-shirt that crossed my path. I assumed that my punk rock lifestyle would consist of spending more time existing within these spaces, rather than spending a lot of time writing about them. And, as expected, that was not the case. While I continue to consider myself a dedicated fan of punk rock, and do continue to attend shows, buy merchandise and remain largely active within the community itself, there is no doubt that these practices have changed with time. These days, there are very specific circumstances that will get me to attend a show on a weeknight, and even more of these qualifications exist if the show is in the middle of winter. And though I would love to buy every album released by all of the bands that I enjoy, it does not always make financial sense to do so when the rent is due. These changes in habit are indicative of a larger understanding about participation within a scene—commitment as a whole tends to change as participants get older (Andes 1998, 215; Bennett 2018; Hodkinson 2013). Several scholars (Bennett 2006; Gregory 2012; Tsitsos 2012), have also demonstrated that involvement within the physical spaces of a scene itself tends to change as participants age, suggesting that while com-

mitment continues as time progresses, behavior within such spaces and sartorial displays of commitment have a tendency to change with time.

In the case of contemporary punk scenes today, most participants considered themselves currently active within their scenes despite the conflicting
obligations of adulthood. This participation was often influenced or affected
by external forces that hinder many from attending shows on a nightly basis
or dedicating a large portion of a paycheck to buying new albums. While
many participants remained active within the subculture well into their twen-
ties and thirties, their change in involvement was noted. Issues such as having to pay a mortgage or living too far from where shows take place were
provided as participants' reasons for not dedicating as much time to attending concerts, especially on weeknights. For instance, in Aaron's interview, he
expressed reasons for his changing participation, but also noted that shows
today are still affordable, and the financial cost of going to local concerts was
still appealing. With many bands selling tickets at lower prices, balancing
adult responsibilities and attending a show now and then is still a possibility:
"Scheduling is very limited, and funds go to a mortgage instead of more
concert tickets and beer, so paying student loans has definitely caught a lot of
it and then a medical fund, mortgages, and stuff, so going to shows frequently enough has dropped down but it's also much more affordable now. It's
nice to see bands that are still keeping their tickets, for the most part, below
like somewhere between $10 and $30 range."

For Jamie, their change in involvement was due to work and not living
near a major city. Because of this, they needed to use public transportation to
get to a show, which made the process of attending a show more complicated. In their explanation, they stated that they have become an "old punk" due
to these challenges:

> I don't go to as many shows as I used to anymore because now I'm kind of like
> I have work in the morning, but also now that I don't live in the city it's . . .
> when I lived in the city it was "oh, I don't have anything to do tonight," "oh,
> there's a show, I guess I'll just go." Now it's like I have to make an effort and
> take a train or whatever, and plan my life around it a little bit more, but I don't
> like going to parties, I don't really like . . . that's my version of going out. I
> like seeing bands perform. I'm an artist, that's their art, that's their baby, that's
> what they're sharing with you, and that's a great experience, and that's why I
> like to go to shows, and it's like you know, so fun. I've been sort of evolving
> into [an] old punk now.

While Jamie acknowledged the ways in which their involvement has changed
with time, they still consider themselves to be part of the scene. Though their
positionality within the scene has changed, attending shows and remaining
active in the community continue to represent a large portion of an identity.

They further expanded upon this sentiment and described how their participation has changed with time due to having a job and a partner:

> It's funny because most of my friends in punk are older, they're in their 30s now, or approaching their 30s. I'm 27, which we joke is sort of when you're creeping into becoming one of us. But it's funny, because I always used to say to myself when I was younger, "I'm never going to be too tired to go to shows," because I would stay out until 2 in the morning, get up at 4 in the morning to open the coffee shop, and it didn't faze me, but yeah, your body changes and you can't handle it, but that's a thing. There are certain things you don't relate to now. If you've been with a partner for a long time, you're not going to relate to getting drunk all the time. If you have your life semi-together, and if you have a regular job, you're maybe not going to relate to "I'm a fuck up, I just can't keep my shit together." It's harder to relate.

Once again, Jamie acknowledged the ways that their commitment to attending shows has changed with time and recognized that there are other obligations that may prevent a scene member from being at a show until the early hours of the morning, only to wake up and go to work a few hours later. In addition, they continued to share more information regarding their involvement, stating that with time, their role in the community has changed from active and engaged participant to one who still remained committed, but did not have as much time to dedicate as before:

> I'm probably less involved now because I don't live in the middle of it anymore, so I'm not quite as like . . . someone was like "oh, there's gonna be a show at this house," and I'm like "I've never heard of that house." I used to know when the houses would disappear and pop up; I used to be on top of that so much. Now I'm like "well, that's not my role in that anymore" because I have a young friend who tries to put on shows and stuff like that, and he was doing it where I used to live and then he moved to Philly and is now trying to do that and I'm like "man, I couldn't do that on top of this 9 to 5 job I have," so you prioritize your time a little bit differently.

Here, we see an example of the ways that the roles change as participants age. While older participants continue to see themselves as active members of their scenes, they look to the younger participants to uphold the DIY practices of organizing and promoting local shows. There is an understanding that younger scene members have fewer responsibilities related to adulthood, and can therefore dedicate more time, effort, and money to preserving the scene. Examples such as these continue to support the notion that participation within a scene is not strictly a trait of youth. Older participants, while their roles may change, continue to identify with their scenes well into adulthood.

Like Jamie, Joe also expressed the difficulty in going to shows on weeknights due to a busy work schedule and a commitment to a full-time job. In a similar fashion, Joe also addressed the impact adulthood has on weeknight show attendance, acknowledging that it is more likely for someone younger to be able to attend such shows due to fewer responsibilities and obligations:

> I know people who are still going [to shows], but I think it's almost kind of weird that people aren't, but then again people get older, people have obligations. I don't think it's that people don't want to be there, but I think it's that people—I work a 9-to-5. I get home at 7:30, I'm exhausted. Getting me to go to a show during the week is probably not going to happen, it's like one night that I'm going out during the week, if that. And then weekend shows. That works out better. . . . When you're younger, you can do these things easily. You're going to school, or you're working a server job. You have a couple bucks, you go to see the show, and then you go home, and you probably don't have to worry about getting up at 6 in the morning. So, I feel like it's more like what comes with growing up, I really hope it's not people being like, "I'm too cool for that." I know people who are much older than me who are still going to shows, who go to Fest, and I think it's important that in a way those people are there because that shows how influential the scene was.

Again, Joe sees the relationship between ageing and a change in show attendance, but remains optimistic that despite these obligations, older participants in the scene are still able to attend shows and support their communities in ways that fit in with the obligations of adulthood. Like Jamie and Joe, Allie also cited a change in her commitment to attending shows, citing her job as the reason for attending fewer shows on weeknights: "I go as long as I know the show is happening. A lot of times I'll find out because I'm so busy with work, I'll find out about a show after it has happened, which is a bummer, but I never stopped going to see bands, from the time I started in high school."

These examples illustrate the ways in which one's involvement in a scene often overlaps with the obligations of adulthood. While participants attended shows as often as possible, and still considered themselves active members within their respective scenes, there exists an understanding that there are extenuating circumstances and responsibilities that may prevent an older scene member from dedicating a large portion of their resources to the scene today. While obligations may be prioritized, scenes today often rely on younger generations to carry on the practices of a DIY scene, with the expectation that younger participants may have fewer commitments that prevent them from dedicating their efforts to keeping a scene alive.

CONCLUSION

In their considerations of their introductions to punk rock, participants addressed their experiences with discovering the music through some of the most accessible ways possible. Thanks to MTV, the radio, and the internet, punk rock was accessible in ways that it was not even a decade prior. With bands like The Offspring, Green Day, and those that subsequently followed, an entirely new generation of youth became the next target audience for punk rock. Because adolescence is a critical time in which identity formation begins, it is very likely that an introduction to punk rock at this time can explain why many participants today credit their current involvement to the bands that served as a gateway into the genre as a whole. Moving forward, many participants developed an understanding of self that associated strongly to the values and norms that exist within punk rock—an objection toward discriminatory practices, and an appreciation for acceptance, open-mindedness, and diversity. By affiliating with others with such likeminded values, participants understood their current involvement within a scene as more than just a location where the music was preferred. Rather, contemporary punk scenes are viewed as sites where the music is a priority, but there exists an understanding that affiliation within a scene provides scene members with a community and a sense of belonging. For those who considered themselves outcasts, or continue to consider themselves outcasts, contemporary punk scenes provide sites where long-term association can provide positive benefits for those involved.

To continue, present day members expressed a longingness to be more active within their scenes but acknowledged that adult obligations must remain a priority. Nonetheless, participants still choose to remain active and continue to communicate with others in their scenes through social media or in-person and expressed an admiration for those who are able to commit so much time and effort into dedicating such contributions to the scene. While participants expressed a desire to attend shows on weeknights, there is an understanding that other obligations outside of their commitment to the scene remain a priority. Because participants view their involvement as such a critical component of an identity, it is difficult to fully justify abandoning such participation in the scene altogether. Furthermore, there is a struggle with the cognitive dissonance that exists between the desire to attend shows and understanding that participation within society can be a deterrent to more involved levels of participation. These considerations reconfirm the fluid participation between spheres of scene involvement and spheres of adulthood and demonstrate that these forces are often the site of struggle for many who wish to spend more time and resources within their scenes.

Chapter Four

DIY and Its Role in Today's Scenes

With popular culture and its continued practice of coopting signifiers of punk, DIY (do-it-yourself) remains as a practice that allows contemporary punk scenes around the world to claim ownership of their commodities and music. Described by Moore (2007) as "commercially independent cultural production," these practices can vary in output and commitment level, and the practice itself emphasizes the ways participants create and produce the commodities that help to contribute to the culture within a scene (438). For instance, this practice might involve putting together a tour and using social media as a means by which to communicate with bands in other cities. It can also involve the creation of goods such as records and t-shirts. As defined by Bennett and Guerra (2018b), DIY is "a form of cultural practice that is often pitched against more mainstream, mass-produced and commodified forms of cultural production" (1). In many cases, DIY becomes a way for groups of people to have direct involvement in the cultures in which they participate, while ridding themselves of the pressure that results from attempting to meet the hegemonic needs of the culture industry (Deibert 2014). In this understanding, DIY becomes an act that gives punk communities the freedom of autonomy in a perpetually hyper-commodified world.

These days, it is not hard to see the influence of punk and punk signifiers across popular culture. Punk fashion, in its myriad forms, was once viewed throughout society as obscene. Its primary goal was to shock and offend, and underscore the alienation felt by a generation of jaded and cynical youth. Safety pins, leather jackets, questionable hairstyles, and makeup choices were all indicative of a lifestyle that stood in opposition to the status quo and hegemonic structures that exist within postmodern society. As time has progressed, however, these commodities and the ways in which they are fashioned have become normalized and expected. A prime example of this cooptation can be observed at the 2013 Met Gala, *Vogue* magazine's themed annual fundraising event for the Metropolitan Museum of Art Costume Institute in New York City. Described as the "Super Bowl of fashion" (Ward 2019), the Met Gala's theme in 2013, titled "PUNK: Chaos to Couture," sought to focus "on the relationship between the punk concept of 'do-it-yourself' and the couture concept of 'made-to-measure'" (PUNK: Chaos to Couture n.d.). Celebrities in attendance were invited to put their own personal spin on this theme, showing up to the Gala donning teased or spiky hair, ripped fishnets, and ball gowns. The entire event represented an amalgamation of what culture industries have concluded about punk—yes, safety pins and ripped clothing will always have an inherent connection to punk fashion, but what about couture ball gowns and the spectacle of the celebrity-studded event itself even remotely speaks to DIY and the autonomous belief systems embodied by so many scenes around the world today?

With the continued cooptation of punk rock and its signifiers by popular culture and fashion runways alike, DIY practice stands in opposition to these systems, allowing participants in scenes around the world to produce albums and music independently of many of these outside forces. More importantly, DIY systems often embrace and reflect inclusive and socially conscious principles that emphasize fair trade practices, equality, and an awareness of environmental issues among others (St. John 2003). The grassroots process of creating a scene's merchandise and investing labor into the production of music allows participants to have a significant investment into how these goods are created and distributed, while also allowing for the focus of the practice to further emphasize the importance of social issues and values within a particular scene. Ethnographic exploration and participant interviews provide firsthand accounts of these practices and confirm that a DIY ethos continues to remain an important element of various punk scenes around the world (Bennett and Guerra 2018a; Griffin 2012; Haenfler 2018; Moore 2007).

In the case of contemporary punk rock, these goods include items such as t-shirts, CDs, records, and posters—the egalitarian ethos behind DIY assumes that anyone can produce these products. In many respects, DIY provides users the opportunity to engage in "the active creation of an alternative culture," wherein this participation seeks to undermine dominant forms of commodity production (Duncombe 1998). As a practice, DIY is not scene-centric. In other words, participants who adopt a DIY ethos through participation in a scene often maintain this worldview in spaces unrelated to these scenes. Furthermore, practices within these external spaces are often influenced by the belief systems that are upheld within DIY (Haenfler 2018).

As a practice, DIY works to help provide a platform by which participants can express ideologies and beliefs that may not be representative of those who work within the music industry at large. Straight edge, a movement which grew to prominence with the Washington D.C. hardcore band Minor Threat, proposed a drug-, alcohol-, and promiscuous sex-free lifestyle as a protest to society's self-indulgent ways and the culture industries that perpetuated these practices. With their DIY record label, Dischord Records, Ian MacKaye and Jeff Nelson of the DC hardcore band Teen Idles (and Minor Threat) used their platform in the early 80s to distribute their own—and their friends'—music. Their philosophies on DIY ethics and self-care appeared antithetical to popular culture's greedy ways and established Minor Threat and the straight edge lifestyle as more "authentic" ways of living (Moore 2010). More contemporary examples of independent punk record labels include Chunksaah Records (Asbury Park/New Brunswick, New Jersey), Epitaph Records (Los Angeles, California), and BYO Records (Los Angeles, California), which function to act as evidence to Frith's (1981) claim that punk record labels "demystified the production process itself—its message was that *anyone* could do it" (159). Similar to independent record labels and the communities within, zine communities offer another example of DIY and the complexities of the practice, and various investigations of this cultural field provide insight into participant subjectivities within the zine community (Kempson 2012, 2015), music exposure and awareness brought about by zine production (Moore 2007), and zine production and significance within feminist spaces (Piano 2003; Piepmeier 2009). Examples such as these demonstrate that with the right tools and a bit of know-how, DIY blurs the consumer-producer line and the myriad ways by which one can contribute provides proof of the egalitarian foundation that upholds DIY today.

Despite punk's recognized place in popular culture, DIY practice continues to allow members the option to design and create goods specifically of interest to these particular scenes. With its emphasis on social awareness and egalitarianism, DIY continues to be a practice that allows producers to contribute their skills in ways that reinforce the community-building ideologies that remain a valuable tenet of punk rock today. While today's punk rock communities embody many of the traditional elements of DIY (including the creation and distribution of goods), the use of social media adds an interesting element to this practice. Rather than solely relying on word-of-mouth and insider knowledge to share information and goods, social media provides bands and fans the platform to promote their goods to a wider audience. For instance, information about shows and band merchandise are often available on a band's Facebook or Instagram accounts, and fans can purchase merchandise directly through these links. As an example, both Fest and Pouzza Fest use their Facebook, Twitter, and Instagram accounts to convey information to their fans regarding performance announcements, ticket sales, and to generally spread awareness of their festivals. Frequently, large announcements regarding the festival's lineups are announced on social media in tandem with an announcement on the festival's website—these locations are often the go-to for fans to find immediate and up-to-date information regarding these events.

Likewise, punk bands wholeheartedly embrace social media to spread awareness of shows, new merchandise, or new music. These platforms offer musicians the option to curate and update these pages in ways that seem appropriate, and they also act as useful intermediaries to bridge the gap between musician and fan. Since these social media pages are usually created and maintained by the bands themselves, fans often have the option to interact with these bands directly through comments, likes, or private messages. Though scenes work to maintain DIY practice for the production of many commodities within their scenes, there is an acceptance that larger forces, such as social media, are at play. As concluded by Thornton (1995), it is unlikely for scenes to exist in (social) media-free bubbles, void of outside influence from the mainstream forces that impact contemporary life at large.

DIY presents a strong departure from the CCCS conclusions about youth culture and the practices within. In their analysis of subcultures, CCCS theorists argued for the subcultural act of "doing nothing," wherein the working-class youth of post-war Britain find activity on the streets by failing to partake in any specific activity at all. The behavior that is identified and explored through interviews, is depicted as juvenile mischief involving activities such as fighting, hanging around with friends, and talking (Corrigan 2006). Though this assumption of "doing nothing" technically results in doing something (as passive as this activity may be), these youthful practices are not viewed as positive contributions to the perpetuation or growth of a youth culture. In the evidence that follows, we see a departure from the CCCS conclusions about youth cultures and a lack of contribution—members of contemporary punk communities maintain an active role in a variety of ways that contribute to the community-building aspects of the scene. These active contributions include music-related undertakings such as creating and producing music and organizing shows and tours, and commodity-related practices such as taking photographs, creating zines, or writing for punk blogs—all of which act to personify the scene's progressive values and egalitarian beliefs regarding participation and inclusion.

WHAT IS DIY?

What is important to note here is the understanding that scenes today emphasize the value of smaller, independently run events that underscore the close connections and socially valued networks that arise from these scenes. Not only do these small-scale shows draw in smaller crowds, the revenue from the shows themselves often reflects the independent nature of smaller shows that are organized through these interconnected networks. Furthermore, we see an understanding that DIY practice gives bands and fans the ability to produce specific merchandise that is appealing to those particular scenes. Seeing value in the possibility of organizing these events and producing these commodities highlights the continuation of DIY practices that operate in translocal scenes today.

While not in a band himself, Jimmy had positive thoughts about DIY and expressed his own perspective which stressed the hard work and dedication that musicians invest order to have autonomous freedom over their music. "The whole punk thing in general is kind of like a not really a huge mainstream thing, so everybody's kind of left to their own devices to make it happen anyways. As far as, a lot of these bands have to self-record themselves and put their music out on their own. That's all happening obviously because there's a group of people for it, but it's not like a huge thing. You just kind of have to do it yourself I guess."

Below, Joe discussed the importance of DIY within his scene. For Joe, putting on shows (again, at a low cost for attendees) and using DIY methods allow scenes to operate independently of external influences, and he hopes for scenes to continue to support the smaller, lesser-known bands who might have to rely more heavily on DIY methods than some of the larger bands that have wider recognition or help from a record label. While we often associate DIY with the production side of a scene, Joe also considered attending these shows a form of DIY, which, for those without the creative abilities and resources can be viewed as a way to participate while also supporting those who organize such events. As with *Punk-O-Rama* and Warped Tour, punk scenes continue to use the low-cost, high-quantity method of music distribution to bring about awareness to the bands that operate today:

> I guess that [DIY] goes with the punk ethos in general, that like, if you can assemble some instruments and have something cool to say, and you don't totally suck, people are going to listen to you. I think that's really unique for the scene, because especially here, I always keep hearing about these bands that keep popping up in Philly, I think that's really cool. You can go see a show for five dollars and see four brand new bands. . . . And that's great because there's a lot of people who need to have their voices heard. I don't really know how other scenes operate since I haven't really been involved in other scenes, but I didn't always listen to smaller bands, I always listened to the more popular things, but as I've moved here I found it, I started listening to smaller up-and-coming bands, that's how it works. It's important not only to support larger bands that get people involved, but it's important that you find those [smaller] bands in the first place.

In this example, we see the ways that low-cost, high-quantity methods are still effective in garnering interest for the music. While bands may not be walking away from the show at the end of the night with a pocketful of money, they likely introduced their music to someone attending the show who was previously unaware of it. With this in mind, musicians perform their music for "the 'right' reasons," which include the opportunity to perform and make connections with others who share similar tastes in music (Haenfler 2014, 87). While a small paycheck may not be desirable when the logistics of touring do not go as planned, viewing this lifestyle as a means to make large amounts of money is not considered an appropriate reason for partaking in these scenes, and is often viewed as antithetical to the value and norms of contemporary scenes today.

Shared spaces and communities of people with likeminded values were two resounding traits of DIY that made the practice commendable for those within the punk scene. In his interview, Eric shared his experiences with DIY punk scenes in his hometown, expressing how DIY practices and a belief in autonomy acted as a common denominator among a variety of different styles of music within these scenes. Currently, Eric plays guitar and sings for a punk band on an independent record label:

> What really made me love it was the fact that there is a like, everyone just does shit without needing anyone else—like the house show scene in Minneapolis was nuts back when I was a kid and big bands will play with small bands like local bands like in a basement. . . . And different genres and it was so cool at that point, where like the catchy punk stuff—which is what I was into—would play with the scariest looking hardcore band I have ever seen and it was just like, wait they are all friends . . . and they were. I thought that was the coolest thing in the world. I was like, this is actually what I have read about, like a music scene that's kind of all-inclusive. It's not about musical taste, it's about ethics behind it. . . . That was always kind of cool.

While DIY may not create the type of mainstream exposure and buzz that a major record label may provide a band or musician, the ways of knowing how to "do" DIY stand out as a form of subcultural capital, which Thornton (1995) defines in this instance as a particular awareness that is "embodied in the form of being 'in the know'" (11). While often associated to the commodity side of scene production, knowledge and the know-how to create such goods can help to establish members as insiders. Being in the know can present itself in a variety of ways and having the knowledge to create and distribute your own music prevail as ways in which bands in today's scenes reinforce their status as members. If you are able to perform, produce, and distribute your own music—and then organize a tour to promote it—the insider knowledge and networking abilities needed to achieve these goals resonate as significant motivators for perpetuating the practice. For Aaron, DIY and its reliance on insider knowledge confers distinction, the Bourdieuian (1984) concept that helps participants "determine not only desirable and undesirable forms of culture but also desirable and undesirable ways of relating to cultural objects, desirable and undesirable strategies of interpretation and styles of consumption" (Jenkins 1992):

> Yeah, the DIY scene is it's pretty much in its title. People kind of find respect in it. "Oh shit, you did that yourself" rather than, "Oh, you got in the studio with Puff Daddy and whoever the fuck else." You know, Beyoncé had like 18 producers and songwriters for every track on her last album or however, many people it was. It's just like the same amount of people whereas these songs or like these five guys or these three guys got together and they put this out, maybe somebody said, "Hey, you might wanna change that," but for the most part, that's where the creation ended. And that's what you got on your album.

In this example, producing an album with a network of well-known celebrities does not confer distinction in the way independently creating your own music would—it takes away from the authenticity of the process, and is not always viewed as a desirable method by which to create and distribute music. Rather, fans and musicians would prefer to create music with other members in the community and proceed to have more input in the end result than decide to work with a celebrity for the name recognition and purpose of popularity. In choosing to proceed in this fashion, participants have "separat[ed] out that which is superior from what which is inferior" (Heath and Potter 2004, 124). While it may be more arduous and labor intensive to record independently and produce a product that may only sell a few dozen copies, the time and effort that go into producing music through these means aligns with the understanding that these scenes can function independently without the help from corporate entities. Furthermore, most punk bands have limited options. If musicians want to create music and share it with the world, their only means of doing so is to produce it independently. Because of this, it is the preferred method, and therefore the superior choice for those who participate in scenes today.

As punk has continued to thrive in spaces out of sight from popular culture, DIY embodies the collaborative and hardworking ethos of those not motivated by fame. The labor itself is viewed as admirable and speaks to an important value that resonates within scenes today. Furthermore, the practice itself can be viewed as a communal approach to determining what scenes from the music and bands that exist within. Here, Andrew describes his experiences with DIY. As an active member in several bands, Andrew viewed the DIY approach as one that allows for creative freedom, but also has its downsides regarding the ways this practice usually does not result in a large paycheck at the end of the night. Regardless, it continues to be a practice that is respected and valued within contemporary punk scenes today:

> To be completely honest a lot of people who take that route become a lot more successful than DIY artists do, but it really exists on the feel-good feeling, in

that we're doing this ourselves, there's nobody else that's going to tell us how to do this, so that makes us feel good that we're doing things our way, and if we can support other people to do things their way, so that they don't have to compromise or change their sound, or dye their hair, or make themselves look a certain way, playing off of their looks or whatever, that's something that we want to do because it makes us feel good too knowing that we're supporting other people. I think the biggest challenges for the DIY scene are just continuing to accept people and understanding that there's only so much that you're going to get back from this. . . . If you're expecting a huge monetary gain, obviously you're doing it wrong; you're in the wrong place. If you're expecting to make a lot of friends, play music the way you want to play music, run shows the way you want to run shows, book tours the way you want to book tours, if you want to play in a scene where all different types are welcomed to join, then you're in the right place. You could book an amazing show where 100 kids turn up in a basement, but if you want the scene to keep going, you've got to give the money to the touring bands, and you've got to give money to the house that held it so that if anything got messed up, they can repair it, or they can buy new equipment, or whatever. You have to kind of accept that you're only going to get out of it as much as you put into it, and sometimes you're not even going to get that much.

Speaking highly of the practice, Adam, who has played in several punk and hardcore bands on the East Coast, viewed DIY as a way to pay it forward to the younger generations of fans who are learning how to support their communities through DIY. He expressed hope that these experiences would encourage others to embrace these practices, and use their own DIY resources to perpetuate local scenes:

In a more precious sense, it's kind of to give back to that experience . . . it was the most fun I ever had. Just trying to replicate that feeling of walking into a sweaty basement and it's like, "wow, this is awesome, I didn't know this existed." You kind of hope that at every show there's some kid who goes, "wow, I didn't know this is a thing." The DIY stuff is kind of not wanting anyone to tell you what to do. Not that I've ever experienced that in music, but I don't think I would like it very much. I'd rather it be good people who are creatively involved [who] make decisions, rather than someone else who is dragging you to a certain direction. You don't want them to have any say in anything.

Adam's experience with DIY speaks to the autonomous nature of the process itself—those who operate their scenes through DIY methods are likely to have creative freedom and the ability to make decisions regarding their music, in contrast to bands who may have to follow contractual agreements with a record label.

Like Adam, Anthony viewed DIY as a practice to be shown to younger generations. Mentioning the ways older generations taught him how to do things in a DIY fashion, Anthony underscored the value in passing down knowledge to those who are new to the scene. Rather than adopting an "every person for themselves" attitude toward using DIY practices, there was a strong belief that these insights should be shared amongst those who have demonstrated an invested interest in working to make a scene successful:

> I think a lot of time you have to learn from your elders, learn from the people who have actually done this for a while, and who have experienced this for a while. And they'll tell you and they'll teach you, because they've experienced it. Our job in general is to teach people who are younger than us, or people that are less experienced than us the morals and ethics because they can learn it in books, but sometimes face-to-face conversations are important. And I think that older people explaining the true ethics and the true morals behind what you're doing, especially in DIY culture, is very important because now you have to understand everything about it because there's a reason why it's DIY.

While DIY is an umbrella term that encapsulates a variety of practices for both fans and producers, contemporary punk scenes view the practice positively, and understand it as a way to maintain to autonomy within their scenes. While it is not always the fastest way to make money and gain fame, it continues to be a prevailing force in allowing scenes to remain more or less self-sufficient. Now more than ever, participants have the methods of production and distribution at their fingertips, meaning that bands and fans can create and assist their scenes in ways that do not involve aid from outside contributors. The know-how involved in using DIY to make these ventures a success confers distinction among participants, as DIY is viewed as a reflection of the insider knowledge one needs in order to become a contributing participant within a scene.

ASK A PUNK: SOCIAL CAPITAL, NETWORKS OF COMMUNITIES, AND THE SPIRIT OF DIY

Because DIY continues to be a way for scene members to maintain autonomy over the production of goods, it prevailed as a prominent theme throughout my conversations with participants. In recent years, investigations into various elements of DIY practice such as DIY punk record labels (Dunn 2012b), DIY show spaces (Culton and Holtzman 2010), and DIY commodity production (Thompson 2004) prove that this method of production continues to be one that helps scenes establish their presence and reinforce the values that remain integral in contemporary punk communities today. One of the ways DIY remains relevant today is through the practice of organizing a show. In many cases, shows and tours are organized by band members themselves, and show organization is often facilitated through a network of other bands and show organizers in other cities. Generally connected through word-of-mouth or social media, participants' knowledge of other scenes and communities in other parts of the country help to perpetuate established lines of communication that operate on smaller levels. Putnam's (2000) social capital is useful to reference here—with the insider knowledge and networks that are used to organize and promote shows and tours, these interactions provide a well-connected system that can exist without major corporate entities such as large music venues or major record labels in order to make these events a reality. Rather than relying on large concert halls and venue spaces, scenes often operate these shows in basements, bars, and art spaces. Furthermore, these networks rely on "norms of reciprocity and trustworthiness," which are crucial when organizing large-scale events such as tours from other parts of the country (Leonard 2008, 224). Justin, who plays in a band, concluded some of the benefits of DIY include allowing bands the freedom to organize and schedule their tours independently:

> Now it's easier than ever to be in a band. Anyone can get a computer or a phone or an iPad or whatever, write a record and put it online. That's amazing. I think that's super important. It's also like where you previously would compete and be like "hey we want to play this show, we're the only band in the area that's even remotely close to this kind of sound." Now it's like well, there's like 50 other bands and 49 of them are willing to bring their friends and family to every single show. There still is compromise but this is also something worth identifying—it's the easiest it's ever been to do whatever you want and find a way to make that work, which I think is a core part of punk rock ethos. . . . But at the same time, if you just want to put your stuff online, go for it. If you just want to book your own tour, you could play houses, you don't have to play venues. You don't have to be on this crazy circuit. You can just find something that works for you. Some people do living room tours. Some people have toured on bikes. The fact that the possibility is out there for you with very little barrier to entry is amazing. I think that's one of the most respectable things about art at this time. Anyone can try to find their voice . . . it just seems like there's so many more options for bands now. You don't have to do all that stuff. You can just do it the best you can. If you have a friend that can help you out, cool. If you think you can do it, cool. If you can't, that's fine.

Justin identified the significance of technology and social media in his thoughts and spoke to the common methods used to create music today. With user-friendly music streaming platforms such as Bandcamp, bands can utilize whatever methods are available to advertise and promote their music at a low cost and with relative ease. Musicians do not need to rely on industry people to record and share music, nor are they beholden to a record label contract with specific creative demands. For many musicians in today's punk community, this freedom allows them to create music whenever and wherever it is possible. The level of commitment is also important to acknowledge here—if creating and playing music is just a hobby, or real life priorities such as work and school keep a band from making music their full-time job, it is still possible to dedicate free time whenever it is available to creating music and sharing it with the community. Punk does not have to be a full-time job. As evidenced here, the methods of creation and distribution within today's punk scenes are fluid, open-ended, and motivated by creativity. There are no set rules or guidelines to production, and the more creative your methods, the better.

Greg echoed similar thoughts as Justin, and he expressed the importance of smaller-scale shows and providing music at a low cost to members within a scene. Highlighting the importance of supporting smaller shows at inexpensive admission prices, Greg reconfirms the ease of access, which was also mentioned in Justin's earlier quote:

> It's cool that you have an alternative, and it's cool that you can look locally and just really see what your peers and what your friends are doing. That's so special to me. I make music, and my friends make music and we communicate that way, and it's kinda nice to not—we don't need bigger bands, we don't need to go to really big, expensive concerts. You can pay like 5 or 10 dollars to see your friend's band play a bar or a basement in Manhattan. I think there's something really special about that. It's something that's really important.

Here, Greg identified the self-sufficient beliefs that exist within his scene regarding organizing, performing, and attending shows. While the larger punk bands do exist, and tickets to see those shows are much more expensive, there is still a sizable and growing demand to continue the practice of organizing shows for inexpensive prices. These shows, which often take place in basements and bars, are advertised by word-of-mouth and social media. Many times, if these shows operate in non-sanctioned spaces (such as basements), any social media posting related to this show will encourage those interested to "ask a punk" for more details. Asking a punk employs the social capital and network of connections addressed previously, with an expectation of "generalized reciprocity" on behalf of participants (Putnam 2000, 134). This practice reinforces an understanding that if the show promoter provides you information on the whereabouts of this show, you will not share this information publicly as to arouse attention from those who could potentially interfere with the show itself. Furthermore, an agreement of trust is also established here: by sharing this information with you, you are agreeing to uphold the norms and values of the scene by behaving in ways that align with the community's values. A result of the closeness of a community itself, generalized reciprocity assumes that long-term investment in the community will keep participants from breaking the rules or going against pre-established norms. Putnam (2000) writes: "If two would-be collaborators are members of a tightly knit community, they are likely to encounter one another in the future—or to hear about one another through the grapevine. Thus, they have reputations at stake that are almost surely worth more than gains from momentary treachery" (136). For many, an understanding of the scene's norms and values act as an unspoken contract between those within a community. If one of these rules were to be broken, say, for example, by sharing the whereabouts of a basement show in a vulnerable location online or becoming violent at a show, there is an understanding that this person has gone against a particular norm within a scene, thereby breaking the unspoken contract regarding acceptable behavior within that particular space. Because punk scenes rely on communicative networks between members within these scenes, and social media allows for instantaneous communication with others, rule-breakers' reputations can be tarnished immediately and their access to the scene can be halted or prevented by others within the community.

While rule breaking can be an issue worth addressing, the majority of participants viewed DIY not as a hassle, but a positive benefit to a community that sees value in creativity. Andrew saw many benefits to embracing DIY show production and the value of having these connect networks within her scene. Because shows are often low-budget, and prices are purposely kept low in the spirt of the DIY ethos, an emphasis is placed on community-building aspects of the practice rather than on leaving the show with a big paycheck. In this quote, he described the common practice of donating most (or a large amount) of the profits made from admission to the touring band(s). The reason for this is to cover the expenses a touring band may accrue due to travel (gas, food, and so on):

> So [punk has] definitely made me a kinder person. I think it's made me a kinder person and it's definitely made me more open-minded and it's definitely made me more generous and willing to share my time and my resources. If ten years ago you would have told me my band's not going to get paid tonight, but we're gonna put all the money toward these touring bands, I would have been like that's not right, that doesn't make any sense—we brought all the kids, so why should they get the money? Now I understand it's kind of a pay-it-forward situation.

Again, the idea of generalized reciprocity is evident here, with the understanding that when the local bands head out on a tour, they will then receive the largest portion of the profits in a pay-it-forward-type situation. He continued this thought, expressing the importance of helping others within the punk community, and hoped that this returned kindness would remain an integral part of today's punk scenes. As evidenced here, the belief in placing community values over a monetary gain and popularity resonates as a way for contemporary punk scenes to maintain autonomy and establish egalitarian values within their scenes:

We put on this show for you so that you can do something good so that kids come and see you because we want you to succeed, and you want us to succeed, so maybe when we come on tour, maybe you'll help us out. And also, once you start helping people, you realize it makes you feel good. As selfish as that is, it makes you feel good to help other people, so you kind of start chasing that feeling as well, thinking how can I help other people? How can I make myself feel good by making them feel good? And selfish as that is.

For scenes today, DIY operates as a free-flowing and subjective practice that can be used by both producers and consumers. Creativity is paramount, and DIY practice within these spaces can manifest itself in a variety of ways. Furthermore, technology is embraced and viewed as a positive avenue by which information can be shared. While technology has helped to blur the boundaries between translocal and virtual distinctions, we see the ways that these platforms are regulated through close-knit communities that rely on the trust and goodwill of others. Largely influenced by the social media and technological platforms that have infiltrated their lives, participants see the ways that these technologies can be used positively for the purpose of sharing information about shows, festivals, and other scene-related events. Though there is an understanding that certain external influences (i.e., social media) exist in subcultural spaces, there is an awareness that certain rules must be followed when communicating information regarding scene-centric events on these platforms. Furthermore, rule following expands beyond the limitations of Facebook, and there are expectations, both spoken and unspoken, that simultaneously work to regulate the behaviors within these spaces. Through the common practice of paying-it-forward, participants in today's scenes recognize that while basement shows may not be the way to financial and musical freedom, they function as sites of trust and agreed-upon behavior. In contrast, rule-breaking behavior often results in threats to one's reputation and may prevent that person from participating in scene-related activities in the future.

SELLING OUT AND THREATS TO DIY

The term "sellout" is one that has a chameleon-like tendency to shift its meaning and significance depending on factors such as context, time, and at whom the term is directed. At some point, any underground artist or musician who receives large-scale attention from a record label or allows their song to air in a television commercial has had claims of selling out hurled their way. What was once a term directed at any musician who allowed their art to be recognized by large audiences, selling out had the ability to cause great damage to, or even ruin, a career (Nicolay 2017). With its ties to authenticity, music fans at large often conflate the two terms as synonymous—if you sold out to a major record label, your values are immediately impacted. No longer were you making music for the sake of making music, but rather, you made it for the money. This conflation had immediate results for Green Day, who were at one time banned from playing Gilman St., the Berkeley, California, club where they got their start following the decision to release *Dookie* on a major record label (Anthony 2015). While it might make sense for today's scenes to have strong beliefs against selling out, evidence suggests that although DIY continues as a popular practice, an understanding exists that fame is not out of the realm of possibility. Furthermore, selling out is not necessarily viewed as an abandonment of scene values or a snub to those that helped a band get to this point. Rather, fame is often viewed as achieving a goal: that your band was successful and talented enough to make a fulltime job out of performing music.

In the last few years, technology and the rise in file sharing and streaming services have motivated music journalists, musicians, and fans alike to re-evaluate their assumptions on what it means for a musician to sell out. With readily available access to music through these platforms, exclusivity and determinants of authenticity become harder to define. Streaming services have democratized music: it takes the same number of steps to access Green Day's latest album on Spotify as it does to access an album by small band that played a local basement show. Because of this, there is continued evidence to suggest that the connotations associated with selling out have changed. As will be explored below, many of those interviewed for this book saw an artist's rise in popularity as a positive thing—more exposure for the band means more money in the long run. And at the end of the day, who doesn't want to make a profit from their art? Furthermore, participants admitted that their own introductions to punk rock were the result of several mainstream avenues by which one can learn about music: MTV and the radio. As long as the band does not change their values or forget the scenes that were supportive before greater attention was directed their way, participants often expressed indifference, and oftentimes support, toward the entire notion of selling out.

Evidence of this can be found in my discussion with Eric. According to Eric, the public opinion on selling out has changed with time, and it is no longer viewed as entirely problematic, nor is it necessarily detrimental to a band's image. He recognized that profit-making is important for anyone trying to make a living from their art, and if a band is able to capitalize on the ability to do so, then they should be able to proceed. On the other hand, bands can take the DIY route if they wish, as the opportunity to create and distribute music today is easier than ever:

> [Bands] can do whatever they want. If they feel comfortable with taking money from a big corporation or shit like that then that's fine. That's none of

anyone's business. It's you. You can decide whether to like them or not again so everyone's in control of themselves in this thing like we said. I think that maybe back in the day that was not cool at all. But now, you don't make any money doing this anyway. So I get it, but at the same time do you really need that money to create it? Like I said, we could record it all ourselves . . . you know what I mean? I understand and if I were put in that situation, I don't know what I'd do. I think that big labels now, major labels are on life support. They've price gouged, they have treated bands terribly and now they're just trying to figure out how to continue.

He continued this line of thinking by providing Against Me! as an example of a band who briefly signed to a major record label (Sire Records, a division of Warner Records) in 2007 (Ozzi 2015) yet remains an active band within today's punk scene. In looking at the band's continued relevance and popularity today, Against Me!'s involvement with a major record label has not impacted their reputation negatively for fans:

Against Me! too is a good example of band that tried to go that route. They got enough money to set themselves up which is what I would always like to do. If there is a way where I could set myself up to run everything, I would totally do it. I would hope that it wouldn't change the mentality of the songwriters which it has sometimes with certain bands, and there's a lot of bands that I don't even know that I used to judge. I am not gonna lie.

Jamie identified their own perspectives on the concept of selling out and made some practical conclusions about the ways that an increase in recognition affords bands the ability to make a living off their work. To someone with little to no personal experience in this field, selling out becomes a catch-all term used by outsiders, and the use of such term demonstrates a failure to understand the level of effort and resources that go into making music:

Even bands signing to majors. That's not really selling out to me. It's very hard to have a career in music. Even when bands sign to major labels sometimes they still can't make that their fulltime job. I don't think people realize, I've had so many friends in bands and they had to juggle their work life, their family life, with this band that makes no money. Most people don't . . . people think that when they're signed to a smaller independent label, like even Fat Wreck [Chords], or No Idea [Records], that you're raking in the big money now because you're on Epitaph [Records]. No, you're not. A lot of those guys still have day jobs. That's not selling out to me, that's you wanting to make your career out of your art. Most people don't get that opportunity. . . . People have to be pragmatic sometimes. You have to eat; you have to keep a roof over your head. That's survival, that's not punk or not punk. You're just trying to get by. Selling out to me is when you have certain ethics and ideas and then you don't stand by them. I'll see guys in bands claim that they're feminists, and they have women's backs, but then they don't. Like when people are calling them out on stuff, and they're like, and they get really defensive and hostile about it. That's selling out to me. That's going against your ideas. You're saying one thing and doing another thing. That's where I, that's my cynical sort of thing about punk. If a band wants to make a career about what they love to do, that's great. I'm happy for them.

What resonates here is the ways in which a change in values indicate the signs of selling out. If a band no longer associates themselves with the core values of a scene, fails to deliver on ideological promises, or uses their newfound platform for a conflicting message, the band is then faced with having lost their credibility with those who were there at the start. For Justin, the issue of selling out was complicated. Referring to selling out as "the most abused oversimplification of anything possible," Justin addressed the ways in which people minimalize the amount of work that goes into making a profit off music:

I also think that phrase is also the most abused oversimplification of anything possible, especially with punk ethos, because I guess the easiest definition that I've always understood, and feel free to correct me if you have a better one, is just when you are no longer doing the thing you are interested in doing solely for the purpose of making money, or gaining fame or success, and that's it. That's kind of where it stops. I think it's always more reasonable than not to see a band bend a little bit, to make sure they can make ends meet.

To continue, Justin spoke toward the notion that directing anger toward a band for making a profit on their music is misguided, claiming that those who use the term do not understand how difficult it is to make a living by touring and recording albums:

People really care when you're like 15 years old and you don't have anything to think about. We all invent problems for ourselves. When you're 15 you don't really have problems besides puberty, and school dances, and no one likes you. Yeah, those are problems and they seem big at the time, but you also . . . I don't have anything real to think about, let me get mad at Rancid for doing a video . . . who gives a shit? That's just the easiest example I can think of . . . I don't think it fucking matters, because honestly even if a band gets big and they're like "oh, fuck off, I'm going to take $10 million." I think the Distillers literally did this. Their website was updated for one day and it was just like "we sold out last night just to get a bajillion dollars, don't listen to us anymore." I'm like whatever, that's fucking funny. I don't care. It doesn't change your whole record to me. Granted if you are a super corporate capitalist person and then you write a record that's a commercial for Ford or something. Yeah, your ethics start to go into question, but it doesn't change the fact that you, at that time, wrote that record that I really like. Also, I don't really give a shit what you're doing.

As evidenced here, contemporary scenes often view a rise in popularity to be a positive thing—as long as one's values remain intact. As participants get older, they begin to understand the amount of work that goes into playing music, and many times, their perspectives on selling out changed. While it is easy to discount a band for making a music video or signing to a major record label, getting older changes this perspective, as participants become more aware of the logistics and motivations behind why bands make these decisions.

For Alex, the notion of selling out perpetuated the assumption that signing to a major record label is a choice made lightly. In addition, it has grown to become a term used by those who do not have the direct experience with producing or distributing music. Thanks to music downloading and streaming, the use value of music as a commodity has decreased, which means that bands have to work harder than ever to make a profit from the music they create:

> Everyone thinks of punk in 1977, and mohawks and leather jackets, and tight pants and all that stuff, but nowadays, it's way more diverse. But people still see that and they're like "oh, that's punk." You can see punk in a Sprint commercial. That's where it gets a little weird to me, but I think it can be done in the right way, it benefits . . . obviously it benefits the companies who are doing it, otherwise they wouldn't do it. But I think it can be a good thing for some people. I try to see the good in it, in other words. As opposed to looking at it as some bullshit thing where this band's a sellout now because you can buy their record at the mall, that kind of thing. I feel that's way too dismissive of something that I feel is a little more nuanced than most people think. I feel like [selling out] is a thing that fans care about more than bands care about. Most bands wouldn't call it selling out, they would call it something else because they're doing something right with their music, and a lot of people are interested in it so they may eventually reach a point where they get to quit their shitty day jobs and just play music full time and not have to worry about anything else. Which in theory is great, but for some reason, a lot of people get upset when that happens. I don't really know why, but I think the thing is, and especially now most people, kids especially, nobody buys records anymore. Everybody just steals them, or shares them, whatever, and you have to have money to go on tour and record albums and if nobody has any money, there's no music. Which is why you see bands with their song in a commercial or something along those lines. Like ten, fifteen years ago, it wouldn't have happened because it was before file sharing and these bands were doing okay, they were doing better than they are now, gas was cheaper and all this other stuff. But they have to supplement their income or else they're not going to be able to survive, and sometimes I think the fans themselves get a little too entitled about that sort of thing where they take ownership of the bands in a weird way, when they shouldn't because it's not their band.

Though possession of scene-specific commodities such as records continues to be a valued practice within scenes today, music streaming and downloading have no doubt impacted the ways fans claim ownership of music. With a perceived devaluation of these goods as ownership shifts from the physical to the digital, it becomes increasingly difficult for musicians to make a profit from their music. For instance, in 2018, artists who posted their music on Spotify earned $0.006 to $0.0084 per stream (Sehgal 2018). In Alex's example, he tries to justify the ways that an artist might see using their song in a commercial as an opportunity and a route to an immediate paycheck. Once again, many within today's scenes understand the economics of digital streaming and demonstrate support for publicity that would result in receiving more than tenths of a cent each time a listener hears their song.

Here, Emily considered the issues with a band gaining popularity, and acknowledges the ways that popular retail stores such as Hot Topic are a gateway for many in the exploration of punk rock:

> I mean, I'm sure some people will sell out. Is it easier because stores like Hot Topic and social media in general, yeah it's definitely easier, but I still think that most people hold true to their roots of where they came from and realize the importance of the community that they built in the years that they've been playing and those people who've been going to shows since the band was doing their first set that's opening for a band that's not even that big and going from that to actually having a following. . . . I don't think that it's a problem, I think it's positive, but people will get greedy because humans are humans and I'm sure some people will sell out because it's the easiest thing to do and the most tempting.

As mentioned above, while participants viewed a band's increased popularity as mostly positive, the concept of selling out was viewed negatively when it resulted in a change of values. When asked about DIY in her Long Island, New York, scene, Emily proceeded to provide some examples of current bands who have either lost or maintained their DIY roots, and she commented on how this change in ethos has affected their relationship with fans. Here, DIY is understood as a positive, uniting practice that helps to reinforce community-building practices. When these practices are sacrificed for fame or mainstream attention, fans lose that relationship with these bands:

> [DIY] brings a community closer together, it also allows punk to stay independent in a sense. I'll use Brand New for an example. Brand New, it's like almost impossible to get tickets for a show on Long Island because they're from there and because they didn't sell out, but they kind of were like, they just went with what their record [label] says to do, and they don't really care as much about their fans as other bands do. Even though Modern Baseball got pretty big, I think they are very attuned to what their fans like, compared to

Brand New for example, who seem to not care as much about where they came from or anything like that. They kind of just have to do what they're told. I mean, they don't have to, but they do. And I think keeping stuff DIY keeps it a more tight-knit community, so not only for the music, but for the people in general and it also allows things to be more flexible, like house shows can happen and stuff like that.

For clarification, following the major success of their 2003 album *Deja Entendu*, Brand New signed to major label Interscope Records to release *The Devil and God Are Raging Inside Me* in 2006. Both albums received positive acclaim from fans and critics alike and made appearances on the *Billboard* 200 charts (Brand New n.d.). In comparison, Modern Baseball, Philadelphia-based band released their 2016 album *Holy Ghost* on Run for Cover Records, a Boston independent record label motivated by "a passion for local punk and hardcore music backboned by DIY ethos and aspirations for an all-inclusive community" (Run for Cover Records n.d.). Again, Emily's thoughts here serve as another example of the importance of maintaining one's values, because any threats to this legitimacy can cause fans to reassess their own relationship with a particular band.

In contrast to Emily's thoughts on Brand New, Jimmy cited Green Day as a prime example of a punk band who, while spending the greater part of the last three decades in the spotlight, have legitimized themselves as a band who has largely stayed true to the values they held well before *Dookie* turned them into overnight pop punk sensations:

I honestly don't care [about selling out]; I think good for them. If you're doing what you like to do it and somebody pays you to do it, I don't see the big deal in that. I was never a huge Green Day fan either, but I could see why people would be like "oh yeah they played here all the time and now they're selling out arenas." I get all that, but you gotta think the band's reaching wider audiences with what they have to say, they're doing it for themselves, they don't need a real job anymore, they don't have to stress about having a job and having to go on tour, this band's my job now. They can support themselves; they can support their families and stuff with that. I think it's cool. Getting opinions out there to wider people. They're reaching so many more people that they have been on the major label than if they were sitting on whatever the hell they were on before.

Like the others, Andrew expressed ambivalence toward the notion of selling out. While more exposure may mean seeing shows in larger venues rather than basements, a general sense of enthusiasm existed about the prospects of punk bands gaining the ability to make money from performing music and sharing their message with a wider audience:

As long as there's no negative attention, it doesn't bother me. The way I see it is literally, like, everyone needs to make a living. And I'm probably going to get to see my favorite band more if they're getting paid for shows, so I don't want to have to see my favorite bands in arenas, but that's not, I just don't think that's happening anytime. So, it doesn't bother me. I don't think I've ever been, like "oh my god." . . . I think that the only thing that ever really does is make a band more accessible, which I think is good, especially if the band doesn't live near you, and it's great if your local band is playing a basement in your city all the time, but bands can't really make a living that way and I think it's kind of unfair for people to get super mad about it. And I really don't think it's that big of an issue as some people think it is, but there's always the people who think they're selling out.

Similar to others who shared their indifference toward the notion of selling out, Greg mentioned the difficulties that arise when attempting to make a living from music. As a current member of several bands on the East Coast, Greg acknowledged the difficulties in balancing responsibilities as a member of a band and the obligations that exist outside of this sphere: "It's really hard to be a musician! If you can make money off that . . . so many musicians have to work odd jobs, or it's really hard to hold onto a job and tour, I would never blame anyone for taking an opportunity like [signing to a major record label]—if someone's really genuinely giving it a shot, and this is how they're gonna do it, why would I blame them for trying something new or outside the box?"

Often used as a term to deride or ridicule a band that has grown in popularity, the concept of selling out is largely a non-issue for members in the scene today. While in previous years, the term itself was loaded with negative associations of celebrity status and the forfeiting of values, selling out is a near non-issue in today's hyper-commodified and branded world. In fact, perceptions of selling out have drastically changed with a shift in generations—today, selling your art to a major company is often viewed positively, as it means you made a profit from this work (Lam 2018). As a generation that is under a great deal of pressure to pay off student loans, health insurance bills, and other debts in an uncertain economy, millennials—who were the largest population interviewed for this book—view the concept of selling out as way to overcome such obstacles (Baab-Muguira 2016; Taylor 2014). Participants were largely supportive of bands who find success in making music—as long as the values and integrity remain intact. Selling out was not viewed as a band's acceptance of the values of the mainstream but was instead understood as a way for a band to use this platform positively. If the band can maintain their integrity in the face of larger paychecks, greater exposure, and the pressing demands of a major record label, then they have succeeded in achieving such goals.

THE AFTERMATH OF SELLING OUT:
WHEN PUNK MEETS THE MAINSTREAM

By in large, fans were mostly ambivalent toward the possibility of a band signing to a major record label and gaining popularity through such means. Several punk bands, including Bad Religion, Jawbreaker, and Rancid all signed to major record labels between the mid-90s and early 2000s, and while not as common now as it was at the peak of punk rock's mainstream popularity, it is an eventuality for some bands to sign to major record labels today. When this happens, these bands bring a renewed awareness to the music and lifestyle itself. When asked about the prevalence of punk rock within mainstream popular culture, Andrew appeared ambivalent toward the possibility, optimistically hoping that mainstream popularity will invite new-comers to explore the more nuanced underground music that exists within scenes today:

> The way that I think about it is anything cool is going to come up in main-stream culture eventually, every single kind of style of music. If it becomes cool, it's going to end up in mainstream culture, whether it's rap or R&B, or punk, or EDM, or dubstep, it's showing up in Taylor Swift songs or stuff like that. It's gonna happen. It's a sign that we're doing something good, and that other people are interested in it. . . . The way I see it as far as [punk] becoming more mainstream, that just means more people will get interested in it. Hope-fully they'll hear Blink-182 on the radio, but then they'll go to Spotify and say, "well what else sounds like Blink-182?" and then they'll find smaller bands they like that they end up supporting. Or they might find out that "oh, I like Blink-182" and you mention that to your friend and your friend says "oh, here's this band that sounds like Blink-182 that's playing at a basement show." So you go to the basement show and you have a great time and you become a fan of punk. So, you know it doesn't bother me that mainstream pop punk bands or stuff like that might lead itself into other kids getting into it, or younger kids getting into it. The more we can diversity the punk scene, the better, because the better-rounded the scene will be, the better it will be to different groups of people within the scene. It's a tough spot to be in because you want people to succeed, and yeah it would be great if we could all support ourselves playing in bands and if you can do that without feeling like you've changed yourself, or you sold out, then awesome, but if you're making a conscious decision to change something to get on the radio, or to get more attention from the media or something like that, and you feel like you're selling out, that's the problem. I can't tell somebody else because they might have just felt like that's the direction their music was naturally progressing in.

Andrew continued his thoughts regarding the ethical issues of selling out and believed that if a band becomes popular and their message and values stay the same, then the band's credibility will remain intact. If the band's message changes, however, and fame becomes a priority over using this platform to raise awareness and evoke change, then selling out becomes problematic:

> So much of punk was built on political statements about [how] we need to support the homeless and we need to support women and end racism and end sexism and we need to get bigots out of here and we need to change people's minds, and those don't necessarily sell very well on mainstream radio. If you started out as this really political, really tough band that was sticking to your ideals, and then all of a sudden, you're playing songs about girls who broke your heart on the radio, then it comes across as not genuine. I do think that mainstream attention can change music. It doesn't necessarily have to. There are definitely punk bands that have gotten famous singing songs about how my girlfriend broke my heart, and that's fine, but their message doesn't change when they get bigger. If your message changes and all of a sudden, you're not talking about these things anymore, then that's a problem that you're getting this mainstream attention. If you're still up there saying like, "the government is bad and here's how we need to change it," and you're not letting it change your message or who you are as people, then I think that's great, then you've really won. I don't know how you did it, but you've won.

Like Andrew, Greg viewed punk's relationship with mainstream popular culture as somewhat of a non-issue. He acknowledged that many within the scene today learned of punk rock through these mainstream methods, and while his own exploration into the music uses more underground methods today, there is an understanding that outlets such as these were integral in introducing so many to the music during adolescence:

> That authenticity thing is kind of hit or miss. I'm not very concerned with it, but it's funny because if you think a band is fake, or pushed by a label, or just a bunch of kids who don't know what they're doing, but you know the parents are paying for it, it kind of bugs you, so I don't know. But at the same time, it's like, no one's born cool. We all heard a Blink-182 song in 5th grade and were like "What's this?" I'm okay making things accessible.

Elizabeth also shared her thoughts on the impact of mainstream culture on punk, and stressed that despite popular culture's interest in punk rock, there continues to be a dedicated group of individuals who remain committed to the DIY efforts of their communities:

> I've never been to Warped Tour, I don't really come to bands through super popular avenues, but I also have been to very few basement shows. I mean, a lot of smaller venues are somewhat DIY just because it's not in someone's basement doesn't mean it's not DIY. I don't think that selling and selling out are the same thing. I know people used to get really up in arms about "this band is selling out because they signed to a major label." It's like if that band wants to make this their living, they probably have to do that. So, I don't think that the DIY scene's ever going to go away, but I think that it's something you

definitely have to try harder to find sometimes. I think it's always going to be there because that's what punk is.

In these examples, we see the ways that those within contemporary punk scenes demonstrate an indifference toward the practices that make the music more available to outsiders—if this attention raises awareness, then many are supportive of this outcome, as it often means that a band now has the ability to make a profit off their music. There is an understanding, however, that participants are discerning when a band is acting under inauthentic premises or changes their values in order to align with the demands of a record label. In those cases, the band's motivations can be questioned.

Unlike those who did not believe signing to a major record label to be a career-ending move, Allie expressed different opinions on this topic. For Allie, the act of signing to a major record label posed a threat to a band's autonomy, as well as to the band's ability to make their own music. Furthermore, the idea of signing to a major record label signified a band's willingness to be told what they can or cannot do with their music, and that, in and of itself, is indicative of the ways a band signs over their autonomy when working with a major label:

> I guess in the 90s when all the bands were starting to be signed, a lot of the times when we heard the first major label release from the band we were always kind of disappointed, it sounded like the spirit was gone, and a lot of those bands ended up getting dropped because they wanted to maintain their way of doing things and the record label didn't want to hear it. It was fine in the 70s when people like The Clash were signed, they maintained their autonomy, but it just seemed like a lot of the bands in the early 90s that got signed lost it. So, I think that's one reason why it's really important. Not to be a purist, because a lot of people are a little too purist I guess, it was a turnoff, but unfortunately if you're working with someone who only cares about how many units they're pushing, you've got to make some compromises and I don't think that compromise is really something that plays a role in what we're listening to.

While punk rock's relationship with mainstream culture has at times proven to be a contentious one, today's punk communities recognize that its existence is inevitable. Similarly, mainstream tastes will continue to coopt various elements of punk culture. Like the concept of selling out, most participants saw the concept of the mainstream as a tool by which more awareness of the genre could occur—discovering bands and learning about punk rock through these mass media was not only a common practice for many members in the scene today, but was viewed as a helpful way for others to gain access. Though this relationship was, for the most part, viewed positively, there still exists an understanding that mainstream outlets can be detrimental to core punk values, which at their most basic, reject hegemonic forces that threaten the authenticity of the genre itself.

POSTERS, PINS, PATCHES, AND PUNK ROCK: HOT TOPIC HAS IT ALL

In the early 2000s, my friends and I would make our way to the King of Prussia Mall where the nearest Hot Topic store was located. We would spend far too much time browsing the selection of band shirts, Goth jewelry, and pop culture paraphernalia displayed to the ceiling on darkly colored walls, and I would always leave the store with new buttons and patches to artfully decorate my backpack. Hot Topic was my first exposure to the commodity side of punk rock—while finding music online and at Best Buy was second nature at this point, locating band t-shirts and patches proved to be more challenging. In 2002, it was much harder to get merchandise from the bands you liked—Bandcamp and Facebook were still years away. Interpunk.com was around at that time, but without a credit card, buying merchandise online only happened if the stars aligned and my parents agreed. Therefore, Hot Topic was the place to go if I wanted a new Saves the Day t-shirt or Dropkick Murphys patch. And while my days of shopping at Hot Topic are now over, I will walk past their windows every now and then to marvel at the pop culture-related references I no longer understand, nostalgic for the old days of perusing their selection for a new band t-shirt or patch for my backpack.

For many teenagers growing up in the early 2000s, Hot Topic was the retailer of choice for alternative fashion, music, and popular culture. Today, the store continues to capitalize on its countercultural appeal and appears to have a monopoly on fandom-friendly merchandise, selling Sailor Moon backpacks alongside purple hair dye and Ice Cube t-shirts. With this wide selection, it is no surprise Hot Topic continues to prevail as a leading retailer for thirteen- to thirty-six-year-olds, who, according to marketing research firm YPulse, consider their products "most unique" (Mejía 2019; YPulse 2018). The retailer encourages customers to embrace their inner fan, giving consumers the ability to choose from an endless variety of music t-shirts, denim, and sweatshirts, Disney jewelry, action figures, and video game-related accessories. A 2003 *Bloomberg* article described Hot Topic as "prid[ing] itself on quickly stocking what its customers crave: hard-to-find fashions coming out of pop culture," which continues to remain true today (Weintraub 2003). While Hot Topic is firmly in the consciousness of every teen interested in memes, anime, and Harry Potter today, the Hot Topic of the early 2000s had an important mission: to act as "gatekeepers" to the counter-cultural commodities that were not as readily available then as they are today (Gallagher 2015).

Though it exists on the opposite side of the spectrum to DIY and independent commodity creation within a scene, Hot Topic frequently appeared as a subject throughout my interviews for this book, and positive associations to the retailer were not uncommon. Like the concept of selling out, Hot Topic was another example of participants' understanding that punk rock and contemporary punk scenes do not exist in media-free bubbles, isolated from the influence of powerful industries and the specter of capitalism looking to profit from a countercultural phenomenon. While it would seem that a hyper-commercialized store such as Hot Topic would be viewed as an infringement on contemporary punk scenes and their ability to maintain autonomy, most participants reacted positively to the notion that Hot Topic provided counter-cultural goods to fans at a time when they were not nearly as accessible as they are today. Furthermore, some credited Hot Topic as a contributor to their own introductions to punk rock, as the store itself was easily found in nearly every mall across the country. When asked about Hot Topic and the ways that the store popularizes various aspects of punk culture and style, Jamie seemed accepting of this practice, and believed that Hot Topic acts as a low-stakes entry into exploration of music and music scenes:

> For me, growing up, Hot Topic was one of the only places I could get stuff like that. I was in rural Pennsylvania. The closest cities were Baltimore—an hour and a half drive, DC was an hour and a half drive, Philly and Pittsburgh were both three-hour drives. It was in the middle of nowhere, and like I said it was before the dawn of the Internet being a crazy accessible thing. That's what I had. I had Hot Topic. That's where I had to get my first band shirt. That was the only place I had. And it's like yeah, Hot Topic's corny, but there's a purpose for it. It's not for you. I always say this to people, especially when dudes complain about boy bands, who say like "this sucks," I'm like "this isn't for you." You are not the demographic for this. Clearly you are not going to get it or understand it. And that's how I feel about Hot Topic. It's for . . . I mean I'll still go in there and I'll buy action figures and stuff. Or I'll see a cool shirt with a cat in a taco or something. I'll go in there from time to time, just to . . . and even then I'll look through the records, the vinyl, and even if it's a small section, I'll be surprised to find some good stuff in there. . . . So kids need to have a way to explore that. So, I do think there's a purpose for it, and I don't decry it.

While Hot Topic may have its detractors, there is no denying the impact that it has had on bringing countercultural commodities to suburban teenagers across the country. Like Jamie, Alex viewed Hot Topic as a place for curious fans to gain exposure to various scenes and did not view the retailer negatively. While the store may not be for everyone, there is an argument to be made for the ways in which Hot Topic raises awareness of counterculture in ways that no other mainstream store has done successfully:

Most people my age hate Hot Topic, for example, but for a lot of kids who are 14, 15, 16, that's their first exposure to alternative culture that they've ever experienced, you know what I mean? It's not the end of the road for them, I mean it might be for some of them, but the fact that kids in suburbia can go to a mall and buy a Descendents record or a Descendents t-shirt is really cool to me. Obviously, it's not perfect, but it's better than the alternative, which is nothing. A lot of people get really upset, and they'll say something like "aw man, Descendents sell their records at Hot Topic now, I can't believe it, I'm so angry." First of all, why do you care? Second of all, some kid might pick up that record and it might change their life. So, I think it's good in a sense that in those situations when that culture, even if it's a small amount of it is being put out there to people who don't normally have access to it, or if they find it on accident. But when brands or companies coopt punk because they think it's hip and they think it'll make them money, that's where I have a problem.

While Hot Topic and its cooptation of subcultural signifiers were received positively or indifferently, Allie viewed the chain as a threat to punk rock's ethos, and provided an example of the ways Hot Topic affected the process of finding new music and purchasing merchandise:

A place like Hot Topic comes and it's a corporation, and it's for profit so someone can get rich. There's a CEO, it's not some dinky little storefront where the guy's just scraping by, and he's doing it because he loves music. Also, from what I've read, not all of the band products that are sold have the approval of the band, and they may not be making a cent from the sale of their product. And that's not something I support at all. As a matter of fact, when I have a student come in with a Hot Topic bag, I give them a little lecture. If you're buying that Ramones t-shirt, no one related to any of those members is seeing a cent from that shirt. How are you supporting the band?

As evidenced in the opinions shared here, Hot Topic, like many other mainstream forces that surround contemporary punk rock, was largely viewed as another means by which outsiders can explore the genre, but was also recognized as an example of a powerful force with the ability to derail the independent efforts of many scenes around the country. For those with no other ways to access the music, Hot Topic serves as a low-stakes way for those interested to learn about what is taking place in the scene today. While it may not serve as an ideal version of what is considered to be punk by the scene itself, there is value in the accessibility Hot Topic offers. And though Hot Topic is just another retail business in the mall and the store operates in the same ways that other large corporate businesses do, participants expressed little opposition to Hot Topic as a corporation who has capitalized on monopolizing the business of counterculture. Because of this, we see further proof that participants within contemporary punk scenes recognize the influence of mainstream outlets such as Hot Topic, and that those who participate within these scenes can coexist in spheres where mainstream forces play a big role in affecting the scenes themselves.

DIY BLOGS, PODCASTS, AND PHOTOGRAPHS: EXAMPLES OF PRACTICE WITHIN TODAY'S SCENES

DIY practice and contributions to a local scene's economy take on a variety of forms. While typical understandings of DIY include the production of music, zines, and t-shirts, today's punk scenes have explored the ways that social and digital media can assist in the production and distribution of these goods. For instance, organizing a show and promoting the event via Facebook and Instagram would be considered a DIY practice in today's scenes, as conveying information about the event to fans through social media is the fastest and easiest way to reach a large audience. Furthermore, the interconnectivity between these audiences reconfirms the contemporary assumption that DIY works as an asset to unite scenes, rather than to divide them: "DIY has now become synonymous with a broader ethos of lifestyle politics that bonds people together in networks of translocal, alternative cultural production" (Bennett and Guerra 2018c, 9). This behavior appears antithetical to the notion that DIY acts as an insular tactic used by scenes as a type of anti-consumerist statement on capitalistic practices and the cooptation of punk rock and its signifiers. Furthermore, the use of social media within a scene reconfirms the "osmotic" relationships that contemporary punk scenes have with external institutions such as media and popular culture (Weinzierl and Muggleton 2003, 7).

Eric, who hosts a podcast that addresses issues within today's punk scenes and often hosts interviews with members from current punk bands, explained how this practice allows him to not only create a product, but also have a direct impact on how this podcast is produced. He also provided information about the web store associated with the podcast, where the merchandise sold is created by hand:

So, now I'm like almost 90 episodes in and I continue to do it, and I like it and if you listen to it, you can hear my ups and my downs and the days when I hate everything and the days when I love everything and I talk about how I get out of my lows and it works. I don't know. It's just interesting and I get to share music and then turned into like a web store where I get to sell shirts and records for only bands that I like. And bands get an insanely great cut of that money with nothing upfront, so like it's another way of like . . . if you're gonna do this and solve things, you need to actually be the person who pays these people, and we do that, and they love it, you know what I mean?

When asked further about the podcast, Eric's response emphasized the importance of social capital in finding people to interview. Through various networks of connections from many years of participating within a scene, and through the connections made via social media and word-of-mouth, Eric uses these relationships to promote guests' music and art:

> It's always people that I know. Or friends of friends . . . that I get to do that, and I only do people that I think would have something interesting to say. It's not just a quick grab for famous people . . . I will do anyone who I think has a story. And now that there's enough of an audience for it, like people listen to it anyway you know what I mean. Obviously, people would like to hear you know, Greg from the Bouncing Souls, but they will also hear Greg, my friend from high school, who did something crazy once. You know what I mean? So, it's all about like you build up trust with an audience of like if they're doing this, it's probably going to be interesting. Sometimes I miss, but hey, I try.

Like Eric, Alex uses social media as a way to contribute to his scene. As the editor of his own blog, where contributors write about their experiences and thoughts on punk, Alex described the goal of the blog, which hopes to generate exposure on issues that face the scene today:

> I wanted to do something a bit different, so I started the site and the site is still so new that it doesn't necessarily have that much of a voice yet, or that much of a central conceit, but for the most part it's essays from a personal standpoint about punk rock and punk rock subculture and stuff not necessarily about the music itself, although we do a lot of music writing and interviews and features and stuff like that. But the biggest part of the site is people writing about their own experiences through . . . whether it's like "this band changed my life" or "I have social anxiety at punk shows and this is how I deal with it," or "I feel weird at punk shows because I'm tall or old," or something like that so that's basically what the site is, and it's been really good, it's been the most gratifying thing I've done so far from a creative standpoint, just because it's really fun to hear people's stories and publish them.

Again, Alex's blog represents another example of the ways in which contemporary punk scenes fail to exist in the "media-free" spaces suggested by the CCCS (Thornton 1995). Rather than remaining isolated from the technologies of modern society or maintaining an us-versus-them approach to the media that surrounds these scenes, participants use these mediums to their advantage, and to raise awareness of the issues that face translocal scenes today. Here, Alex explains the motivations behind the blog in more detail, and how it serves as a platform for voices within the scene: "In my case, I think it's important because we're talking about stuff that other people aren't talking about. You know, it's not just 'here's an album I'm really excited about,' it's 'hey, this thing is happening in our scene and it's problematic.' Let's talk about it."

The active participation in DIY is not relegated to bands and those with large platforms or audiences—anyone can help out in ways that they deem appropriate. For Alex, his blog could serve dual purpose in providing information about the music-related topics within the scene, but also served to address some of the larger, more pressing social issues that often arise. Furthermore, Alex encourages others to partake in contributions with the hopes that those who submit articles will help to diversify the voices within the scene itself.

Below, Greg described his own contributions to DIY practice, and provided some information on an artist collective that he and a friend organized together:

> I started [the artist collective] with my best friend from college, and in college we would start clubs together. I'm more practical and he'll have bigger ideas and kind of get all the people together. So I had this idea to make it about bands, like "oh all of our bands will put out a comp or something" and we have a lot of friends who are visual artists and friends who do video, so we do two shows a year. . . . During the day we have all our artist friends selling their posters and screen prints, whatever they might make. We have acoustic acts and poets during the day, and at night we had bands. My rule is 20-minute sets, so we had eight bands in three hours. It was crazy.

In this example, Emily describes her experiences with taking photos for bands, citing this practice as a way "to help them out." Rather than passively attending a show, Emily explained that her participation is an active contribution to creating goods for a scene:

> So when [the band] played at one of the venues out east, since I'm a photographer, they were like "Do you want to take pictures?" and I'm like "sure" so I went on stage when they were playing and I took a bunch of pictures and videos for them. And I guess I'm like more involved that way, not because I'm necessarily a person that has to take photos at shows because I don't, but my friends are like "hey can you do this for us." . . . So I'm surrounded by people that play or work for the shows, so knowing them I guess I'm more there to not only see the show, but also to help them out.

For Jamie, their involvement with DIY consisted of creating crafts to sell at the Punk Rock Flea Market, which is held twice a year in Philadelphia. Like other participants, this contribution was a way to be a part of the community, but was not necessarily a long-term practice that required total dedication and commitment:

I still like to be involved. . . . I'll draw stuff from time to time. Not that Punk Rock Flea Market really is a thing in this, I mean, it is part of the community, but it's a way to help R5 [Productions] raise money, so last year I got a table for the first time and sold crafts and stuff, and I'm gonna do that again, and I'm working on stuff, so I guess it's an artistic DIY kind of thing. It's not punk music, but it's punk ethics. It's part of that community still all the same. I always think about how I don't have to worry about school or juggling five jobs or whatever and I want to get back into learning music again. My friends and I always joke about starting bands, but we never do. It's one of those things we always talked about and I always entertained the idea.

In all of these examples, we see a range of practices and levels of commitment to DIY. The notion that participants both "help out" and contribute when possible is important to consider. CCCS theorists argued that participation within a subculture was an all-or-nothing practice. In contrast, we see here that commitment can fall on a spectrum of dedication. While some efforts such as creating a blog or hosting a podcast may be more time consuming than other practices, the varied levels of involvement explored here demonstrate the ways in which contributions can be "fleeting" (Hodkinson 2002, 31) or "wax and wane" due to other obligations outside of one's participation within a scene (Andes 1998, 228).

COMMITTING TO DIY: SUPPORTING A LOCAL SCENE THROUGH DIY

With regards to commitment, many participants recognized the amount of effort it takes to promote a band or tour the country without the help of a major record label, and despite these challenges, participants often had a positive view of the concept. In Anthony's interview, he discussed the ways that DIY can seem appealing, as it allows for total independence and control over a person's art. Furthermore, he mentioned that DIY can have its setbacks, as it often requires a lot of hard work, dedication, and money. DIY can often seem appealing to some people, but to those with other commitments outside of the band, it can become a very time-consuming and arduous task:

It's definitely something you can do, but it's harder. It's a lot of work. How much of your life do you have to dedicate to being DIY? In college, maybe it's a little different. Maybe in college you have that little bit of extra time, but once now you have obligations and you have things that you have to do, I think that's why a lot of bands break up, that's why a lot of people fall out of it and that's why a lot of people stop being DIY is because it's a lot of work and if you don't delegate that work to somebody that can help you and create a symbiotic relationship between a record label and you or something else, then eventually it's going to overtake your life and you're not going to have the time to do the things you need to do in your regular life. So I think DIY is very appealing because younger people want to express themselves and they want to do it in a way that they want to do it, but as you get older I feel that DIY gets a little bit harder to accomplish with all the obligations that you have in your life. Because everybody gets more obligations as you get older.

Andrew provided an optimistic view of DIY and suggested that today's community is willing to help younger generations who wish to commit to the punk scene. He stressed the imperfections within the community, and the willingness of older participants to help those who want to be a part of the scene. In this sense, there's an understanding that older generations are "paying it forward" for younger generations. By helping newcomers to the scene understand the logistics of organizing a show, or working to keep a community afloat, older participants reevaluate their own positions within the scene, and pass these duties on to those who may have the time and the desire to organize shows:

> No one has any clue, especially when you first start out, you're not going to have any clue what you're doing, you're not going to be very good, you're going to make mistakes, that's fine. It doesn't matter. This isn't *The Voice*; this isn't *American Idol*. You can make mistakes. As long as you keep going, you're gonna get better. As long as you keep surrounding yourself with people that make you feel good, and you have a good time playing music together, you're gonna get better as a band, and you'll figure it out as you go. And if you ever have any questions, find an older punk in the scene who's nice to you, and I promise, if they're an older, nice punk, and you come up to them with questions, I promise they will be your mentor. Because older, nice punks always want younger punks to come in, and they want to help them out, and they want to support them. So, if you feel out of place, find an older punk who looks like you, and makes you feel comfortable, and ask them for advice and they'll help you out.

DIY knowledge was viewed as information that should be passed down to younger members within the scene. For Andrew, taking on more responsibilities within the scene meant using such knowledge to ensure that shows were booked and organized. Furthermore, there is an understanding that the punk community works together to benefit everyone, and not just the individual:

> Now that I'm kind of one of the older people in the scene, your role goes from being show-goer and band member, a lot of people as they get older take on bigger roles as far as setting up shows, booking bands, booking tours, stuff like that, so I would say I've definitely taken on some of those aspects. I've put on shows in Brooklyn before, I've put on shows in Pennsylvania before, near where I went to college, so that's definitely something that I've done. I would say too when I first started out I was a lot more selfish, I kind of only thought about my band and myself and now that I'm a little bit older, I think about other bands, I promote other bands way more than I did when I was younger.

In a specific example, Andrew discussed the New Brunswick, New Jersey, punk scene, which, for many years has thrived as a scene where a contemporary punk community continues to exist in basements and bars throughout the college town. Home to punk bands such as The Bouncing Souls, The Gaslight Anthem, and Lifetime among other, smaller local bands, New Brunswick plays a significant part in the history of contemporary punk rock, especially on the East Coast. Andrew, who spent a great deal of time organizing, performing, and attending shows in the vicinity, described the efforts of college students and locals who work together to ensure that the scene continues, especially if resident turnover is high due to the amount of scene members who are in New Brunswick for a short few years while attending the University:

> When punk houses shut down in New Brunswick because kids graduate college, you'll see that next year it'll start up again because two of those kids did stay in the house, or the kids who were in that house contacted other people who wanted to run shows, and said "you should move into our house and take our basement." It's kind of the passing of the torch, and that's how DIY is going to survive as well. It's just passing the torch onto younger people as they're coming up. The basement community in New Brunswick . . . it's been a staple in New Jersey music since I moved here, and since I moved to North Jersey in 2007, 2008. So it's been around for a really long time and the reason that it keeps going is people keep teaching the younger generation how to do it, and then the younger generation takes it on and passes it down.

In order for a scene to survive such high turnover, it is important for necessary skills to be shared among those within the scene. By introducing newer participants to the procedures and by helping them along the way, younger generations of fans can continue to pool their resources to keep the scene from becoming nonexistent. The community-minded effort serves an important purpose in acknowledging the varied efforts that come together to make a scene successful. Below, Andrew acknowledged these efforts, and stressed the importance of continuing to make scenes accessible to outsiders and younger members:

> I think what it comes down to is, we need to keep bringing in young kids who feel left out. We need to keep bringing them in, because they're the ones who are going to keep DIY going, and they're the ones who are going to keep punk culture and the punk community going, so we need to play all-ages shows and bring those kids in and show them that we can do this together. You don't need to sell 20 tickets at $10 apiece and sucker all your friends into coming to this dumb bar. You can come here, and they can pay $5 to see a whole bunch of bands and have a great time. So, bringing those kids in, showing them the ropes, and then kind of letting them take the reins from us as they get older.

By selling tickets for lower prices and making these shows all-ages, there exist few exclusionary practices that prevent outsiders from exploring their local scenes. Such practices, which support and uphold contemporary punk rock's values of inclusion, represent a continued effort to use DIY as a means to remain autonomous and support others' creative endeavors. To continue, Andrew identified the ways individuals, including himself, use their own resources to promote and support the current efforts of bands within his scene:

> When a band you like, or a band that you're friends with puts out a CD or puts out whatever, they're going on tour, I'm sharing it on groups, I'm putting it on Twitter, I'm putting it on my Facebook, I'm trying to get other people to listen to it in my car with me and stuff like that, whereas when I was younger there was maybe one or two bands that I would really push. Now it's . . . there are lots of bands I want to push because I think they're good and I think they're doing something important.

In this example, we see the ways that social media prevails as an important component to establishing communicative networks within scenes today. Social media such as Facebook and Twitter are often used enthusiastically as an easily accessed method to distribute and share information regarding issues within the scene. Again, this type of involvement demonstrates the ways that scenes today operate as spaces that exist within the greater forces that influence society at large.

In his own experiences with DIY, Eric shared some of the ways that his band used their own resources to tour and play music. Below, Eric mentions *Book Your Own Fucking Life (BYOFL)*, which was a resource for bands to network with others in a pre-social media era (Jolly 2018; Warwick 2019). Officially created in 1992 through the efforts of *Maximum Rocknroll*, a zine dedicated to DIY scenes and the music within, *Book Your Own Fucking Life* provided helpful resources on "bands, distributors, record labels, record and book stores, radio stations, promoters, venues, and zines," and gave bands the connections to network and tour using these DIY methods (Thompson 2004, 104). *Book Your Own Fucking Life* originally existed in print, but can now be found online as well:

> The amount of control we had over that we had over everything, nobody will ever tell you what to do for better or worse. And I've learned a lot and I am now too old for it to have sunk in, I thought that was really cool where like if you want to make a shirt, just go make a shirt. How do you do it? I don't know. Try. Just do it and like that sort of how it is with everything, and you know I was sending cassette demos through there's a site called *Book Your Own Fucking Life* and like sending out my shitty high school band cassette demos everywhere. It was just like a full-time hobby for me since I got into this until today. It's crazy. That whole thing, it was always really cool to me and like we

always did everything ourselves and it was always kind of a pain in the ass, but
I guess you got to have something to do. And I chose that because, again,
direct control over everything is always awesome.

As evidenced here, DIY practice allows bands and fans to make decisions
regarding the trajectory of their communities. By creating and selling the
goods that exist within these spaces, participants can maintain the norms that
they wish to see represented in their scenes today. While this is largely a
positive effort, and those who participate within these scenes see the autonomy as a means to creative freedom, too much entitlement can cause a rift
within these communities, which occur when scene members take advantage
of such democratic practices, and do not abide by the implicit and explicit
rules that may exist, such as buying a band's album, rather than illegally
downloading it for free.

Though the majority of scene members today do not see their scenes as
something worth taking advantage of, there always exist the few that see
little value in the creative efforts that come from a scene, while equating such
efforts with little monetary value. Though this may seem problematic, most
of those involved scenes today recognize the hard work and effort that are
associated with using DIY as a practice. Because of this, most participants
are willing to spend their money on albums, shows, and merchandise, because this is a direct way by which fans can help to support their scenes.

CONCLUSION

Contemporary punk scenes and their relationship with DIY demonstrate an
important intersection between autonomous production and mainstream influence. While using DIY methods prevail as the ideal way to create merchandise and music, scene members are not blind to the external forces that
commodify and popularize various aspects of punk rock. Furthermore, there
is an understanding that these forces are inevitable within society today and
exist as an influence in the creation and production of the goods that exist
within a scene. As an example of such an influence, Hot Topic was viewed as
a force that has coopted many elements of punk culture with time but was
considered a non-issue for participants who continue to use their own skills
and resources to maintain a scene through creative endeavors. For some, Hot
Topic was a gateway to punk rock, as it represented yet another easily accessible method by which to explore a curated representation of the current
trends in punk rock culture.

Like Hot Topic, the notion of selling out was one that frequently prevailed, but once again, was viewed an irrelevant issue for scenes today.
While it may seem contradictory, many participants praised and even supported scene members who found a way to make a profit from their music.

Because such an opportunity for bands was often an exception, rather than a norm, there was an appreciation for those bands that were able to spread awareness of their music and the values within. Selling out only became problematic when participants' felt that the band's values had changed—if signing to a major record label meant a change in values for the band, it was then equated to an abandonment of the scene altogether.

While some of the larger external forces such as retail stores and major record labels remained as continued spheres of influence within scenes today, participants felt largely optimistic about the persistence of their scenes, and the efforts of those who participate today. Aside from the obvious practices of DIY music and commodity production, interconnected networks of likeminded participants used their efforts and connections to help one another navigate the process participating in the scene. Through such communicative networks, social capital was used by participants as a way to reinforce scene values and distinguish those who are willing to abide by such belief systems. These networks also functioned as a means by which local scenes evolve into translocal scenes—social media allows for interactions between scenes in different locations, and because of this, bands can use these contacts to promote their music and tour. With such efforts, today's scenes continue to exist as autonomous entities amidst the external forces that find novelty in the various elements of the contemporary punk lifestyle.

Chapter Five

Support Your Local Scene

Participatory Culture, Consumption Practices, and
Navigating Involvement in the Scene Today

A common theme throughout my conversations with participants in today's punk scene is the leveling of roles and responsibilities when it comes to creating the goods that confer scene affiliation—everyone has an opportunity to take part in their scene in any manner deemed appropriate by the scene at large. As explored in chapter 4, DIY continues to flourish as a common practice within scenes today, and the types of practice within can vary not only in levels of commitment, but also in content—creating music confers the same amount of subcultural value as taking photos or writing for a blog. In doing so, these practices help to keep a scene afloat, and act as a way for communities to maintain their autonomy.

Playing in a band is one example of a DIY practice that proved to be a significant way by which scene members displayed their commitment and dedication. Of the fourteen interviews I conducted, six participants played in one band or more at the time of their interview. Participants' duties within their bands varied, and each person I interviewed shared different stories regarding the levels of commitment and time dedicated to practicing, touring, and creating new music. While playing in a band was a valued practice, it was not considered a fulltime endeavor—participants shared their experiences of having to navigate a commitment to a band and several external obligations, including jobs and relationships. While there was repeated conversation surrounding the level of commitment being in a band requires, those who shared their stories with me depicted a largely optimistic view of what it means to be in a punk band within the scene today. In many ways, the band represents a community within a community—an "idealized" site where band members develop close knit relationships with the others in the band and view their participation as a larger contribution to their understanding of an identity (Shank 1994, 140).

Like belonging in a band, the ownership of band merchandise prevailed as an important component of an involvement in scenes today. Participants shared their experiences with buying merchandise and believed their commitment to be demonstrated by the possession of such goods. While not a tangible object, attendance at shows prevailed as a common way for participants to express their commitment to the scene, and frequent attendance was valued as a way to outwardly demonstrate a continued effort to participate in the physical spaces that exist within scenes today.

This chapter will focus on two separate practices within scenes today: playing in a band and buying merchandise. While both practices embody different responsibilities on behalf of the person completing the action, these involvements are critical in the perpetuation of a scene and rely on both groups of participants to follow through with the obligations of their roles in order for a scene to be successful. Participants who play in bands today shared their experiences with the interpersonal dynamics that impact some of the decisions regarding the band's musical and creative trajectories, and those who consider themselves fans expressed an enthusiastic commitment to buying merchandise, listening to new music, and generally supporting the scenes in which they are involved.

PARTICIPATORY CULTURE AND MEANING MAKING

As evidenced in chapter 4, fans place great value in the opportunity to create the goods and commodities that are of specific interest to those within the scene today. While these commodities can include tangible items such as t-shirts and beer cozies, the ability to create music is a highly respected practice. With help from social media, reaching audiences is easier than ever—platforms Facebook and Instagram help bands share their music and inform fans of upcoming shows, and Spotify and Bandcamp provide listeners with immediate access to new music. These affordances dissolve the boundaries between fans and musicians—with immediate access to the music and the bands themselves, social media helps to perpetuate the democratic nature of contemporary punk scenes today. In many cases, band members shared their experiences in attending other friends' shows out of support for their music. The creation of music was not viewed competitively—participants actively supported their friends' endeavors and were willing to share their own resources to raise awareness, help out, and generally support those within the community. In doing so, contemporary punk communities view those within their scenes "as equals with whom they can build a larger community that benefits them all" (Baym 2011, 22). There is little emphasis on competition, and both bands and fans alike see opportunity in using their skills and resources in collaboration with one another to create scenes where equality and prevails as the norm.

With this mindset, contemporary scenes become "communities based on sharing," where an emphasis is placed on passing along insider knowledge and resources to others within the community (van Poecke and Michael 2016). For instance, rather than expecting everyone to bring all of their instruments and amps to a show, bands will often share gear in order to assist with easing the transition between performances. Another common practice involves the use of social capital to spread knowledge about scenes in various locations. Translocal relationships between bands are made via social media and through continued face-to-face interactions, and these networks help bands who wish to organize a tour identify who to contact in a particular city about putting together a show. While these practices are not specific to contemporary punk scenes and the concept of sharing can be observed in communities around the world, these efforts are integral in preserving the autonomy that punk scenes appreciate today.

Because contemporary punk scenes value their autonomy and the democratic nature of DIY, little distinction is made between producers and consumers. Participatory culture and the investigation of the role fans play in creating their cultures help to explain the ways communities collaborate with one another to create meaning. According to Jenkins (1992), participatory culture stresses "fans as active producers and manipulators of meanings" (23). Because this process is undertaken by those within the community, fans also play a role in the production side of scene construction, thereby making the separation between producers and consumers challenging to define (Baym 2011). In the case of contemporary punk scenes, bands and fans act as the active producers of the content they wish to see distributed throughout their communities. Through music, meaning is made. Chapter 2 addressed some of the common social issues that face scenes today, and included topics such as diversity, combatting racism, sexism, and homophobia, and the continued belief that scenes should be inclusive. When these issues are addressed in the music and throughout the physical and digital platforms that exist within these spaces, scenes give meaning to these issues. With that, these issues then become community-centered topics and by raising awareness, scenes can actively work to address the problems that face their scenes today.

I'M IN THE BAND: THE FLUID DYNAMICS OF COMMITMENT AND BAND DEDICATION

As mentioned previously, six of the fourteen interviews conducted for this book included participants who play in bands. While levels of commitment varied, and bands were in different stages of producing music, touring, or playing shows, there was a larger understanding that commitment was an important element in making a band successful, however that success is defined. For Eric, playing in a band was an important part of his experience within today's scene, and it was important that those who play in the band also saw the endeavor as a commitment as well. Through social media, Eric connected with others who played music, and described how he maintains the success of his band, despite adding or losing members:

> I always liked being in bands, like all I ever want to do is be in a band, so I just moved to the city from my town and just went on message boards, looking for people and like ran into people and I slowly started meeting people that I got along with through being in bands. . . . You know it's just like wait a minute, I can't be in a band with some crazy guy who writes all the songs who will just be like fuck this, I don't wanna do it anymore. So that's how I formed my band. I was like "I need to be the one who is in direct control of that." I guess I'm a control freak, because if nobody wants to do it, but I still do, why start a new band?

The issue of commitment was a common theme throughout these interviews, as participants acknowledged the level of dedication it takes to play in a band and have some success. Again, because autonomy is such a critical element in the composition of today's scenes, it was important for those within these scenes to have control over the ways their band operates. Eric mentioned ways an understanding of autonomy influences his own band's work, and addressed the ways the band's endeavors are with cost in mind: "We go around in this [van], which is ours, we own, pretty much recording our next record on our own. You know what I mean? Back to back . . . because I don't think—I've never cared about like super polished radio recording type things and we're just like 'why don't we just do it like we always did before?' It saves money. Yeah, it's all about being like stingy. So that you have more for other things. And that's what we've done." Similarly, Justin described the feasibility of being in a band today. Similar to Eric's thoughts on the cost of production, Justin emphasized the ways that technology has facilitated in making music production more accessible. Participants do not need to spend lots of money on expensive technology to record, nor do they need to invest a lot of money in the production of the music. Rather, it can be done at home with a computer and can be shared online within minutes: "Now it's easier than ever to be in a band. Anyone can just get a computer or a phone or an iPad or whatever, write a record and put it online and 'oh, these are all my thoughts and feelings.' That's amazing. I think that's super important."

Justin provided a specific example of this practice, citing Bomb the Music Industry! and Jeff Rosenstock as evidence of the ways these technologies afford fans and musicians the opportunity to create their music with low barriers to accessibility:

> Bomb the Music Industry! was just Jeff [Rosenstock] with an iPad, or his guitar and his iPod and a drum machine, and he just wrote the things he wanted to, and in his first record you can hear the beeps and the buzzing that come with all the plug-ins that he was using the trial versions of, and it doesn't matter, no one cared. No one was like, "man, that would have been such a good song, but then you hear the buzzing because he didn't pay for the full version of the plugin on that guitar." It's just funny that he did that, but nothing stopped him from doing that. That's awesome.

Justin's example provides evidence to the notion that today's scenes find novelty in the creative process. While more popular musicians may be criticized for taking the least expensive route to produce their music, there is value in evidence (as in the case of Bomb the Music Industry!) that the music was created by the musicians themselves. By creating and producing music, musicians reaffirm the notion that today's scenes value the process and consider it an important way to maintain control over the means themselves.

While it is important to maintain control over the production and distribution of music, there are also explicit and implicit norms that impact the way bands operate while on tour. As a member of several bands, Andrew spent a significant amount of time performing and creating music. According to Andrew, in order for a community to maintain its DIY approach, commitment involves an element of working constructively with others in order to achieve these goals. For Andrew, DIY allows freedom in the creation of music, and gives musicians the ability to share their music in ways that make sense to them—it involves balancing creative freedom and managing expectations of money and celebrity:

> If you're expecting a huge monetary gain, obviously you're doing [DIY] wrong, you're in the wrong place. If you're expecting to make a lot of friends, play music the way you want to play music, run shows the way you want to run shows, book tours the way you want to book tours, if you want to play in a scene where all different types are welcomed to join, then you're in the right place. You have to settle almost. But when you think about what you're settling for, as artistic freedom and the ability to do things the way that you want to, and to support other people who are chasing after their own artistic freedom, then it's very fulfilling. But if you think of it in dollars and cents, you're screwing yourself. You're not going to be happy. . . . If you want to

make money on a DIY tour, you have to be prepared to sleep on somebody's floor, or in the van, and understand that you're not going to be staying in cushy hotels. You have to understand that you're going to be playing basement shows, or maybe bar shows where not a lot of people show up, but the people who do show are going to be into it. And if you're more worried about being in front of a packed house than playing for actual people who enjoy what you're doing, again, the DIY scene is not for you.

While not exactly the most glamorous way to tour, there is an understanding that touring in a van and playing shows in basements prevail as culturally relevant for contemporary punk scenes—more value is placed on doing it the "right way," which involves prioritizing creativity and hard work over luxury or immediate recognition. Participants within these scenes do not ridicule others for taking the least expensive route. In fact, there is tremendous value in no value—the more cheaply you can tour or create music, the better.

Like the dynamics of any small group, being in a band is a complex practice and relies on a set of communicative skills that are required in order for the band to be successful. Band participation relies on the qualities of small group communication, where participants recognize that the dynamics of involvement require commitment, organization between members, and a shared understanding of goals (DeVito 2014; Wood 2017). For many, participation in a band provided a second family and the ability to form close bonds with others who share in the passion of creating music. As a member of several bands, Andrew acknowledged the family-like structure of band participation, recognizing that a bond exists between himself and those members:

> Well, when you're in a ska band, there's like 6 of you, or 7 of you, or 8 of you, so it's almost like you're in a small gang. There's always somebody that you can call or you can carpool with and it's really fun and you really get to know people when you're traveling, when you do stuff like that or you travel together and stuff. Some of the people I've been in bands with, we might talk once a year, but there's still this very strong emotional bond that I have for them because we've been through these things together and we've played music together.

Like Andrew, Anthony also found this sense of belonging by participating in a band at a young age. As the drummer in a band today, Anthony saw parallels from his time participating in the middle school band and in his current band—both groups provided Anthony with a sense of community and the opportunity to collaborate with others:

> I think that back then I was subconsciously wanting to be a part of a community and I saw what it felt like to be a part of a band, through middle school and through being in a middle school band and you start to experience how moving it is, it's not even just about the product of what you're making. I

mean, it is in a sense, it's the collaboration of all these people who are basically inputting their energy into these instruments and making it together and I think that music affects people in such a deep level, you know? Back then I subconsciously think I felt it. I didn't really understand what was happening, but I felt good. It felt like I was doing something that would move me and make me feel a certain way.

To continue, Anthony emphasized the "responsibility" that comes with being in a band. Here, he mentions the importance of his bandmates' interests, acknowledging that their band is a group effort, and if one member cannot make the commitment, then it has adverse effects on other members in the band. Below, Anthony described the ways in which dedication and hard work presented themselves as important values to have in order to be successful, however this success is defined, in a punk band today:

And it's funny because one of my favorite things about being in a band, and making music with people is not only just I've always loved getting to know people and really getting to know somebody, like when you're in a band with somebody, it's honestly one of the deepest relationships you can possibly have with somebody, other than an intimate relationship because you're going to see them in emotional times, you're going to see them every week, you're making a schedule, you're putting your life on hold once a week or doing basically making a responsibility to, you know, it's not only for me if I don't show up to band practice, now I'm keeping the people that I'm doing this with from progressing, and if I'm doing that, it's like a relationship it's like anything else.

The language that Anthony uses in his discussion of his obligations in playing with his band reiterates the ways that those who play in punk bands today see their endeavors as valuable. Furthermore, there is an understanding between members that commitment is equal throughout—if one member of the band does not dedicate a similar level of commitment as the others, this can prove to be problematic for the other members. Finding musicians with likeminded thoughts on commitment is crucial because tensions can arise if one member, for example, fails to show up to practice. Anthony's example serves as evidence of equity theory within a small group, which emphasizes that those in interpersonal relationships prefer there to be an equal level of commitment within this relationship, as opposed to an unequal balance of commitment between members (Fine and Holyfield 1996; Wood 2017).

In his interview, Greg stressed the difficulty that came with being in a band, but recognized the importance of having the drive and dedication that ultimately produce good art. If this philosophy is not adopted by all members in the band, the dynamics of this relationship can be impacted in negative ways: "The only thing as far as being in a band is that—not to complain too much—but it's hard and I kind of imagine it's always hard to do art stuff, and

I think it's good in a way because everyone would do it and it wouldn't be—I think it's good that artists have to be a little bit hungry, you have to work really hard, you have to care a lot. I think that's really important in making good art and authentic art, or important art."

In his interview, Adam shared the story of how he joined a band, and how his commitment to the band and the scene consumed a lot of his free time, especially with regards to the writing process. Again, evidence of commitment is prevalent here, as Adam emphasized the importance of practicing and communicating with others in his band:

> Honestly, I—we were at a party where [the band] played . . . the three of them, before I joined the band, and it was a friend of ours house, he was having a show and I saw them play and it was a lot of fun and all my friends were really into it and I felt like that too, and then they asked me to play and I was like, sounds like fun. I hadn't played music in a long time. I had started my own band at some point . . . and I was starting to think "oh, I should probably grow up," and then they asked me to play in it and I was like "okay I'll do this." It's a lot of fun and I don't regret it. As they all know, I love writing songs and terrible lyrics. It's kind of all I do in my free time. I just write. I mean, look around, there's nothing but guitars and shit everywhere. The writing process is good, and I love performing and meeting people and doing well. It's not fun when you don't do well. Practicing a lot helps.

For Justin, belonging in a band required a great deal of commitment and know-how. While scene members may join a band for a variety of reasons, the success of the band involves dedication, but also an understanding of how to market this band within the scene. Through various social networks, a band can collect their money and resources and use these connections to help their band succeed. If the band is not well-connected, however, it will be more difficult to raise awareness or generate a fanbase:

> There are a lot of elements to being in a band and being productive. You actually have to be really good at a lot of things to be effective, which is not easy. And why so many bands fall short is because, sure, you can play guitar really well and you can write a catchy hook for a song, but can you market yourself? Do you know how to make a good band name? Do you know how to make enticing cover art? Do you have a friend who will take your promo photos? Do you have $300 to go do it? Do have the money to get a record pressed? All that stuff can get in the way, but it' just seems like there's so many more options for bands now. You don't have to do all that stuff. You can just do the best you can. If you have a friend that can help you out—cool. If you think you can do it—cool. If you can't, that's fine.

With these connections, managing a band's success becomes easier. If these resources are unavailable, however, a band can operate in whatever way is most beneficial for those who are in the band itself. While knowing others within the scene can be viewed as beneficial, it is not a requirement.

As explored in chapter 3, participants often associate themselves with various scenes during adolescence, and with time, this in-group membership and scene affiliation often changes—obligations such as jobs, relationships, and schooling all play a role in the amount of time one can commit to participation within a scene. While such involvement may change with time, older fans continue to see their affiliation with a scene as a large part of an identity. In many cases, participants have to navigate a balance between their participation in a band and the obligations that take time from this practice. When discussing his commitment to his own band, Justin expressed a change in the way this commitment is articulated. As he has gained more experience playing in bands, Justin believed it important to have a job, and in most cases, claimed that being in a band full time was an unrealistic expectation:

> We're kind of running this [band] on our own time . . . especially when you're first starting a band, and you're trying to make it a thing, and it's a lot more accessible now than it ever has been for anyone to make a record. It's harder to stand out and you're like, is there a certain path I'm supposed to follow, and we're all at the point now where we don't have to do that. First of all, we just know better, so we're not going to waste our time and our money on endless pursuits of merch and record deals and XYZ. Stuff that doesn't really exist that frequently. And we can kind of run on our own pace, which is awesome. We all work and that's got to be a fulltime commitment for everyone because you gotta pay the bills, but we can still play shows.

Like any understanding of participation within a scene, playing in a band also involves a level of commitment and dedication. The relationships between band members relied on shared understandings and a vision of a particular goal, and when these visions were not met, conflict was a likely result. Because of this, participants who play in bands acknowledged the dynamics that exist within these spaces and recognized the importance of clear communication with other band members. As with others who were interviewed in this book, many participants understood that their involvement in a band was not a full-time endeavor. While that is desirable, there was a realistic understanding that real-world obligations were a priority.

THE OWNERSHIP OF BAND MERCHANDISE AND THE OUTWARD DISPLAY OF ONE'S COMMITMENT TO THE SCENE

As I sit writing this book, I am entirely aware of the perplexing relationship that exists between punk rock and punk rock "stuff." One quick glance around my apartment and this is evident to anyone who walks through the door. Several bookshelves contain far too many books that chronicle various punk histories and topics. Whole Ikea storage units are filled from end to end with vinyl. A pile of band shirts sits atop my dresser, and there is no denying I own multiple shirts from many bands (thank you, Bouncing Souls and Nothington). Dozens of concert tickets fill scrapbooks, and the organization and framing of show posters is considered an art form. As it stands, one might argue that my entire experience within punk rock is merely a culmination of the punk-related goods that have accumulated over the years. And though DIY had a hand in producing some of these goods, it is likely to assume that larger capitalist forces were at play at some point during the production and distribution of many of these items.

My experience of years of commodity collecting is not unique. Band merchandise continues to be an enormous source of subcultural capital within scenes today. A quick search of any current punk band's Facebook page will lead you to the merchandise promised land. Standard band merchandise websites often include t-shirts, hoodies, and albums (both CD and vinyl). However, in recent years, bands have taken the commodification of their products to the next level. If you want a t-shirt, they probably have 3 or 4 different styles to sell you. If you are looking for a baseball cap, beer koozie, or knitted throw blanket, the Menzingers have you covered. If you are in the market for a new pair of sunglasses, a baby onesie, or logoed Christmas stocking, a quick visit to Social Distortion's online merch store will deliver the merchandise. With these examples among countless others, it is very clear that today's punk communities are very committed to the scene-related goods that can be bought online or at shows. While not everyone may see the need for a Social Distortion virgin candle or a bag of Bouncing Souls "Stoked" coffee blend, the demand for these goods within today's punk scene exists. These goods not only act as the manifestation of subcultural capital, but the acquisition of these goods demonstrates a level of commitment and dedication by participants who continue to build their collections with this merchandise.

For many, the dedication to the ownership of these goods equates to the physical manifestation of commitment and participation within a punk scene. The act of publicly announcing ownership of such commodities, or through the act of wearing this merchandise in spaces where ownership is culturally relevant (like at a concert or festival, for example) helps to confirm an insider status within the scene through the display of knowledge of relevant bands in appropriate settings. Because of this, fans use the ownership of punk-centric commodities to reaffirm insider status and demonstrate an awareness of the culturally relevant knowledge in the scene today. In my interviews, participants viewed their consumption habits positively—ownership of goods was understood as a way to support a band, and there was little, if any resistance to acquiring scene-related merchandise, other than perhaps a lack of funds to do so. While commitment is often explored in terms of time dedicated to scene involvement, I argue that commitment can also be understood as it relates to the purchasing habits of those within the scene today. Furthermore, consumption habits did not align with the CCCS approach to commodification in youth cultures, which understood consumption habits in these communities as a means to stylistically rebel against the status quo. Instead, goods today are often purchased as a means to fit in, demonstrate insider knowledge, and to relate to others within the scene.

For his second indicator of subcultural substance, commitment, Hodkinson (2002) raised issue with the Chicago and Birmingham Schools, who believed that commitment to a subculture was an all-or-nothing practice. Instead, Hodkinson argues that commitment within subcultures involved accounting "for a considerable proportion of free time, friendship patterns, shopping routes, collections of commodities, going-out habits and even Internet use" (31). In other words, commitment involved dedication in a variety of ways, and participants can partake and demonstrate commitment through various forms and levels of dedication. For any scene, commitment can manifest itself in a variety of manners and levels. Postsubcultural theory frequently suggests the "fluid" nature of participation, which allows for ingroup acceptance of a range of commitment practices which can be based on the ownership tangible items (such as fashion and music merchandise) or awareness of insider knowledge of the scene itself (Force 2009). Though this range of commitment varied from person to person, and presented itself in a variety of ways, members within today's punk scenes viewed participation to be up to the individual.

For those who participate within a scene today, commitment within that particular community can be a large strain on one's time and money. With time, these outward displays of involvement through fashion tend to change. Bennett's (2006) research on aging fans of punk rock supported this hypothesis—as fans age, commitment tend to be embodied internally, rather than externally through physical manifestation of fashion statements tied to that particular scene. Davis (2006) argued that it is possible to maintain one's identity within a scene as time progresses—doing so creates a "synthesized identity" (64) wherein one's participation evolves in ways that accommodate both in-scene and out-of-scene practices. While evidence suggests that there may be a shift in one's outward display of a punk "appearance," band merchandise continues to be a thriving business—one that is enthusiastically supported by many participants within the scene today.

CONSUMPTION HABITS AND SUBCULTURAL THEORY

Since the beginning days of cultural youth studies, the relationship between consumption habits and subcultural participation has been an abundant topic of investigation. Early CCCS theorists, who argued that post-war UK subcultures has purposeful and deliberate consumption habits, also asserted that these specific stylistic choices were a way for youth to subvert the status quo and hegemonic structures that existed in their everyday lives (Hebdige 1988). Fashion prevailed as an important subcultural characteristic for the CCCS; it was understood as vital for the establishment of one's identity, but only if the commodities served a particular purpose and conveyed a distinct message in establishing oneself as resistant to the consumerist system of commodification. In making these choices, youth cultures sought to distance themselves, but never fully escape, from the "parent" culture, or the dominant forces that exist within society (Clarke et al. 2006). Because there is no true way to escape this system, CCCS emphasized ways youth cultures practiced "appropriation and reinterpretation" (Debies-Carl 2013, 116) of various signifiers, with a goal of reestablishing meaning of that object. An example of this can be witnessed in Hebdige's (1988) observations of punk subcultures in the United Kingdom which highlighted the importance youths placed on subcultural appropriation, and the practice of taking everyday objects such as safety pins and garbage bags and transforming them into fashion statements meant to shock and confuse. While some of these consumption practices (specifically those made by punks) may have raised a few eyebrows in the process, they prevailed as an interesting contradiction with which to contend—while subcultures were viewed as resistant forces to dominant ideologies, their participation within a capitalist system was inevitable.

Some of the more recent postmodern approaches to youth cultures and consumption have grappled with this juxtaposition and have since posited for a redefinition of the ways in which this relationship is embodied and enacted by those within specific cultural groupings. Postsubcultural theorists found fault within the CCCS conclusions, claiming that subcultural identity is not entirely dependent on one's purposeful semiotic reinterpretation of commodities and the resulting antiauthoritarian message about dominant society at large.

Today, conspicuous and purposeful consumption remain as important distinguishing characteristics of any subcultural group, and the practice works to distinguish members as unique and distinct from others (Heath and Potter 2004; Hodkinson 2002; Schouten and McAlexander 1995). Participants actively accumulate subcultural capital in order to help establish identities among peers, and commodities such as record collections, posters, and band t-shirts act as indicators of cultural substance and insider knowledge (Thornton 1995). These goods offer participants the ability to see themselves as part of a scene, yet also distinct from others. In addition, subcultural capital functions as a means by which ways of knowing distinguish those who truly "get" the various elements of a subculture from those who lack the insider status, knowledge, and understanding of the various nuances of that group

(Moore 2010). These possessions help the owner to reassert their involvement within a scene and convey to others their insider knowledge. Similarly, these commodities act as physical manifestations of participation and dedication and serve as a testament to one's commitment to a scene.

Rather than engaging in the appropriation and reconfiguration of goods as argued by the CCCS, commodities in the contemporary punk scene are purchased with little, if any, resistance to the process by which it was created. Once again, participants acknowledge their relationship with these larger forces, and while DIY is often a method by which to mitigate some of the negative influences of the capitalist world that surrounds them, buying merchandise and spending money on scene-related experiences continue to remain a popular practice within scenes today. As discussed in chapters 3 and 4, those who participate within contemporary punk scenes today were highly influenced (and likely introduced to the music itself) by the mass market commodification of various punk elements. Therefore, participants do not see this relationship as overwhelmingly problematic. Rather, easier access to these commodities was accepted and embraced.

GO TO THE SHOW! SUPPORTING A LOCAL SCENE AND ATTENDING SHOWS

With regards to spending habits, many participants felt it very important to support their local punk scenes through purchases of all kinds. By doing so, participants have the ability to play a role in making a scene thrive, supporting the bands they like, and express dedication to the values that exist within these communities. While the purchase of tangible items is a common practice within the scene, there was also an understanding that supporting the local scene-specific businesses, such as music venues and record stores, was also a way for commitment to be demonstrated. Likewise, there is the belief among many contemporary punk scenes that attending such shows and supporting friends who may be in these bands demonstrates one's commitment to the scene. For many, attending shows was viewed as a must—it is the most direct, immediate way by which you can demonstrate your support for the bands within the scene today.

For example, Elizabeth described the motivations behind supporting a local punk scene in New Jersey, as support for local venues often translates into support for local music. Here, Elizabeth cited two New Jersey–based venues known within the scene for hosting punk shows: The Court Tavern in New Brunswick, and the Asbury Lanes in Asbury Park. While both venues have closed in recent years and are now operating under different management, these venues continue to be sites where punk shows occur (though not as frequently as in the past):

> Well, I think for one thing it's really important, especially since I like a lot of
> local bands, in like a legitimate support local business way, like, I'm in New
> Jersey, the Court Tavern was one of my favorite venues in the world, it shut
> down, now it's coming back, but it's probably not going to be the same. The
> [Asbury] Lanes is closing for renovations, so I think that in terms of the
> people, it's really important literally to support them by going to shows be-
> cause it's something you want to keep alive.

In many of these spaces, costs of a show are meant as a way to provide
some money to the bands that played the show and possibly to those who
helped to organize the show, and one of the common themes among shows
that take place in venues such as these is the low price point. While it is not
uncommon to find punk shows with tickets costing $30 and up or shows that
take place in large amphitheater-type settings, the allure of a smaller show in
a venue such as a basement or a bar is the opportunity to experience the
music in a more intimate, dedicated setting. Once again, this practice can be
viewed as a common norm within today's scenes—more emphasis is placed
on the show itself, rather than the profit at the end of the night. The enthusiastic support for such spaces affirms the notion that an "inter-dependent
relationship" exists between the spaces themselves and those who attend
(Green 2018, 75). If scenes do not support these venues and continue to
attend shows in these spaces, these venues become threatened. To stay true to
this spirit, low admission prices were viewed as an outstanding trait of today's scenes. In his interview, Joe explained why this practice is an important element of his scene. Here, we see evidence of the value of this practice.
While the cheaper prices may be alluring, there is also an understanding that
attending such shows demonstrates support for the bands that play these
shows:

> You should go to lots of DIY shows, support local bands, that's something I
> didn't do enough growing up, I sort of only went to what I heard about that
> was more mainstream. Go to $5 Punk Night, see your friend's band, not that
> they'll become the next big thing, because it's not what it's really about, but
> it's . . . I feel like you have to do it, but I don't want to say that's what you
> have to do because you might end up liking it.

He continued this thought by explaining why attending smaller shows is such
a critical component of participation today. While this was not always a
practice for Joe, attending smaller shows provides a way for him to find new
music. Here, Joe discusses Everybody Hits, a DIY space in Philadelphia that
operates as a batting cage by day and a DIY punk show space by night,
located in the Northern Liberties section of Philadelphia, Pennsylvania. After
The Golden Tea House, a DIY show space in West Philadelphia, closed in
2015, Everybody Hits became a popular venue for local punk shows:

> I went to a really cool show at Everybody Hits . . . it's what happened since Golden Tea House has gone, Guild Shows started doing stuff there. It's a batting cage on Girard. So after they're done being a batting cage, it becomes an afterhours venue, and I saw, I'm trying to remember all the bands. It was March, Rat Boys, Sundials, and some other bands, and they were all pretty great. I went for Sundials, but I checked out Rat Boys. I never listened to, whatever the fourth band was, I was really into it. Normally I wouldn't. I'd be like "alright, I'm off to see the Menzingers," and they're headlining, they're touring with the Holy Mess, or some other band we already know, and it's neat when you go to like the smaller bands, because you're likely going to like what you hear.

In his explanation, we see a change in dedication—while Joe may have attended shows in the past, doing so involved seeing more popular or familiar bands that likely performed at larger venue spaces. With the prevalence of smaller DIY venues in Philadelphia, it is possible for fans to have access to smaller venues and basement shows nearly every day of the week. Because of this, smaller venues and cheaply priced shows afford the opportunity for low-stakes exploration of other bands. Jamie expressed a similar sentiment with regards to supporting a local scene. In their opinion, Jamie believed that supporting a scene was something that both bands and fans have to do. If shows are not attended and these bands are not supported, the scene itself will fail to exist: "If you love [the scene], then that's what you gotta do. If people don't go to shows and don't buy the records, then people can't really make the music function. It's not like I've got to be like 'oh I have to keep up punk,' but it's just what I've always done. It's been such a big part of my life since as long as I can remember. It's just like what I do now. It comes naturally, you don't even think about it." In this description, attending shows is viewed as a habit and a requisite component of an involvement within a scene. For many, attending a show occurred on a regular basis, and was not a practice that occurred sporadically or inconsistently. Participants expressed the importance of habitually attending shows and demonstrating their continued loyalty to their scenes through this practice. In Emily's experiences attending shows, she described the ways in which the community aspect of attending shows became a major motivator in her continued participation within the scene on Long Island:

> I became friends with a few people who are in different bands on Long Island, and really into the punk scene, and I became, I don't know, I really enjoyed going and one of the first things I picked up on is even though at first I wasn't super into all the music I was hearing, but the camaraderie and the vibes that you get at these punk shows are . . . it's hard to describe, but it's just like a big gathering of people and everyone is mostly happy to be there, and they just I don't know, it's just really hard to get, it's hard to not like being there. . . . I would say most of the bands I've found from going to shows. So, you go see

someone you like and you like someone who opened for them, and then you go
see them, and make friends with their people. So I really think shows is the
way. Sometimes I look stuff up, like if I'm trying to find, for example an all-
girl band who's really rare, LGBT bands are not super, super common, so
sometimes I literally search "queer punk bands" and try to find stuff that way,
but mostly I get new stuff from connections at shows I'm already seeing.

Like others who shared their experiences in attending local shows, Andrew found shows to be a place where repeated involvement from dedicated
scene members was common. In his example, shows can be a place for
interaction with other scene members, attending a show means relationships
are likely to develop. Furthermore, these shows prevailed as a location where
it was likely that likeminded tastes among attendees help to facilitate relationships between others:

There's a lot of reasons why you go to shows. You go for the music, obviously. You go, I mean, once you're part of the community, you can show up to a
show and know, "oh this band is playing so I know Jeffy and Joey and Margaret are all going to be there." So, you know that you're going to have friends
and even if you don't necessarily have friends there, there's a possibility that
you're going to make new friends based on the fact that you're there to see this
band.

What is important to note here is that smaller shows at these venues
provide community members with established networks of likeminded others. While it is possible to go to a show alone, there is a strong possibility that
you will know others, or at least recognize attendees who have attended other
shows in the area. The awareness of others is often facilitated by social
media, where local Facebook groups and event pages help to connect members digitally, oftentimes before participants even meet one another in person. In Aaron's discussion of his own experiences of attending shows, he
provided an example of a common norm that is practiced within scenes
today. He emphasized the importance of attending a show on time in order to
see all of the bands performing—not just the headliners:

I got myself back into going to shows early and I've been yelling at a lot of
people lately that they're like, "Oh, I always call a venue to see what time the
headliners are going on." Fuck you, don't do that, just go. Like this band is
putting their shit out there for people to hear. Ninety nine percent of the time,
the opening band is there because that headlining band actually likes them, it's
something you're going to like. Or their record label, if they're on one, thinks
that's a good pair, so I've been seeing a lot of good openers, I guess. I swear
every time I see a new show, I get into a new artist.

In explaining the practice of attending a show early, Aaron stressed why doing so is important. While it may be tempting to arrive at a show just in time to see the headliner, showing up early or on time to a show benefits both the musicians and attendees, and can be an opportunity to learn about new music and support those bands at the same time. Attending a show on time demonstrates an example of the ways that dedication is performed—while this is not an example of dedication that directly correlates to spending money, attending a show in time to see the opening bands demonstrates an understanding of a valued norm within this particular community.

Though some participants discussed their attendance at shows and the significance of continuing this practice, attendance at festivals also provided some insight into the ways that attendance demonstrates such commitment. As mentioned in previous chapters, Fest acts as a location where fans from around the world come to experience the festival and interact with others in the community. In Elizabeth's interview, she discussed attending Fest for the first time, and considered the ways that Fest reflects some of the community values that are so evident in scenes today. In this quotation, Elizabeth identified several instances where physical presence equates to a demonstration of commitment within her scene. In their exploration of DIY spaces in a Long Island, New York, scene, Culton and Holtzman (2018) argue that participation in such DIY spaces was most resonant when participants took part in the DIY elements of a scene and demonstrated a prolonged commitment to such practices. Below, Elizabeth's discussion of Fest exemplifies this assumption:

> Fest—it's going to be my first time. I'm super excited. I've always wanted to go, but it didn't make sense when I was in school, and I only graduated like a year and a half ago, and I couldn't go last year and I really, really, really regretted it. When tickets went on sale I didn't want to go yet, and then I decided before October I wanted to go, but it was too late, and I was so mad. And just seeing how many bands there are and what a community there is, with Fest specifically was really cool. So that's definitely a part of it—the community. I think that, and just shows in general, I really think that I would say it started with the physical and emotional release of seeing someone up there yelling about something you care about. It's equal parts emotional and physical being at a show, but also the community and all the friends. Like I literally moved to New Jersey because of the music scene because that was where all my friends were, like literally almost everyone I know here is someone that I've met at a show and I hardly ever go to shows alone anymore and when I do now I usually make friends, and I really think that's just the biggest part for me is like where I found my people which is super corny, but it's true.

In their study of leisure activities and the groups that form around such practices, Fine and Holyfield (1996) contend that while the primary activities of such groups are important for group cohesion, the activities themselves are not enough to keep these groups unified. Therefore, members of such groups must feel their involvement is worthwhile and appreciated by others. In the case of contemporary punk rock, while the music itself remains a binding factor between scene members, ownership as merchandise and in-person involvement in places such as festivals are viewed as examples of the ways in which members envision their involvement as valued by others.

Attendance at Fest prevailed as a relevant topic in Joe's interview as well. As an annual attendee of Fest, Joe described the importance of attending Fest each year, and how the active social media community surrounding Fest influenced his decision to attend:

> I've only been to Fest twice and this will be my third year. For me, I've wanted to go at least since Fest 8. I first heard about maybe around Fest 7, and I was in college and I couldn't convince my parents because it would always happen around finals, at least for my school. And it just . . . I couldn't either convince them or be ballsy enough to fucking do it. But my first Fest was Fest 12, I kind of was . . . I was going through school and I was trying to figure out what I was doing, and I wasn't really too keen on college anymore, and I wanted to just start working. And in between that, finding a job, I was like I'm just going to go to Fest because I don't really have any obligations, and I went with a couple people I knew from the internet, like a message board, and I only met a couple people, maybe a handful, and I just added a whole bunch of people on Facebook. . . . I met all those people and it was unreal. It was, I don't know, every five minutes I walked into someone I knew, and it was like, I never felt like that before. I felt important, or at least I felt recognized in a way.

For today's punk communities, show and festival attendance prevailed as significant ways to demonstrate commitment in scenes today. Furthermore, such locations are viewed as spaces where a physical presence helps to reinforce an insider status within the community. Show attendance was viewed as a critical way for participants to support their favorite bands, and there was an understanding that if shows are not attended, the scene would struggle to succeed. Low-priced shows at small bars and venues continue to be commonplace, and members of the community view this practice as an effective and low-stakes way to explore new music and support friends' bands. Likewise, local shows and punk-centric festivals prevailed as sites where a sense of community was established with others who have like-minded values and similar tastes in music.

BUYING GOODS AND SPENDING MONEY

As I have mentioned, buying merchandise is a hobby that occupies nearly all realms of my life—the limit for too many band t-shirts does not exist, no matter what a modest apartment closet might say. For many of those interviewed, the act of buying merchandise was a similar experience, so much so that many participants expressed some concern with their spending habits on scene-related merchandise. Participants discussed buying various types of merchandise, which included goods such as t-shirts, albums, and posters. For instance, Jimmy described a recent trip to a popular California record store chain, Amoeba Records:

> I actually have a million t-shirts, a million records. I buy mostly from shows, because there's not a lot of good record stores around where I'm at. Down in San Diego there's a new place that just opened that I really want to go check out, but I just haven't had the time yet. I've been to Amoeba [Music] in LA and San Francisco, and stuff. But mostly from shows. I came back with a lot of stuff from Fest last year. I was just looking at it all, like "oh my god why did I buy so much stuff?"

Here, Jimmy noted that most of his purchases did occur at shows and bought most of his merchandise directly from the bands. This was a common theme throughout many participants' interviews. Like Jimmy, Emily expressed exasperation at some of her spending habits with regards to buying merchandise, though she noted that buying merchandise at shows was a frequent practice: "Sometimes I will force myself to not bring my wallet, because I know that I can't afford anything, but almost always when I go to a show, whether it be a small show something like that, I'll usually buy a poster and/or a shirt. I have many posters, I'm sure, as you understand, [and] I have a lot of shirts." While there was some reflexivity on the process of buying merchandise at shows, and perhaps some buyer's remorse to go along with it, there was a greater understanding that buying band merchandise was a large part of investing in the scene. These goods were viewed to have long-term use value and represented ways for members within these communities to help their scenes succeed.

Another common theme that arose was the dedication to a band and merchandise purchasing habits. For both Elizabeth and Aaron, spending habits varied based on interest within a particular band. In this quotation, Elizabeth described her purchasing behaviors, and noted that her dedication depends on whether or not she likes the band:

> I have some t-shirts, I'm a big t-shirt person, but not until I really like your band, and I'm unemployed right now until next week. Financially I'm not at a great place and I'm usually more likely to buy your album on Bandcamp, but I'll also listen to you on Spotify. Like I'm the person, [that] once I'm into your band I will buy everything you do. Like I'll buy every song you put out, I'll buy all your t-shirts, whatever. But, because my money is little, I definitely have to work my way to that point. Usually using the internet.

Elizabeth's quotation provides some insight into the ways that these purchasing decisions are made. While it is not possible to buy every item from every punk band in existence today, dedication to a band will likely mean spending a lot on their merchandise. Spotify and Bandcamp have prevailed as helpful tools in assisting with this process, as they afford users the ability to sample a band's music before making any purchases. Bandcamp is a website that allows fans to "discover amazing new music and directly support the artists who make it" (Bandcamp n.d.). On a band's particular Bandcamp page, for instance, fans can listen to music and purchase albums, audio downloads, or other merchandise directly through the website and bands, in return, make a profit from the website. In some instances, there is also the option for a band to allow listeners to "pay what you wish," and determine their own price for the music on a band's page. For many, the Bandcamp website can be a way for fans to gain access to new music without having to spend a lot of money. Unlike Spotify, who only offers fractions of a cent each time their songs are played, Bandcamp gives artists 85 percent of the share of profits and represents the ways technology and social media have facilitated in allowing fans to directly gain access to the music they wish to enjoy (Ratliff 2016). With the fan's freedom to determine whether or not to purchase an album after streaming it through Bandcamp, websites such as these can influence how much merchandise one buys.

In his interview, Aaron also mentioned Bandcamp. For Aaron, the streaming website helped him make decisions regarding his own purchasing habits:

> I guess it's kind of how much I actually like the band, if I want to support and have that, like yeah, I've gotten that whole kind of collection from that band or going back like, "Oh shit, they re-released. That was like a major influence on me when I was younger. I've gotta have that album." Yeah, other than that, I'm not buying too many CDs lately unless it's a band that's small if I actually don't have. . . . It's pretty awesome, if I've just discovered a shit ton of music through Bandcamp and something I got on those. It's good stuff.

While digital downloading remained a popular practice among participants and granted fans power in determining what merchandise to purchase, some expressed varying opinions on the difference between buying mp3s versus buying physical commodities such as vinyl or CDs. For Allie, it was important to purchase the physical copy of an album, and to purchase it from an independent record store or directly from the musician at a show: "I don't own an iPhone or an iPad or an mp3 player. I buy it in an independent store, or there really aren't that many people selling things at the shows I've been to, but I have bought stuff at shows. But generally, I go to independent record stores and I choose to buy vinyl over CD if I can. Or I'll buy directly from the record label, if I can't find it in the store."

Similar to the practice of attending shows at small music venues that persist as relevant within the scene, supporting independent record stores also prevailed as a way for participants to ensure their money was going directly to those with the most investment within these communities. Like Allie, Jamie expressed a similar sentiment, adding that the practice of listening to a physical copy of an album becomes more of an experience than simply streaming it from a website such as Spotify or Bandcamp. Furthermore, commodities such as vinyl records, as physical embodiments of the live music experience, are viewed to hold higher value in terms of subcultural capital as "[vinyl's] value as an object is heightened and legitimated due to its connection to the actual music" (Geraghty 2014).

Jamie also supported a preference for physical formats over digital, as listening to music on vinyl provided an experience that cannot be replicated with a music streaming platform. To add, Jamie specifically emphasizes preference for vinyl over CD which supports the evidence that shows that not only has vinyl made a tremendous comeback in the last decade, it continues to be a preferred method in the music listening experience (Rosenblatt 2018):

> Any physical format I buy anymore is vinyl exclusively because I have a record player. And it's an experience for me. You have to get up to physically flip a record, so that for me is different than when I put Spotify on and I'm just doing work around the house. . . . It also makes you thoughtful of what you're buying. Even Spotify, you take it for granted sometimes. So that's why I still really like vinyl . . . it's a way for me to also purchase your band's music, support the band, without buying a t-shirt because I have a million of those.

In what Bartmanski and Woodward (2018) describe as a "labor- and care-intensive artefact," (173) the ownership of vinyl signifies a level of dedication that cannot be attributed to digital streaming and downloading. There is a greater amount of labor that goes into the process of acquiring, listening to, and maintaining a record collection than into streaming songs on Spotify. While both methods offer fans the opportunity to support their favorite bands and contribute to their scenes, any practice that requires a greater level of labor will be viewed as a more committed level of dedication within the community.

As it is evidenced, the ownership of music provided several functions within punk communities today. Digital streaming platforms afforded fans the opportunity to explore new music and sample albums before purchasing, and websites such as Bandcamp helped to provide musicians with a direct link to their fans and vice versa. While these sites offer fans immediate access to the music, greater value was placed on the more labor-intensive practices of music acquisition. Supporting local record stores or purchasing vinyl acted as ways for participants to directly support their scenes and give their money to those who are most passionate about the goods that are distributed within these spaces. Furthermore, these practices were viewed as most legitimate, as the hobby of collecting and curating a record collection requires more labor, commitment, and insider knowledge than simply streaming an album online.

Buying Directly from the Band vs. Buying Online

Buying albums and streaming music both represented ways of showing commitment within scenes today. Often, both of these practices are used simultaneously—in some cases, fans can stream the album before the album is released. Streaming also offers fans the ability to listen to a band's music before making the decision to purchase. While sites like Spotify and Bandcamp make it more difficult for fans to commit to a purchase, they are very helpful when considering a band's exposure to new audiences. Though streaming sites have impacted sales of music as a whole, and as of 2018 exist as the music industry's largest source of revenue (Ball and Auchard 2018), today's punk scenes continued to see value in ownership of the physical versions of an album. When asked about his own habits, Justin underscored the need to buy physical albums directly from bands—either through their website or at a show. Preordering merchandise was a topic that came up, and Justin explained the reasons for supporting such a practice, which included the understanding that doing so helps to promote a band who might be in the early stages of producing albums or touring:

> As a consumer, I think I do everything. The one thing I don't really do, I don't usually buy digital. I don't like just mp3s or whatever. I just don't do that, unless it's something I cannot get. I always, if it's up to me, I try to buy from bands at the shows, and I always try and tip. That's super important to me. I will preorder records, I think that's really important, especially if it's a band's first record on a label, I think that's incredibly important.

Though this topic did not come up in any other interviews, Justin briefly mentioned the practice of tipping. A common practice among touring bands, providing a tip jar at the merch table gives fans the opportunity to help out with the costs of touring, even if they are tipping just a few dollars. It offers another way for fans to support their scenes and demonstrate a commitment to seeing these communities thrive. When asked to explain the reasons behind preordering an album from a band, Justin explained his motivations, stating that making these early purchases can reflect positively on a band whose record label invested a lot of time and money into:

> Because it's like you're a label, you just threw $5,000 or $10,000 out, 5,000 man hours promoting or working on this record, what's it's going to look like to you if your new band announces their preorder on Twitter and Facebook and stuff and they get three orders? Versus they get like 100? Versus they get 500 orders? That stuff's super important. . . . I definitely buy from . . . I do try to buy from bands . . . but at the same time the independent labels, I'll usually

just try to buy from them too. I buy a lot of vinyl. In many cases I'll buy vinyl and download mp3s legally or illegally, I don't really care. As far as t-shirts go, I have a t-shirt problem. Always buying merch from bands, always buying t-shirts. I don't really buy stickers, pins, patches, anything that piles up. I have ten years of that stuff in various Ikea Expedit drawers in my apartment and at my parents' house, so I'm done doing that. Also, those are like freebies for other people. But yeah, also if a band I've played with before, or if [a band] I'm friends with guestlists me, I always try and buy from them that night. I think it's easier in the punk scene than any other one to control where your dollar goes—if you're just throwing away your dollar, what's the point?

As many of those within the scene (myself included) can attest to, these commodities can at times become a source of frustration. With bands' and record labels' abilities to create and distribute their own merchandise and sell it directly to the consumer, these goods can pile up quickly. As Justin explains, many of the smaller, more cheaply produced items such as stickers, patches, and pins can quickly accumulate, and become devalued as they sit in a drawer untouched. While all of these goods can become a challenging task to maintain, it was still important to support the scene via these purchases. Later in the interview, Justin discussed the significance of buying merchandise from a band, as it often provides a source of immediate income for bands who are touring and playing shows. These purchases will often determine whether or not a band returns to that particular city—if the show is not very profitable, it is unlikely that they may return in the future:

And I think that bands are more transparent about [making money], and it's not like "hey we made $300 in merch tonight," no one's posting that online . . . but at the same time you can tell when a band is doing well on tour versus when they're not. You see how many people are at their merch table, you can see how likely they are to come back to that city. A lot of responsible band managers and merch people will be logging who is selling what in what cities, if this is a city worth coming back to. I think it's been shallow and immature to be like "well, they should just come back here if they want to play here, they shouldn't come back here if they're not making money." That shouldn't have any effect, but have you ever bought gasoline for a car? Or fed yourself? That stuff all matters, and me buying a shirt might be the reason that they come back to this city in another year versus them maybe never again, yeah, it's a no-brainer for me. In a way, I think that the community that's buying stuff . . . and I also understand that not everyone's going to be able to afford that stuff, they were barely able to get to the show anyway, and they snuck into the show anyway just so they can be there. I think that's primarily the most important thing, but then the next most important thing is being sure these bands are taken care of.

For Justin, buying this merchandise was more significant than the ownership itself. It was a direct action that immediately impacted the band's ability

to continue making music. In contrast, Adam's perspective on buying merchandise differed from Justin's, as Adam stated he does not preorder merchandise like Justin. However, Adam did describe the purchases he does
make, and, like the others, admitted that these are usually made at shows he
attends:

> A lot of times I don't get to see the bands I really want to see, so I'll just end
> up ordering something online like if a record comes out. I don't usually
> preorder anything because I don't know what it sounds like, if I hate it maybe.
> But whenever I preorder something, and I've heard it before and I just order a
> record, I usually get a t-shirt or something too, if it's something I want. When I
> go to shows I usually buy something from the band, even if it's just a CD. I
> don't buy cassettes, but I try to buy something or take one of their stickers and
> put it some place it's not supposed to be so that other people see it. I definitely
> try to buy merch to at least support the band if not because I want it.

Though it is not always possible to support a band by directly buying
merchandise at a show, there is an understanding that making these purchases, in whatever way they are made, is a determining factor in whether or
not a band succeeds with their craft. Like the ownership of vinyl, purchasing
merchandise directly from a band at a show was prioritized over making
these purchases online, though both practices are viewed as supportive ways
to contribute to the success of a band.

CONCLUSION

As evidenced in the interviews conducted here, fans have yet to abandon
their scenes because of the relationship to the forces that assist in the commodification process. In fact, many do not see the relationship to be problematic, but instead endorse ethical production and distribution whenever possible. As a result of this movement toward ethical consumption, awareness of
the issue within today's scenes has become a prominent topic within scenes
around the world. Because t-shirts are one of the major merchandise options
that most bands sell, there is a growing concern for those who create these
shirts and the ways in which this labor is exploited. Punk Ethics, a UK
collective that works to raise awareness about sweatshop labor and its connections to the t-shirts that are often sold by bands today, currently works to
advocate for bands and the scene at large to consider using ethical practices
in the creation of their merchandise. Their 2019 campaign, called Punks
Against Sweatshops, encourages today's scenes to adopt fair trade practices
and to consider the source of their clothing when designing merchandise
(Punks Against Sweatshops n.d.). Rather than resisting the practice of consumerism altogether or using anti-consumption ideology as a means to speak

out against this process, many participants today actively purchase merchandise, and use these goods to both support a particular identity, with many envisioning these purchases as a long-term investment in their communities. As argued by Force (2009), "As a subculture operating in overlapping physical and social space with dominant culture, punk refracts more than rejects consumerism despite its oft-attributed resistance to it" (296). While it may seem more likely for today's punk communities to reject consumerism as a whole, efforts are often rerouted, as in the case of Punks Against Sweatshops, to align with more ethical and socially conscious ideologies that currently exist within the scene.

In the last four chapters, I have explored the various ways that participants demonstrate commitment to their scenes. As it is demonstrated, commitment can manifest itself in a variety of ways, which include an adherence to scene rules, dedication to playing in a band, or pursuing DIY ventures to further the scene's mission. Belonging in a band presents its own sets of challenges for those who wish to operate using a DIY method. While this method is preferred, significant levels of commitment and communication are required in order for a band to be successful in doing so. While band membership is one way to demonstrate commitment to a scene, other ways are also accepted, if playing music is not ideal. For example, adherence to the scene's values demonstrates commitment—if you can agree to follow the spoken and unspoken rules that exist in the digital and real spaces in which a scene operates, you have proven an acceptance of the insider knowledge that is required in order to consider oneself a member of this community. Actively working within a scene to tackle the various social issues that confront scenes today also reaffirms one's commitment to the larger causes, and in some cases, this activism is assisted by merchandise and the music that is created within the scene. Because commitment is understood on a spectrum of levels, one's actions do not have to involve the organization of large-scale movements, but rather, any small amount of effort, such as donating money or attending a show, is viewed as acceptable participation in the efforts to combat some of the issues facing scenes today. These grassroots efforts are emblematic of the varied and welcomed ways in which participants can display their commitment within their scenes, and through the ownership of merchandise participants, demonstrate their own commitment to the lasting impact of their scenes. DIY music production and an involvement in a punk band act as a way for participants to obtain autonomy of the creation process.

Chapter Six

God Save the Scene

Concluding Thoughts and the Future of Contemporary Punk Scenes in America

It's 2019. Warped Tour will hang up its Vans for the last time this summer, and MTV hasn't had a relevant punk rock moment in nearly two decades. And yet, despite the death of punk in the eyes of the pop culture forces that served as the gateway for many to bands like Blink-182, Green Day, Jawbreaker, Bad Religion, and many more, thriving communities continue to exist worldwide. They exist in basements, backyards, and at festivals, where watching a favorite band perform is only a small part of the overall punk experience. Today, information on such goings on is never privileged just to an exclusive group, but is instead posted far and wide on social media—hashtagged, tagged, and shared with anyone within that social sphere. Merchandise is not just available at the show—music, t-shirts, hoodies, and other logoed products are readily available on any band's Facebook page, Bandcamp, or merch websites. Members commit to their scenes by respecting a DIY ethos, and by supporting their friends' artistic endeavors by attending shows and buying merchandise. And moving forward, it is unlikely to assume that contemporary punk scenes will stop using their platforms in constructive ways—as a style of music that was built on the belief that the status quo should be challenged, today's scenes have narrowed their sights on issues that directly affect those within their communities right now.

Knowing this, what can be determined about the future for contemporary punk scenes in America? With regards to punk rock's future, there exists an optimism about the future of these scenes. The community itself continues to thrive in both physical and digital spaces, and the well-connected networks that exist within these locations provide useful communities of support to

149

those who identify as members. Jamie, in discussing the future of their scene, remained optimistic that those who are committed today will continue to uphold the values of inclusion. Today's scenes are not focused on the outward sartorial expression of rebelliousness as much as they are focused on transforming their communities into places where constructive action can be used to make a positive effort to combat some of the worn-out stereotypes of punk. There is value in awareness, and a value in making a positive effort to improve the scene moving forward today:

[Punk] is not about safety pins and liberty spikes and that crap. It's not about being an ignorant dude. So, I want that to be what happens in the future. I want the scene to sustain itself. I want smaller bands to be able to sustain themselves, and it's a lot harder now in the dawn of the internet where everyone feels entitled to free music. It's really hard, I hope maybe there will be more DIY spaces that aren't someone's house, so that cops won't shut it down, and that everyone can go, and it's not a bar. Shows shouldn't have to be at seedy bars. . . . I do hope that people make good on their intentions to make it all-inclusive for everybody. So that's the future I hope for it, in that it progresses and does not regress because there's this section of dudes that are trying to fight the PC police and they're trying to beat us back twenty years again. I hope there's more of those attitudes and that becomes the norm and not the reaction, and that safe spaces continue to grow and flourish. So that's my future. That we'd all feel comfortable going to shows and no one has to worry about being assaulted, or feeling like, "oh, well, I guess I'm the only person of color in the room."

Like many others, Andrew expressed many thoughts on the presence of inclusion and diversity moving forward for today's punk scene. He had high hopes for his scene but recognized specific instances of change that still need to be made. Below, Andrew's quote addressed the problematic approach of the Shiragirl Stage at the Warped Tour, which, during the run of the festival, operated as a stage dedicated exclusively to female bands and musicians, with an objective "to get more girl band representation" at Warped Tour (Gil Kaufman 2018). Below, Andrew explained the complications of dedicating a stage exclusively to women, and how this practice existed as an example of a perpetuating of a gender bias within the punk community at large:

I want [the scene] to be the melting pot that we were promised, that America was going to be, and hasn't quite become yet. Because, you know, we're still very, as American culture as a whole, or society as a whole, there's still this pocket, this area is white, and this area is black and in this area there's a lot of Koreans or whatever. There's still very much segregation in that, and I feel like too there's still segregation in punk at that . . . you know, of course Warped Tour is a terrible example, but with something with Warped Tour where they're like "well, we're gonna put all the bands with girls on the Shiragirl stage." Why? Only women are gonna go to that now, you know that.

I don't want "female-fronted" to be a genre. I think it's a nice thing to add on to say, like a female-fronted powerviolence band, female-fronted mopey indie rock band. I want all of us to kind of blend together and to hang out and be happy with one another, that we can make all these friendships. I want an end to the hush-hush covering it up when people assault each other, or when people rape somebody else, I want an end to that. I want people to feel comfortable and to be happy, and to not think when they show up to the show, "is somebody going to pick a fight with me? Am I going to be the only Asian girl there?" I want people to feel comfortable and to be happy and to have this safe place where they can release those emotions and to be a part of this crowd and to feel this catharsis of, you know, my week sucked, and all this shit in my life isn't necessarily going in the right way, but right now, in this moment, I feel better. I feel okay about what's going on and I know that I'm gonna make it to next week, I know I'm gonna make it until two weeks from now when I go to my next show, I'm gonna survive this because I've been part of this and I have this community that supports me.

In his discussion of an outlook for punk's future, Andrew mentioned the importance of acceptance and the hope that those who attend shows will not feel threatened by others at the show. To continue this thought, Andrew expanded on the idea of inclusion, and addressed the issues with punk culture and its infamous relationship with a narrow demographic of fans. For Andrew, having a greater diversity in representation within the punk community today will help future generations of participants feel accepted within the scene. Such representation and inclusion can only come about if scenes actively take part in addressing these issues and working toward diversifying their spaces:

So now we need to start getting more of that going on from every single group imaginable so that everybody has a place in punk, and everybody has somebody to look up to and somebody to idolize and want to be part of. . . . This is the same as customer service practically. I just have to be nice and do my job and be confident and then I'll be fine, and that's really what it is, but if you don't have that person who looks like you, to look up to, then it makes it so much more difficult. So, the more people that we can get involved for younger people to look up to of different races, and sexual identities, and gender identities, and all that kind of stuff, the more of that we can get, the better our scene is gonna be. Even within the last couple of years, there's been such a big change in how many women I see on stage, and how many I see at shows. That alone just within maybe the last five years has changed a lot for me personally, so that is very encouraging, and it should go without saying, but the more women that are on stage, the more will be in the audience.

With regards to acknowledging the wider range of diversity within punk scenes today, Alex remained optimistic, citing several bands that are doing their part to take on the male-dominated worldview of punk rock today.

Downtown Boys, whose mission is to "topple the white-cis-het hegemony and draft a new history," as written on their Bandcamp page (Downtown Boys n.d.), represent a current punk band that uses their platform to actively address issues of representation within the scene. Similarly, G.L.O.S.S., which stands for Girls Living Outside Society's Shit, is another example of a current band whose 2016 EP *Trans Day of Revenge* is described as "bringing feminism to a scene notoriously dominated by men, and challenging authority in under eight minutes" (Weiss n.d.). Alex's discussion of these bands helped to exemplify both the popularity of these bands, and the community's acceptance of people from backgrounds different from their own. When asked about his thoughts on punk rock's future, Alex provided an optimistic understanding of the subculture, and used both Downtown Boys and G.L.O.S.S as examples of punk rock's move toward prioritizing a wider range of voices:

> I think [punk's future] is bright. I think it's really exciting now, just because at least I feel it's more diverse now than it ever has been, both in terms of the music and in terms of the people playing it. Just because as society has progressed and become more accepting of different kinds of people, punk rock for the most part has always been like that, with a few exceptions, but now you see bands that are writing songs about . . . one of my favorite records this year is the Downtown Boys record. All of their songs are super political and they're writing about what it's like being a person of color in punk and being a woman in punk. There's a hardcore band called G.L.O.S.S. They're made up of all transgender people, and they're singing super hyper-aggressively about what their lives are like and how fucking grim and dire their lives are, and what they're going through, and it's so interesting and so affecting in so many ways. And I feel like more of that is happening now, and that's going to be kind of the new thing, as opposed to . . . I mean there's going to be those people over here, and there's going to be the white dude punk over here and that's still going to exist always, but I feel like as society is progressing, punk is progressing in an even more outward way than it would have been even five years ago, which is awesome. It's really exciting. I know a lot of jaded really jaded people, and it's just like "what's the point?" If you don't like it, do something else. Listen to something else. If you're just going to be angry about stuff, and not like angry in a productive way, just like, angry because things aren't what they used to be or whatever . . . listen, the world's moving on with or without you, so you can stay on or you can get off and it's entirely up to you.

In his thoughts on the present state of the scene, Alex addressed the ways that he sees members within his scene take an active, rather than a passive, approach to solving the problems that face the community today. While there will always exist a contingent of punk rock fans who do not see purpose in actively addressing such issues, it is evident that many of those who participate today hope to use their anger and frustration toward productive means. Like Alex, Greg echoed a similar sentiment regarding the push for diversity within scenes today. There exists an understanding that punk rock has the opportunity to be a voice of change, that criticism can be constructive, and that advocating for change can result in a positive outcome:

> I think there's even like a rift or a difference between what's an old punk and what's a new punk. I think that older punks, there's like an "I don't give a fuck" attitude, like the Dwarves are very much about shock rock, and stuff like that. None of that appeals to me. I don't get that. It's cool that other people do. Now, I think there's such a big movement in the punk rock community to be more socially conscious, to be more feminist, to be more aware of trans issues. I think there's a big push too in bands that aren't just like dudes, and obviously I'm guilty of that, a lot of people are because it's just easy to play with your guy friends, but you see bands like Chumped or Cayetana, or Worriers, or people like RVIVR, people really like that it's just not dudes.

Here, Greg addressed the diverging perspectives that we are seeing in punk today. As addressed in previous chapters, punk is at a crossroads— should it be a site of offense and exclusion, or should progressive efforts work to combat these old approaches to the punk rock message? While there will always be a contingent of fans who believe the former, I see significant evidence that suggests that punk rock has taken on a renewed responsibility to be a platform for productive efforts to rid the genre of some very old and exclusionary practices that contributed little to the advancement of punk rock. Joe repeated this sentiment in his thoughts, and cited some other examples of bands that actively use their platforms to advocate for change within the scene today:

> I think bands like War on Women, or Cayetana, are probably going to become a lot bigger. Hopefully the way that the scene's going, that there's a lot more accepting of a scene, more open, more female bands, more female-fronted bands, queer bands. There's already a ton right now, Worriers are a good example of a queer band. Because those are important issues and I already have a couple friends who are always raving about these bands. Against Me! is another good example. They're veterans at this point. They've sort of paved the way in a way, or at least in this era of the scene. So, hopefully we see a lot more Against Me! and we see a lot more Worriers, a lot more War on Women. And it becomes . . . I think it's important there's a lot of songs about introspection and relationships and such, but it's time for a change of pace in a way.

For both Emily and Allie, there were many positive aspects about today's punk scene that they hoped would continue on in the future. Emily expressed a desire for things in her scene to remain the same, reinforcing the importance of a tight-knit community and the values that emerge from such a dynamic:

This might sound weird, but I kind of wish it would just stay the same. I know that might be wanting failure in some sense, but not at the same time, because I think that the level that it's at is great. If it grows, that's awesome too, but I also think that the fact that it's such a tight-knit community falls where it does because it's not being played on the radio and everyone is listening to it, and everyone is like "oh my god, I love this," but people actually work really hard to where they're getting and appreciate it more I suppose.

Like many others, Allie hoped to see the political message of punk rock continue to be a priority and expressed a desire for the music itself to remain aggressive: "I think it's going to keep going, as far as being politically aware. I think there's still going to be stuff to be angry about and fight against. So, I think it will keep on going. It's not going to sound like Taylor Swift. I don't see it evolving too much, because I notice when I listen to a lot of new bands, they're talking about new topics, but musically I don't think it evolves a great deal."

By in large, participants expressed hesitant optimism regarding the future of their scenes. Many of those interviewed hoped to see more progress with regards to inclusion and provided several examples of current bands that were actively working to make these changes evident. There was an understanding that in some instances, punk rock activism takes on little action—it often manifests itself as outspoken dissent and hostility rather than proactive work toward change. With younger generations of scene members learning the ropes from later generations who represent these progressive stances, it is likely to conclude that contemporary punk rock scenes will continue to thrive and use a range of DIY efforts to work toward becoming more inclusive sites of representation and diversity.

CONCLUDING THOUGHTS

It's interesting to see what people make of us. That's the thing, I was walking here [to the interview] and people were looking at me funny, you know, normie folks and their families. Tattoos and piercings, it's interesting to see what people think of . . . because some people still think punk is the Sex Pistols, when everyone, most of us, you say "Sex Pistols" and we all laugh. I have never met anyone outside of high school that ever had liberty spikes. It's interesting to see what people think of us. People don't realize . . . I was talking to someone and they were like "I didn't realize most punk dudes now are just chubby guys with beards." . . . It's funny to me. I even have friends that are normie looking, but they love punk music and they're just as punk as me, just because they don't dress a certain way. They love the music; they go to the shows. People think it's fashion. It's silly when I'm like "it's not a way of life," but yes, it is. (Jamie, personal communication)

In the introduction to this book I briefly outlined the historical approaches to investigating subcultures and scenes. Early subcultural theory viewed youth cultures as groupings of adolescents that fit specific parameters, with a focus on prioritizing class status and fashion. While the CCCS was integral in justifying legitimate sociological exploration into youth cultures as a whole, their all-or-nothing binaries and methodological approaches oversimplified the complex and consistently changing characteristics of these cultural groups. Moving forward, postsubcultural theory branched off from these perspectives, asserting that involvement within a subculture (or scene, neo-tribe, and so on) was a more complex, subjective, and reflexive process than originally concluded by the CCCS. Indicators such as fashion, commitment, and personal spending habits were addressed by postsubcultural theorists as unique traits that presented themselves through fluid and varied ways. In the literature that emerged, postsubcultural theorists investigated an expansive range of communities centered around shared interests in music, art, technology, and an extensive range of hobbies. From these investigations, we can further understand the subjective and wide-ranging characteristics that qualify participation within scenes today.

While identity has always had a connection to an affiliation within a particular scene, those within today's punk communities recognize their affiliation as an important part of an identity. Values that one abides by within these spaces often transcend into other realms of life, and the values that one upholds within scene involvement often transcend between these punk-centric spaces and other aspects of everyday life. Furthermore, this shared understanding of values and interests translated into a sense of belonging for many. This sense of belonging manifested itself through the connections made with others within the scene, and were supported by shared interests in bands, social issues, and current events. Though there is great value placed on the attendance of events such as shows and festivals, these interactions were just as important in the digital spaces that operate to connect members through Facebook groups, private chat groups, Instagram pages, and so on. With social media used as a common means to stay connected, local and physical scenes coalesce with one another in digital circles where shared interests are explored across a range of platforms. As evidenced in the interviews I conducted with members throughout the scene today, contemporary punk scenes see value in the immediacy of social media, as such contact allows for social capital and communicative networks to keep scenes connected.

I believe that this particular generation of punk rock exhibits specific traits that are not explored at length within the postsubcultural field today. As prevalent in my interactions, participants learned of punk rock through very specific and common ways—either through a mainstream route such as MTV or through friends and family. Introductory bands did not include the time-honored mainstays such as the Sex Pistols or the Clash, but instead included bands like Green Day and the Offspring, suggesting that an entirely new generation of listeners was drawn to the genre as a result of vastly different circumstances. In addition, scenes today place an overwhelming emphasis on the importance of inclusion and representation. Their scenes are not viewed insular entities where high levels of gatekeeping prevent outsiders from participating. Rather, participants encourage outsiders to join their scenes, and hope that the low barrier to entry will introduce more fans to the nuances of punk culture. While a low barrier to entry exists, there is a prioritized understanding that those who participate demonstrate perceived likeminded positions on various social issues. Social networks between these scenes are encouraged and are used to alert others to those who choose to engage in rule breaking behavior, whether it consists of physical behavior such as fighting or ideological behavior such as sexism or racism.

While it may seem that punk rock and notions of authenticity go hand in hand, current concerns with authenticity come across as trivial and largely nonexistent, as we see a greater emphasis within these communities placed on the productive use of various platforms to address issues that face scenes today. The indifference toward authenticity is a likely result of time and place—current economic situations have made millennials largely apathetic toward the notion of selling out. Instead, scenes wish to focus their efforts on immediate issues that demand the most attention. As a result, resources and DIY efforts are often used to directly focus on some of these issues, and rather than adopting an antiauthoritarian stance toward intangible issues that are uncontrollable, there is an emphasis toward proactively addressing issues that face scenes today through grassroots movement and communicative networks, with special attention paid toward addressing these issues at the microlevel.

Indeed, today's contemporary punk scenes are similar to and still resemble older generations of punk in some ways—largely in terms of musical style, perhaps—but these scenes lack many of the signifying traits upon which punk rock was founded and as a result, they have truly distanced themselves from the Mohawk-wearing, class-rebelling structure that informed much of the original subcultural literature of the CCCS theorists. When looking at the evidence presented here, there is very little that can be considered "revived" or "modified" about today's punk scene. Instead, contemporary punk scenes exist as fluid and amorphous spaces where involvement and commitment are determined by the participant, but also influenced by the existing ideologies and belief systems that are shared among the majority of those who partake in contributing to the scene. While conceptualizations of fluid participation exist throughout postsubcultural literature, today's punk communities provide a prominent example of the importance of perceived shared beliefs among members.

All of these traits are indicative of the "osmotic" relationships that exist between contemporary punk scenes and the external environments that exist within society today (Weinzierl and Muggleton 2003, 7). Contemporary punk scenes do not exist as insular, exclusive sites where external influences do not make an impact. Rather, today's scenes operate within several spheres of influence, which include forces such as popular culture and the internet. While it may seem that these forces would be a source of contention for scenes today, there is an understanding that there is no escaping the capitalist forces that exist to influence various components of scene preservation today. Efforts such as DIY production are used as a way to remain autonomous despite these forces, but there is an awareness, and at times an acceptance, that such forces will influence or invade these spaces, and participants acknowledged their own involvement and relationship with the greater powers of modern society.

Moving forward, I would like to underscore the need for more empirical study of contemporary punk scenes in America today. Punk rock, as a genre, has always prevailed as a lifestyle worthy of investigation, and today's scenes are sites of continued efforts of the individuals who identify as part of these communities. Specifically, I would suggest more in-depth study of the contemporary punk rock scene's relationship with DIY practice, both the commodity production and music-making process. Ethnographic study of this relationship would help us see the ways that current participants use their efforts, connections, and resources to create these goods as a means to control the narrative of punk rock today. Investigation into the commodification of contemporary punk scenes as a whole would provide valuable insight into current understandings of fashion, expression, and outward displays of a perceived insider status. I also suggest further investigation into the conflicting opinions on what it means to be a member within a contemporary punk scene. While all of my participants offered similar perspectives on what punk rock's message and present goals were, it is obvious from these examples that there are others within such scenes that do not believe punk rock to be a site of progressive ideas and inclusivity. Further exploration of these perspectives would offer a more well-rounded understanding of the motivations for holding such ideologies and the justifications for doing so.

References

"About Feed the Scene." n.d. https://www.feedthescene.com/about.

Al-Attas, Jai. 2009. "One Nine Nine Four." YouTube video. Los Angeles: Robot Academy.

Allooh, Noah N., Christina M. Rummell, and Ronald F. Levant. 2013. "'Emo' Culture and Gender Norms in Late Adolescents and Young Adults." *Boyhood Studies* 7 (1): 21–42. https://doi.org/10.3149/thy.0701.21.

Andes, Linda. 1998. "Growing up Punk: Meaning and Commitment Careers in a Contemporary Youth Subculture." In *Youth Culture: Identity in a Postmodern World*, edited by Jonathon S. Epstein, 212–31. Oxford: Wiley-Blackwell.

Anthony, David. 2014. "The Perfect Music Festival for People Who Hate Music Festivals." *A.V. Club*. https://music.avclub.com/the-perfect-music-festival-for-people-who-hate-music-fe-1798273851.

———. 2015. "Green Day Got its Cred Back, Is No Longer Banned from 924 Gilman Street." *A.V. Club*. https://news.avclub.com/green-day-got-its-cred-back-is-no-longer-banned-from-9-1798279753.

Anthony, David, Kyle Ryan, and Jason Heller. 2014. "A Beginner's Guide to the Bouncy Buzz of Pop-Punk." *A.V. Club*. https://music.avclub.com/a-beginner-s-guide-to-the-bouncy-buzz-of-pop-punk-1798268060.

———. 2017. "A Beginner's Guide to the Bouncy Buzz of Pop-Punk: From Buzzcocks to Blink-182 and Beyond." *A.V. Club*. http://www.avclub.com/article/beginners-guide-bouncy-buzz-pop-punk-201853.

Arnett, Jeffrey Jensen. 2007. "Suffering, Selfish, Slackers? Myths and Reality about Emerging Adults." *Journal of Youth and Adolescence* 36 (1): 23–29. https://doi.org/10.1007/s10964-006-9157-z.

Aswad, Jem. 2011. "Screeching Weasel Singer Hits Two Women at Band's SXSW Gig." *Billboard*. https://www.billboard.com/articles/columns/viral-v%09ideos/472506/screeching-weasel-singer-hits-two-women-at-bands-sxsw-gig.

Aubin, Paul. 2011. "Screeching Weasel Members Resign." *PunkNews*. Accessed May 9, 2016. https://www.punknews.org/article/42026/screeching-weasel-members-resign.

Azerrad, Michael. 1992. "Grunge City: The Seattle Scene." *Rolling Stone*. Accessed June 4, 2019. https://www.rollingstone.com/music/music-news/grunge-city-the-seattle-scene-250071/.

———. 2001. *Our Band Could Be Your Life: Scenes from the American Indie Underground 1981–1991*. New York, NY: Back Bay Books.

Baab-Muguira, Catherine. 2016. "Millennials Are Totally Cool with Selling Out." *Quartz*. https://qz.com/751171/millennials-are-totally-cool-with-selling-out/.

Baker, Sarah, Andy Bennett, and Jodie Taylor, ed. 2013. *Redefining Mainstream Popular Music*. New York, NY: Routledge.

Ball, Tom, and Eric Auchard. 2018. "Music Streaming Overtakes Physical Sales for the First Time." Reuters. https://www.reuters.com/article/music-sales/music-streaming-overtakes-physical-sales-for-the-first-time-industry-body-idUSL8N1S143H.

Bandcamp. n.d. "About Us." Bandcamp.

Bartmanski, Dominik, and Ian Woodward. 2018. "Vinyl Record: A Cultural Icon." *Consumption Markets & Culture* 21 (2): 171–77. https://doi.org/10.1080/10253866.2016.1212709.

Baxter, Leslie A., and Earl R. Babbie. 2003. *The Basics of Communication Research*. Belmont, CA: Wadsworth.

Baym, Nancy K. 2011. "The Swedish Model: Balancing Markets and Gifts in the Music Industry." *Popular Communication* 9 (1): 22–38. https://doi.org/10.1080/15405702.2011.536680.

Beedham, Tom. 2016. "Pizza, Poutine, and Punk: Meet the Founder of Montreal's Infamous Pouzza Fest." Vice. https://www.vice.com/en_ca/article/rkqvw9/pouzza-fest-hugo-mudie-interview-2016?utm_source=viceadwordsca&utm_medium=cpc.

Before the Party. n.d. "Before the Party Upgrade." Accessed June 6, 2019. http://beforetheparty.jxrticketing.com/upgrades/15271-atlanta-ga-october-27th.

Bennett, Andy. 1999. "Subcultures or Neo-Tribes? Rethinking the Relationship between Youth, Style, and Musical Taste." *Sociology* 33 (3): 599–617. https://doi.org/10.1177/S0038038599000371.

———. 2004. "Consolidating the Music Scenes Perspective." *Poetics* 32 (3–4): 223–34. https://doi.org/10.1016/j.poetic.2004.05.004.

———. 2006. "Punk's Not Dead: The Continuing Significance of Punk Rock for an Older Generation of Fans." *Sociology* 40 (2): 219–35.

———. 2011. "The Continuing Importance of the 'Cultural' in the Study of Youth." *Youth Studies Australia* 30 (3): 27–33.

Bennett, Andy. 2018. "Popular Music Scenes and Aging Bodies." *Journal of Aging Studies* 45 (January): 49–53. https://doi.org/10.1016/j.jaging.2018.01.007.

Bennett, Andy, and Paula Guerra, ed. 2018a. *DIY Cultures and Underground Music Scenes*. New York, NY: Routledge.

———. 2018b. "Introduction." In *DIY Cultures and Underground Music*, edited by Andy Bennett and Paula Guerra, 1–6. New York, NY: Routledge.

———. 2018c. "Rethinking DIY Culture in a Post-Industrial and Global Context." In *DIY Cultures and Underground Music*, edited by Andy Bennett and Paula Guerra, 7–18. New York, NY: Routledge.

Bienstock, Richard. 2014. "How The Offspring's Smash Defeated the Majors." *Rolling Stone*. https://www.rollingstone.com/music/music-news/the-offsprings-smash-the-little-punk-lp-that-defeated-the-majors-189742/.

Bourdieu, Pierre. 1984. *Distinction: A Social Critique on the Judgement of Taste*. Cambridge, MA: Harvard.

Brand New. n.d. "Brand New." Billboard. Accessed June 4, 2019. https://www.billboard.com/music/brand-%0D%0Anew/chart-history/billboard-200%0D%0A.

Breidahl, Karen N., Nils Holtug, and Kristian Kongshøj. 2018. "Do Shared Values Promote Social Cohesion? If so, Which? Evidence from Denmark." *European Political Science Review* 10 (1): 97–118. https://doi.org/10.1017/S1755773916000266.

Brown, Andy R. 2003. "Heavy Metal and Subcultural Theory: A Paradigmatic Case of Neglect?" In *The Post-Subcultures Reader*, edited by David Muggleton and Rupert Weinzierl, 209–22. New York, NY: Berg.

Brown, August. 2018. "End of the Warped Tour: What the Loss of Rock's 'Cheap, Scruffy' Roadshow Means for the Concert Biz." *Los Angeles Times*. https://www.latimes.com/entertainment/music/la-et-ms-warped-tour-20180614-story.html.

Burnett, Stephanie, Catherine Sebastian, Kathrin Cohen Kadosh, and Sarah Jayne Blakemore. 2011. "The Social Brain in Adolescence: Evidence from Functional Magnetic Resonance Imaging and Behavioural Studies." *Neuroscience and Biobehavioral Reviews* 35 (8): 1654–64. https://doi.org/10.1016/j.neubiorev.2010.10.011.

Bury, Rhiannon. 2003. "'The X-Files,' Online Fan Culture, and the David Duchovny Estrogen Brigades." In *The Post-Subcultures Reader*, edited by David Muggleton and Rupert Weinzierl, 269–83. New York, NY: Berg.

Cateforis, Theo. 2011. "Introduction." In *Are We Not New Wave? Modern Pop at the Turn of the 1980s*, edited by Theo Cateforis, 1–16. Ann Arbor, MI: University of Michigan Press.

Chuang, Lisa M., and John P. Hart. 2008. "Suburban American Punks and the Musical Rhetoric of Green Day's 'Jesus of Suburbia.'" *Communication Studies* 59 (3): 183–201.

Clark, Dylan. 2003. "The Death and Life of Punk, the Last Subculture." In *The Post-Subcultures Reader*, edited by David Muggleton and Rupert Weinzierl, 223–36. New York, NY: Berg.

Clarke, John, Stuart Hall, Tony Jefferson, and Brian Roberts. 2006. "Subcultures, Cultures, and Class." In *Resistance through Rituals: Youth Subcultures in Post-War Britain*, edited by Stuart Hall and Tony Jefferson, 3–59. New York, NY: Routledge.

Cohen, Sara. 1995. "Sounding out the City: Music and the Sensuous Production of Place." *Transactions of the Institute of British Geographers* 20 (4): 434–46. https://doi.org/10.2307/622974.

Cohen, Stanley. 2002. *Folk Devils and Moral Panics: The Creation of the Mods and Rockers*. 3rd ed. New York, NY: Routledge.

Cole, Shu Tian, and Steven F. Illum. 2006. "Examining the Mediating Role of Festival Visitors' Satisfaction in the Relationship between Service Quality and Behavioral Intentions." *Journal of Vacation Marketing* 12 (2): 160–73. https://doi.org/10.1177/1356766706062156.

Cormany, Diane L. 2015. "Coachella Fans, Online and Translocal." *Journal of Popular Music Studies* 27 (2): 184–98. https://doi.org/10.1111/jpms.12120.

Corrigan, Paul. 2006. "Doing Nothing." In *Resistance through Rituals: Youth Subcultures in Post-War Britain*, edited by Stuart Hall and Tony Jefferson, 153–56. New York, NY: Routledge.

Culton, Kenneth R., and Ben Holtzman. 2010. "The Growth and Disruption of a 'Free Space': Examining a Suburban Do It Yourself (DIY) Punk Scene." *Space and Culture* 13 (3): 270–84. https://doi.org/10.1177/1206331210365258.

D'Angelo, J. 2004. "How Green Day's *Dookie* Fertilized a Punk-Rock Revival." MTV. http://www.mtv.com/news/1491001/how-green-days-dookie-fertilized-a-punk-rock-revival/.

Davis, Joanna R. 2006. "Growing Up Punk: Negotiating Aging Identity in a Local Music Scene." *Symbolic Interaction* 29 (1): 63–69. https://doi.org/10.1525/si.2006.29.1.63.

———. 2012. "Punk, Ageing, and the Expectations of Adult Life." In *Ageing and Youth Cultures: Music, Style, and Identity*, edited by Paul Hodkinson and Andy Bennett, 105–18. London: Berg.

Debies-Carl, Jeffrey S. 2013. "Are the Kids Alright? A Critique and Agenda for Taking Youth Cultures Seriously." *Social Science Information* 52 (1): 110–33. https://doi.org/10.1177/0539018412466636.

———. 2015. "Print Is Dead: The Promise and Peril of Online Media for Subcultural Resistance." *Journal of Contemporary Ethnography* 44 (6): 679–708. https://doi.org/10.1177/0891241614546553.

Deibert, Ron. 2014. "Foreward." In *DIY Citizenship: Critical Making and Social Media*, edited by Matt Ratto and Megan Boler, ix–x. Cambridge, MA: The MIT Press.

DeVito, Joseph A. 2014. *Essentials of Human Communication*. Eighth. Pearson.

Downtown Boys. n.d. "Downtown Boys." Bandcamp. Accessed June 14, 2019. https://downtownboys.bandcamp.com/.

Drass, Jessica Masino. 2016. "Creating a Culture of Connection: A Postmodern Punk Rock Approach to Art Therapy." *Art Therapy* 33 (3): 138–43. https://doi.org/10.1080/07421656.2016.1199244.

Drissel, David. 2016. "Anarchist Punks Resisting Gentrification." *The International Journal of the Humanities: Annual Review* 8 (10): 19–44. https://doi.org/10.18848/1447-9508/cgp/v08i10/42992.

Driver, Christopher, and Andy Bennett. 2015. "Music Scenes, Space and the Body." *Cultural Sociology* 9 (1): 99–115. https://doi.org/10.1177/1749975514546234.

Duncombe, Stephen. 1998. "Let's All Be Alienated Together: Zines and the Making of Underground Community." In *Generations of Youth: Youth Cultures and History in Twentieth-Century America*, edited by Joe Alan Austin and Michael Willard, 427–51. New York, NY: NYU Press.

Dunn, Kevin. 2012a. "Anarcho-Punk and Resistance in Everyday Life." *Punk & Post Punk* 1 (2): 201–18. https://doi.org/10.1386/punk.1.2.201_1.

———. 2012b. "'If It Ain't Cheap, It Ain't Punk': Walter Benjamin's Progressive Cultural Production and DIY Punk." *Popular Music* 24 (2): 217–37.

Epitaph Records: The Offspring. n.d. "Epitaph Records: The Offspring." Epitaph Records. http://www.epitaph.com/artists/artist/54/.

Fine, Gary Alan, and Lori Holyfield. 1996. "Secrecy, Trust, and Dangerous Leisure: Generating Group Cohesion in Voluntary Organizations." *Social Psychology Quarterly* 59 (1): 22–38.

Force, William Ryan. 2009. "Consumption Styles and the Fluid Complexity of Punk Authenticity." *Symbolic Interaction* 32 (4): 289–309. https://doi.org/10.1525/si.2009.32.4.289.

Fox, Kathryn Joan. 1987. "Real Punks and Pretenders: The Social Organization of a Counterculture." *Journal of Contemporary Ethnography* 16 (3): 344–70.

Frith, Simon. 1981. *Sound Effects: Youth, Leisure, and the Politics of Rock'n'Roll*. New York, NY: Pantheon Books.

Gallagher, Brendan. 2015. "Why Did We Ever Shop at Hot Topic?" Complex. https://www.complex.com/style/2015/03/why-did-we-ever-shop-at-hot-topic .

Gee, James Paul. 2011. *An Introduction to Discourse Analysis: Theory and Method*. 3rd ed. New York, NY: Routledge.

Geraghty, Lincoln. 2014. "It's Not All about the Music: Online Fan Communities and Collecting Hard Rock Café Pins." In "Material Fan Culture," edited by Bob Rehak, special issue, *Transformative Works and Cultures*, no. 16. http://dx.doi.org.ezproxy.snhu.edu/10.3983/twc.2014.0492.

Glass, Pepper G. 2012. "Doing Scene: Identity, Space, and the Interactional Accomplishment of Youth Culture." *Journal of Contemporary Ethnography* 41 (6): 695–716. https://doi.org/10.1177/0891241612454104.

Green, Ben. 2016. "'I Always Remember That Moment': Peak Music Experiences as Epiphanies." *Sociology* 50 (2): 333–48. https://doi.org/10.1177/0038038514565835.

Green Day. n.d. "Green Day." Billboard. Accessed November 20, 2014. http://www.billboard.com/artist/303108/green-day/chart?f=305.

Green Day—Grammy. n.d. "Green Day—Grammy." Grammy. Accessed November 20, 2014. https://www.grammy.com/grammys/artists/green-day.

Green, Katie Victoria. 2018. "Trying to Have Fun in 'No Fun City': Legal and Illegal Strategies for Creating Punk Spaces in Vancouver, British Columbia." *Punk & Post Punk* 7 (1): 75–92. https://doi.org/10.1386/punk.7.1.75_1.

Gregory, Julie. 2012. "Ageing Rave Women's Post-Scene Narratives." In *Ageing and Youth Cultures: Music, Style, and Identity*, edited by Paul Hodkinson and Andy Bennett, 37–51. London: Berg.

Griffin, Naomi. 2012. "Gendered Performance and Performing Gender in the DIY Punk and Hardcore Music Scene." *Journal of International Women's Studies* 13 (2): 66–81.

Haenfler, Ross. 2004. "Rethinking Subcultural Resistance: Core Values of the Straight Edge Movement." *Journal of Contemporary Ethnography* 33 (4): 406–36. https://doi.org/10.1177/0891241603259809.

———. 2006. *Straight Edge: Clean-Living Youth, Hardcore Punk, and Social Change*. New Brunswick, NJ: Rutgers University Press.

———. 2012. "More than Xs on My Hands: Older Straight Edgers and the Meaning of Styles." In *Ageing and Youth Cultures: Music, Style and Identity*, edited by Andy Bennett and Paul Hodkinson, 9–23. London: Berg.

———. 2014. *Subcultures: The Basics*. New York: Routledge.

———. 2018. "The Entrepreneurial (Straight) Edge: How Participation in DIY Music Cultures Translates to Work and Careers." *Cultural Sociology* 12 (2): 174–92. https://doi.org/10.1177/1749975517700774.

Hagerty, Bonnie M., Reg A. Williams, James C. Coyne, and Margaret R. Early. 1996. "Sense of Belonging and Indicators of Social and Psychological Functioning." *Archives of Psychiatric Nursing* 10 (4): 235–44. https://doi.org/10.1016/S0883-9417(96)80029-X.

Hall, Stuart, and Tony Jefferson. 2006. *Resistance through Rituals: Youth Subcultures in Post-War Britain*. Edited by Stuart Hall and Tony Jefferson. New York, NY: Routledge.

Hancock, Black Hawk, and Michael J. Lorr. 2013. "More than Just a Soundtrack: Toward a Technology of the Collective in Hardcore Punk." *Journal of Contemporary Ethnography* 42 (3): 320–46. https://doi.org/10.1177/0891241612465652.

Hannerz, Erik. 2013. "The Positioning of the Mainstream in Punk." In *Redefining Mainstream Popular Music*, edited by Sarah Baker, Andy Bennett, and Jodie Taylor, 50–60. New York, NY: Routledge.

Harris, Keith. 2000. "'Roots'?: The Relationship between the Global and the Local within the Extreme Metal Scene." *Popular Music* 19 (1): 13–30. http://www.jstor.org/stable/853709.

———. 2014. "1994: The 40 Best Records from Mainstream Alternative's Greatest Year." *Rolling Stone*. Accessed May 17, 2019. https://www.rollingstone.com/music/music-lists/1994-the-40-best-records-from-mainstream-alternatives-greatest-year-29203/green-day-dookie-4-169404/.

Heath, Joseph, and Andrew Potter. 2004. *Nation of Rebels: Why Counterculture Became Consumer Culture*. New York: Harper Business.

Heath, Sue. 2004. "Peer-Shared Households, Quai-Communes and Neo-Tribes." *Current Sociology* 52 (2): 161–79. https://doi.org/https://doi.org/10.1177/0011392104041799.

Hebdige, Dick. 1988. *Subculture: The Meaning of Style*. New York, NY: Routledge.

Hodkinson, Paul. 2002. *Goth: Identity, Style and Subculture*. London: Bloomsbury.

———. 2004. "Translocal Connections in the Goth Scene." In *Music Scenes: Local, Translocal, and Virtual*, edited by Andy Bennett and Richard A. Peterson, 131–48. Nashville, TN: Vanderbilt University Press.

———. 2011. "Ageing in a Spectacular 'Youth Culture': Continuity, Change and Community amongst Older Goths." *British Journal of Sociology* 62 (2): 262–82. https://doi.org/10.1111/j.1468-4446.2011.01364.x.

———. 2013. "Spectacular Youth Cultures and Ageing: Beyond Refusing to Grow Up." *Sociology Compass* 7 (1): 13–22. https://doi.org/10.1111/soc4.12008.

Hopeless Romantics Club. n.d. "Hopeless Romantics Club." Accessed June 9, 2019. https://www.bouncingsouls.com/club.

Hotels. n.d. "Hotels." Fest 18. Accessed June 12, 2019. https://www.thefestfl.com/hotels.

Huber, Alison. 2013. "Mainstream as Metaphor: Imagining Dominant Culture." In *Redefining Mainstream Popular Music*, edited by Sarah Baker, Andy Bennett, and Jodie Taylor, 3–13. New York, NY: Routledge.

Interpunk.com. n.d. "Interpunk.com." Accessed April 11, 2016. http://www.interpunk.com/.

Jenkins, Henry. 1992. *Textual Poachers: Television Fans & Participatory Culture*. New York, NY: Routledge.

Jolly, Nathan. 2018. "Book Your Own Fucking Life: The Pre-Internet Guide that Connected the Indie Scene." The Industry Observer. https://theindustryobserver.thebrag.com/book-your-own-fucking-life-the-pre-internet-guide-that-connected-the-indie-scene/.

Kai, Alyssa. 2014. "If Punk Is the Ultimate Anti-Establishment Scene, Why Is It Still Run by All These White Men?" *The Guardian*. Accessed May 22, 2019. https://www.theguardian.com/commentisfree/2014/nov/09/transgender-punk-inclusivity-men.

Kaufman, Gil. 2018. "Shiragirl Talks Hitting the Road for Final Warped Tour, Shares Punk Pop Anthem." Billboard. Accessed January 14, 2019. https://www.billboard.com/articles/columns/rock/8458910/shiragirl-summers-comin-new-song-warped-tour.

Kaufman, Spencer. 2018. "Warped Tour to Return to Three Cities in 2019 to Celebrate 25th Anniversary." Consequence of Sound. Accessed January 19, 2019. https://consequenceofsound.net/2018/12/warped-tour-return-2019-25th-anniversary/.

Kempson, Michelle. 2012. "'I Just Call Myself a DIY Feminist': The Subjectivity, Subculture and the Feminist Zine." University of Warwick. http://webcat.warwick.ac.uk/record=b2624168~S1.

———. 2015. "'I Sometimes Wonder Whether I'm an Outsider': Negotiating Belonging in Zine Subculture." *Sociology* 49 (6): 1081–95. https://doi.org/10.1177/0038038514565834.

King, Joseph P. 2014. "A Man of Peace in a World of Mayhem." Facebook. https://www.facebook.com/permalink.php?story_fbid=728402553886697&id=100001508771758.

———. 2018. "Weaselfest and the Weasel Debacle." Facebook. https://www.facebook.com/note.php?note_id=154567054603586.

Klein, Gabriele. 2003. "Image, Body, and Performativity: The Constitution of Subcultural Practice in the Globalized World of Pop." In *The Post-Subcultures Reader*, edited by David Muggleton and Rupert Weinzierl, 41–49. Oxford: Berg.

Knopper, Steve. 2018. "'It Was 11 Guys on a Bus, and Then Me': Women on the Warped Tour." *New York Times*. https://www.nytimes.com/2018/06/21/arts/music/warped-tour-women.html.

Kruse, Holly. 1993. "Subcultural Identity in Alternative Music Culture." *Popular Music* 12 (1): 33–41. https://doi.org/10.1017/S026114300000533X.

Lam, Bourree. 2018. "Generation Sell Out." Refinery29. https://www.refinery29.com/en-us/2018/08/205859/selling-out-millennials-why.

Lane, Daniel S., and Sonya Dal Cin. 2018. "Sharing beyond Slacktivism: The Effect of Socially Observable Prosocial Media Sharing on Subsequent Offline Helping Behavior." *Information Communication and Society* 21 (11): 1523–40. https://doi.org/10.1080/1369118X.2017.1340496.

Lecaro, Lina. 2017. "Why Both Sides Are Wrong about The Dickies' Offensive Warped Tour Rant." *LA Weekly*. https://www.laweekly.com/music/the-dickies-warped-tour-rant-was-safer-scenes-right-to-heckle-leonard-graves-phillips-8397230.

Leonard, Madeleine. 2008. "Social and Subcultural Capital among Teenagers in Northern Ireland." *Youth & Society* 40 (2): 224–44.

Lorentzen, Anne. 2009. "Cities in the Experience Economy." *European Planning Studies* 17 (6): 829–45. https://doi.org/10.1080/09654310902793986.

Maffesoli, Michel. 1996. *The Time of the Tribes: The Decline of Individualism in Mass Society*. London: Sage.

Marin, Rick. 1992. "Grunge: A Success Story." *New York Times*. Accessed June 1, 2019. https://www.nytimes.com/1992/11/15/style/grunge-a-success-story.html.

Martins, Chris. 2012. "MTV Kills 'Headbangers Ball,' Host Says Network Neglects Rock." SPIN. Accessed April 25, 2016. http://www.spin.com/2012/09/mtv-kills-headbangers-ball-host-says-network-neglects-rock/

Maslow, Abraham. H. 1962. *Toward A Psychology of Being*. New York, NY: von Nostrand Reinhold.

McCormack, Karen M. 2017. "Inclusion and Identity in the Mountain Biking Community: Can Subcultural Identity and Inclusivity Coexist?" *Sociology of Sport Journal* 34 (4): 344–53. https://doi.org/10.1123/ssj.2016-0160.

McDowell, Amy D. 2017. "Aggressive and Loving Men: Gender Hegemony in Christian Hardcore Punk." *Gender and Society* 31 (2): 223–44. https://doi.org/10.1177/0891243217694824.

———. 2018. "'Christian but Not Religious': Being Church as Christian Hardcore Punk." *Sociology of Religion: A Quarterly Review* 79 (1): 58–77. https://doi.org/10.1093/socrel/srx033.

Mckenty, Finn. 2019. "Video Game Soundtracks that Shaped Punk and Metal." YouTube. Accessed June 10, 2019. https://www.youtube.com/watch?v=EDKEU8U5eJQ.

Mejía, Paula. 2019. "Hot Topic Is Still Hot." *New York Times*. Accessed May 8, 2019. https://www.nytimes.com/2019/04/06/style/hot-topic-stores.html?smtyp=cur&smid=tw-nytimes.

Menapace, Brendan. 2018. "Tony Hawk Ranks His Video Game Soundtracks." Vice. Accessed June 3, 2019. https://www.vice.com/en_us/article/yw7dy5/rank-your-records-tony-hawk.

Miner, Dylan, and Estrella Torrez. 2012. "Turning Point: Claiming the University as a Punk Space." In *Punkademics: The Basement Show in the Ivory Tower*, edited by Zack Furness, 27–35. Brooklyn, NY: Minor Compositions.

Mitchum, Rob, and Diego Garcia-Olano. 2018. "Tracking the Gender Balance of This Year's Music Festival Lineups." Pitchfork. Retrieved from https://pitchfork.com/features/festival-report/tracking-the-gender-balance-of-this-years-music-festival-lineups/

Moore, Allan. 2002. "Authenticity as Authentication." *Popular Music* 21 (2): 209–23. https://doi.org/10.1017/s0261143002002131.

Moore, Ryan. 2004. "Postmodernism and Punk Subculture: Cultures of Authenticity and Deconstruction." *The Communication Review* 7 (3): 305–27. https://doi.org/10.1080/10714420490492238.

———. 2007. "Friends Don't Let Friends Listen to Corporate Rock: Punk as a Field of Cultural Production." *Journal of Contemporary Ethnography* 36 (4): 438–74. https://doi.org/10.1177/0891241607303520.

———. 2010. *Sells Like Teen Spirit: Music, Youth Culture, and Social Crisis*. New York, NY: NYU Press.

Nicolay, Franz. 2017. "The Rise and Decline of the 'Sellout.'" Slate. https://slate.com/culture/2017/07/the-history-of-calling-artists-sellouts.html.

Nirvana—Grammy. n.d. "Nirvana—Grammy." Grammy. Accessed November 20, 2014. https://www.grammy.com/grammys/artists/nirvana.

North, Adrian C., David J. Hargreaves, and Susan A. O'Neill. 2000. "The Importance of Music to Adolescents." *British Journal of Educational Psychology* 70: 255–72. https://doi.org/10.1037/h0094049.

O'Brien, S. F., and K. L. Bierman. 1988. "Conceptions and Perceived Influence of Peer Groups: Interviews with Preadolescents and Adolescents." *Child Development* 59 (5): 1360–65. https://doi.org/10.1111/j.1467-8624.1988.tb01504.x.

Ozzi, Dan. 2015. "Major Label Debut: Punk's 'Sell Out' Albums Revisited." Noisey. http://noisey.vice.com/blog/major-label-debut-punks-sell-out-albums-revisited.

Ozzi, Dan, and Jonah Bayer. 2017. "The Shape of Punk to Comp." Noisey. https://noisey.vice.com/en_us/article/a37dzz/the-shape-of-punk-to-comp-v24n8.

Pelly, Jenn. 2018. "Punk's Not Dead? How Vans Warped Tour Jumped the Shark." *The Guardian.* https://www.theguardian.com/music/2018/aug/15/punks-not-dead-how-vans-warped-tour-jumped-the-shark.

Peterson, Richard A., and Andy Bennett. 2004. "Introducing Music Scenes." In *Music Scenes: Local, Translocal, and Virtual*, edited by Andy Bennett and Richard A. Peterson, 1–15. Nashville, TN: Vanderbilt University Press.

Piano, Doreen. 2003. "Resisting Subjects: DIY Feminism and the Politics of Style in Subcultural Production." In *The Post-Subcultures Reader*, edited by David Muggleton and Rupert Weinzierl, 253–65. Oxford: Berg.

Piepenbring, Dan. 2017. "A Punk Band that Knows 'The Bar Is Low' for Straight White Men." *The New Yorker.* https://www.newyorker.com/culture/culture-desk/a-punk-band-that-knows-the-bar-is-low-for-straight-white-men.

Piepmeier, Alison. 2009. *Girl Zines: Making Media, Doing Feminism*. New York, NY: NYU Press.

Pirkey, Melissa Fletcher. 2015. "People Like Me: Shared Belief, False Consensus, and the Experience of Community." *Qualitative Sociology* 38 (2): 139–64. https://doi.org/10.1007/s11133-015-9303-6.

Poecke, Niels van, and Janna Michael. 2016. "Bringing the Banjo Back to Life: The Field of Dutch Independent Folk Music as Participatory Culture." *First Monday* 21 (3). https://doi.org/10.5210/fm.v0i0.6385

Portwood-Stacer, Laura. 2012. "Anti-Consumption as Tactical Resistance: Anarchists, Subculture and Activist Strategy." *Journal of Consumer Culture* 12 (1): 87–105.

Potter, Shawna. 2017. "Let's Not Mistake The Dickies' Onstage Warped Tour Rant for Anything but Misogyny." Vice. Accessed May 28, 2019. https://www.vice.com/en_us/article/mbaa4q/war-on-women-on-the-dickies-warped-tour-rant.

"Pouzza Grand Slam." n.d. Pouzza Fest. https://pouzzafest.com/en/baseball-tournament/.

Prinz, Jesse. 2014. "The Aesthetics of Punk Rock." *Philosophy Compass*, 9 (9): 583–93.

"PUNK: Chaos to Couture." n.d. https://www.metmuseum.org/exhibitions/listings/2013/punk.

Punk Voter. n.d. "Punk Voter." Accessed June 12, 2019. https://www.punkvoter.com/.

Punks Against Sweatshops. n.d. "Punks Against Sweatshops" Punk Ethics. Accessed June 18, 2019. https://www.punkethics.com/punksagainstsweatshops/.

Putnam, Robert D. 2000. *Bowling Alone: The Collapse and Revival of American Community.* New York, NY: Simon & Schuster.

R13 Ramones Print Tee. n.d. "R13 Ramones Print Tee." Nordstrom. Accessed June 6, 2019. https://shop.nordstrom.com/s/r13-ramones-print-tee/5151735?origin=keywordsearch-personalizedsort&breadcrumb=Home%2FAll Results&color=washed black.

Ratliff, Ben. 2016. "Is Bandcamp the Holy Grail of Online Record Stores?" *New York Times*, August 19, 2016. https://www.nytimes.com/2016/08/20/arts/music/bandcamp-shopping-for-music.html.

Red, Magdelana. 2014. "Who Are the 'Emos' Anyway? Youth Violence in Mexico City and the Myth of the Revolution." *Journal of Popular Music Studies* 26 (1): 101–20. https://doi.org/10.1111/jpms.12062.

Reia, Jhessica. 2014. "Napster and Beyond: How Online Music Can Transform the Dynamics of Musical Production and Consumption in DIY Subcultures." *First Monday* 19 (10). https://doi.org/http://dx.doi.org/10.5210/fm.v19i10.5552.

Rife, Katie. 2017. "The Dickies Frontman Splits Punk Community with Misogynistic Onstage Rant." A.V. Club. https://news.avclub.com/the-dickies-frontman-splits-punk-community-with-misogyn-1798263841.

Robards, Brady, and Andy Bennett. 2011. "MyTribe: Post-Subcultural Manifestations of Belonging on Social Network Sites." *Sociology* 45 (2): 303–17.

Roche, Jason. 2013. "The Bad Religion Album Everyone Hated." LA Weekly. https://www.laweekly.com/music/the-bad-religion-album-everyone-hated-4167413.

Rosenberg, Morris, and B. Claire McCullough. 1981. "Mattering: Inferred Significance and Mental Health among Adolescents." *Research in Community Mental Health* 2: 163–82.

Rosenblatt, Bill. 2018. "Vinyl Is Bigger than We Thought. Much Bigger." *Forbes*. https://www.forbes.com/sites/billrosenblatt/2018/09/18/vinyl-is-bigger-than-we-thought-much-bigger/#74cf8d3b1c9c.

Run for Cover Records. n.d. "Run for Cover Records." Accessed May 20, 2019. http://www.runforcoverrecords.com/info.

"Safe Space." n.d. https://pouzzafest.com/en/safe-space/.

Schilt, Kristin. 2004. "'Riot Grrl Is . . . ': The Contestation Over Meaning in a Music Scene." In *Music Scenes: Local, Translocal, and Virtual*, edited by Andy Bennett and Richard A. Peterson, 115–30. Nashville, TN: Vanderbilt University Press.

Schmidt, Rodney. 2017. "The Fall of American Punk-Rock Music." Culture Trip. Accessed January 11, 2019. https://theculturetrip.com/north-america/usa/articles/the-fall-of-american-punk-rock-music/.

Schouten, John W., and James H. McAlexander. 1995. "Subcultures of Consumption: An Ethnography of the New Bikers." *Journal of Consumer Research* 22 (1): 43. https://doi.org/10.1086/209434.

Sehgal, Kabir. (2018). "Spotify and Apple Music Should Become Record Labels So Musicians Can Make a Fair Living." CNBC. https://www.cnbc.com/2018/01/26/how-spotify-apple-music-can-pay-musicians-more-commentary.html.

Shank, Barry. 1994. *Dissonant Identities: The Rock'N'Roll Scene in Austin, Texas.* Hanover, NH: University Press of New England.

Share of Total Music Album Consumption in the United States in 2018, by Genre. 2018. Statista. Accessed May 29, 2019. https://www.statista.com/statistics/310746/share-music-album-sales-us-genre/.

Sheppard, Oliver. 2012. "The Many Deaths of Punk" Souciant. http://souciant.com/2012/10/the-many-deaths-of-punk.

Shildrick, Tracy, and Robert MacDonald. 2006. "In Defence of Subculture: Young People, Leisure and Social Divisions." *Journal of Youth Studies* 9 (2): 125–40. https://doi.org/10.1080/13676260600635599.

Sklar, Monica. 2013. *Punk Style.* London: Bloomsbury.

Sklar, Monica, and Marilyn DeLong. 2012. "Punk Dress in the Workplace: Aesthetic Expression and Accommodation." *Clothing and Textiles Research Journal* 30 4: 285–99.

Sklar, Monica, and Mary Kate Donahue. 2018. "Process over Product: The 1990s United States Hardcore and Emo Subcultures and DIY Consumerism." *Punk & Post Punk* 7 (2): 155–80. https://doi.org/10.1386/punk.7.2.155_1.

Social Impact. n.d. "Social Impact." Fest 18. Accessed June 18, 2019. https://thefestfl.com/social-impact.

SPIN. 1994. "The Year Punk Broke," November 1994.

St. John, Graham. 2003. "Post-Rave Technotribalism and the Carnival of Protest." In *The Post-Subcultures Reader*, edited by David Muggleton and Rupert Weinzierl, 62–82. New York, NY: Berg.

Stewart, Francis. 2017. "This Is [Not] the A.L.F.?: Anarchism, Punk Rock and Animal Advocacy." *Punk & Post Punk* 5 (3): 227–45. https://doi.org/10.1386/punk.5.3.227_1.

Taylor, Astra. 2014. "How to Get a Whole Generation to Sell Out." Creativetime Reports. http://creativetimereports.org/2014/04/11/astra-taylor-how-to-get-a-whole-generation-to-sell-out-student-debt/.

Thompson, Stacy. 2004. *Punk Productions: Unfinished Business*. Albany, NY: State University of New York Press.

Thornton, Sarah. 1995. *Club Cultures: Music, Media, and Subcultural Capital*. Oxford: Blackwell Publishers.

Torkelson, Jason. 2010. "Life after (Straightedge) Subculture." *Qualitative Sociology* 33 (3): 257–74. https://doi.org/10.1007/s11133-010-9153-1.

Torrez, Estrella. 2012. "Punk Pedagogy: Education for Liberation and Love." In *Punkademics: The Basement Show in the Ivory Tower*, edited by Zack Furness, 27–35. Brooklyn, NY: Minor Compositions.

Traber, Daniel S. 2012. "L.A.'s 'White Minority': Punk and the Contradictions of Self-Marginalization." In *Punkademics: The Basement Show in the Ivory Tower*, edited by Zack Furness, 157–78. Brooklyn, NY: Minor Compositions

Trnka, Radek, Martin Kuška, Karel Balcar, and Peter Tavel. 2018. "Understanding Death, Suicide and Self-Injury among Adherents of the Emo Youth Subculture: A Qualitative Study." *Death Studies* 42 (6): 337–45. https://doi.org/10.1080/07481187.2017.1340066.

Tsitsos, Bill. 2012. "Slamdancing, Ageing, and Belonging." In *Ageing and Youth Cultures: Music, Style, and Identity*, edited by Paul Hodkinson and Andy Bennett, 66–78. London: Berg.

Ueno, Toshiya. 2003. "Unlearning to Raver: Techno-Party as the Contact Zone in Trans-Local Formations." In *The Post-Subcultures Reader*, edited by David Muggleton and Rupert Weinzierl, 101–17. New York, NY: Berg.

Vorobjovas-Pinta, Oskaras. 2018. "Gay Neo-Tribes: Exploration of Travel Behavior and Space." *Annals of Tourism Research* 72: 1–19.

Ward, Maria. 2019. "André Leon Talley Explains the Significance of the Met Gala." *Vogue*. https://www.vogue.com/article/what-is-the-met-gala-things-to-know-andre-leon-talley.

Warwick, Kevin. 2019. "The Story of the DIY Publication that Kept Bands on the Road for Decades." Noisey. https://www.vice.com/en_us/article/ywyzpm/the-story-of-the-diy-publication-that-kept-bands-on-the-road-for-decades?utm_source=nt.

Weintraub, Arlene. 2003. "Hotter than a Pair of Vinyl Jeans." *Bloomberg Business Week*. Accessed April 22, 2016.

Weinzierl, Rupert, and David Muggleton. (2003). "What is 'Post-subcultural Studies' Anyway?" In *The Post-Subcultures Reader*, edited by David Muggleton and Rupert Weinzierl, 3–23. New York, NY: Berg.

Weiss, Alex. n.d. "G.L.O.S.S. Frontwoman Talks Punk Rock Feminism: Bust Interview." Bust. Accessed January 28, 2019. https://bust.com/music/16802-hardcore-band-g-l-o-s-s-frontwoman-talks-punk-rock-feminism-bust-interview.html.

Wheaton, Belinda. 2000. "'Just Do It': Consumption, Commitment, and Identity in the Windsurfing Subculture." *Sociology of Sport Journal* 17 (3): 254–74.

Widdicombe, Sue, and Rob Wooffitt. 1990. "'Being' versus 'Doing' Punk: On Achieving Authenticity as a Member." *Journal of Language and Social Psychology* 9 (4): 257–77.

Williams, J. Patrick. 2006. "Authentic Identities: Straightedge Subculture, Music, and the Internet." *Journal of Contemporary Ethnography*, 35 (2): 173–200.

Witt, Stephen. 2015. *How Music Got Free: The End of an Industry, The Turn of the Century, and the Patient Zero of Piracy.* New York, NY: Penguin Random House.

Wood, Julia T. 2017. *Communication Mosaics.* Boston, MA: Cengage Learning.

YPulse. 2018. "Gen Z & Millennials Think This Clothing Brand Has More Unique Styles than Nike." Accessed May 29, 2019. https://www.ypulse.com/post/view/gen-z-millennials-think-this-clothing-brands-has-more-unique-styles-than-ni.

Index

life: band membership juggled with, 123; discovery and changing, 155–156; DIY complicated by, 116–117; live performances amid, 82, 83–84; punk and facets of, 58; scenes and way of, 154; scene values into, 155
Lifetime, 118
liner notes, 65
live performances: aging influencing attendance, 82–83; attendance of, 58, 59, 81, 91, 95; collective identities from attending, 28, 76; commitment and attendance of, 124, 135, 140; for community building, 75, 98; digital media and, 113; DIY and, 91, 95; friends and shared values at, 53–54; inclusivity and attending, 44–45; insider knowledge and locations of, 59–60, 97–98; punk thriving with, 149; relationships developed at, 138, 139; scenes and small, 90–91; scene support for thriving, 135–136, 137; as smaller-scale and lower-cost, 97–98; social media and, 6, 38, 89–90, 124; support for, 136–139; translocal scenes equal to, 155; work, distance and attendance of, 82, 83–84
low barriers to entry, 40, 96; as accessibility, 33, 35–36, 156; windsurfing subculture with, 55

MacKaye, Ian, 9, 89
mainstream culture. *See* popular culture
males: CCCS on urban, class-based, 16; PC police fought by, 150; The Warped Tour dominated by, 35
March, 137
marketing: band membership and, 130; social media for, 6, 38, 90, 124
media: CCCS and, 16, 114; discovery through, 109; youth recognizing influence of, 14. *See also* social media
The Menzingers, 4, 77, 132, 137
merchandise: Bandcamp for selling, 71, 110, 141, 142, 149; bands with, 6; CCCS not aligning with punk, 132; CDs as, 18, 67, 119, 132, 142, 146; Coachella and, 13; commitment and band, 124, 131, 132, 134; consumption

and festival, 11; contemporary punk and spending on, 82; dedication to bands and purchasing, 141, 145–146, 146; DIY for scene, 88, 90–91, 92, 95; Facebook for selling, 132, 144, 149; group valuing benefits of, 55, 139; Hot Topic for counterculture, 25, 26, 104, 110–113; inclusion and purchasing, 44–45, 59; insider knowledge on, 59–60, 92; Interpunk.com for, 67–68; podcasts promoting, 113–114; Punks Against Sweatshops and, 146; punk thriving with, 149; purchase of, 140–141, 146; scene membership and, 18, 134, 141; social media for promoting, 89–90, 124; Spotify and cheap, 104, 141; as subcultural capital, 132, 134; Twitter for selling, 144; types of, 132
Midtown, 2
The Mighty Mighty Bosstones, 10, 69
Millencolin, 1, 70
millennials, 106, 156
Minor Threat, 71, 89
Modern Baseball, 104
Mods, 15
Montreal, Canada, 11, 12, 13
morals, 30–31
Motion City Soundtrack, 10
mountain biking, 54–55
The Movielife, 2
MTV: band awareness by, 8; contemporary punk aired by, 64; as cool arbiter, 3; discovery through, 10; insider knowledge via, 26, 111–113, 120; Mudhoney popularized by, 8; Pearl Jam popularized by, 8; pop punk and mid-2000 on, 10; punk rock and, 5; punk thriving and lack on, 149; Soundgarden popularized by, 8
Mudhoney, 8
Mudie, Hugo, 13
Mumford and Sons, 52
music: Bandcamp for streaming, 96, 124, 142, 143; bands and hyper-commodification of, 77; CD collections of, 2, 39, 64, 70–73; commitment and pre-order of, 144, 145; community and love of, 81; compilations of smaller

About the Author

Ellen M. Bernhard is a lecturer in Chestnut Hill College's Communication Department in Philadelphia, Pennsylvania. Her research interests include contemporary punk rock scenes in America, punk rock music festivals, issues of scene identity, and the impact of social media on fans of the genre. She received her PhD from Drexel University in 2016.